THE WINES OF ARGENTINA, CHILE AND LATIN AMERICA

Christopher Fielden has been in the wine trade since leaving school over forty years ago and his travels have taken him to more than a hundred different countries. On his first trip to South America, thirty years ago, he arrived in French Guiana by dugout canoe and has been fascinated by the continent ever since.

Within the trade he has launched a number of wines on the British market, including Jacob's Creek from Australia and Marqués de Cacéres from Rioja. He has been President of the national Wine and Spirit Association and a Trustee for two terms of the Wine and Spirit Education Trust. He has had a wide and varied career, which has included a time selling Scotch whisky all over the world and more than four years as the France-based sales director of a leading Burgundy producer.

For over ten years he had a column in *Decanter* and has written ten books on wine-related subjects, including Burgundy, Alsace and wine fraud. He also contributed to *The Oxford Companion to Wine*. He used to have a regular wine spot on national radio and has lectured on wines from Beijing to Memphis.

In real life he is a clergy spouse in Wiltshire, where he is deeply involved with rural life.

FABER BOOKS ON WINE

Series Editor: Julian Jeffs

THE WINES OF ARGENTINA, CHILE AND LATIN AMERICA

CHRISTOPHER FIELDEN

faber and faber
LONDON·NEW YORK

First published in 2001
by Faber and Faber Limited
3 Queen Square London WC1N 3AU
Published in the United States by Faber and Faber Inc.,
An affiliate of Farrar, Straus and Giroux, New York

Typeset by Steven Gardiner Ltd, Cambridge
Printed in England by Clays Ltd, St Ives plc

A CIP record for this book
is available from the British Library

ISBN 0-571-19267-X

2 4 6 8 10 9 7 5 3 1

To Ann, with thanks for all her support

USA

MEXICO

Mexico

North Atlantic

CENTRAL
AMERICA

Caracas

VENEZUELA GUIANA
COLOMBIA   FRENCH GUIANA
Bogota
SURINAM
ECUADOR
Quito

PERU   BRAZIL   Recife
Lima

La Paz
BOLIVIA

Pacific Ocean

PARAGUAY
Rio de
Janeiro

Santiago   URUGUAY
CHILE   Buenos Aires
ARGENTINA

South Atlantic

 Main wine growing areas

General map

Contents

―――――

Acknowledgements

━━━━━━━

I would like to thank all those who have helped me with this book. It would be invidious for me to mention them all by name, for I would be sure to miss some out but these include:

Those writers who have gone before me, and whose works I have consulted.

Those who received me so kindly and patiently showed me their vineyards, wineries and wines.

Those who helped me on my travels. In some countries, it was really a voyage into the unknown and, on three occasions, I would have come to a complete halt if I had not come across the right person at the right time:

In Brazil, Senhor Manuel Jesús Buj, Production Director of Allied Domecq at Garibaldi.

In Paraguay, Corlia Truter and her family, from Colonia Independencia.

In Venezuela, an unknown young girl from the Polar Group at Barquísimeto Airport.

I would also like to thank a few other individuals:

Pedro Olaechea of Viña Tacama in Peru for devoting so much time to me in Peru; fellow writer, Ivan Bluske, for showing me Tarija, in Bolivia.

Cecilia Rázquin, of ProMendoza, Argentina. I was her first foreign visitor and no one could have been more helpful then, and in finding me statistics afterwards.

Sue Crabtree, who saw me through the worst moments of my trip and whom I abandoned.

Julie West, who researched the chapter on Cuba for me and

ACKNOWLEDGEMENTS

Natalia Solís, who tried hard to keep me up to date on how I should use my computer and who read my proofs for me.

To the thief, who stole all at Caracas Airport, I hope he made something of my notes and nothing of my money and passport.

Introduction

'Begin at the beginning', the King said,
gravely, 'and go on till you come to the end:
then stop.'
Lewis Carroll, *Alice's Adventures in Wonderland*, 1865

In an over-populated world, does one have to justify the creation of a new being? If the world is that of wine-books, I feel that the answer has to be, 'Yes!' What justification can I give then for this book? First of all, it must be realised that the countries of Latin America are both important producers and consumers of wine. Of the 25 largest wine-producing countries, 17 come from Europe and five from Latin America; that leaves just three places for the rest of the world. Of the 10 countries with the largest per capita consumption of wine, eight come from Europe and two from Latin America. Wine then is important not just as a crop within the region; it is also an important part of the regular diet of many of the countries of Latin America. The subject is therefore broad enough to justify a book.

Equally important is the growing role that wines from these countries play in the open markets of the United States, the UK and other countries. The wines of Chile are no longer considered to be novelty items; those of Argentina are broadly available and both Mexico and Uruguay are creating niches for themselves. The matter of surprise is that there are so few books on the subject of the wines of Latin America. Until last year, the leading book in English on the wines of Chile appeared almost 20 years ago. Whilst one on those of Argentina has recently appeared in the United States, it has found no publisher in England. Indeed, even in the countries concerned, outside technical works, there is very little available for the reader

I

interested in wine. It is not that the wines of Latin America are newcomers. *Monseigneur le Vin*, published by French wine-merchants Nicolas in 1924 gives production statistics not just, as you might expect, for the vineyards in the Americas of Chile and Argentina, but also for those of Brazil, Bolivia, Uruguay, Peru and Mexico.

Interestingly, I have in front of me some wine-lists from Harvey's, the fine wine merchants from Bristol: that of 1962 includes one Chilean wine – a Valparaiso Tinto at 7/6d; that of 1976 contains no wines from South America at all. However, I can remember from my early days in the wine trade in Liverpool in the 1960s buying bottles of Undurraga and Concha y Toro as 'novelty' wines for tasting. I hope that this book will fill some of the undoubted gap in current wine knowledge that exists.

Why is it a book on the wines of Latin America and not just on, for example, those of Chile or Argentina? Here I must admit a great debt. To celebrate the 500th anniversary of the first arrival in America of Christopher Columbus, the Spanish government published a book entitled *La Viticultura Americana y sus Raíces* ('American Viticulture and its Roots'). This gave the background to all those countries in the Americas, North and South, where there are vineyards and full details of their history and composition. This did not speak much of the wines; indeed, in some of the countries the grapes grown were just for table consumption. On the other hand it clearly showed the progress of the vine through the Americas. The scope of this book is somewhat different. First, the United States and Canada are omitted because they are plainly not Latin American countries, though a case might be made for the inclusion of some American wineries from the south-west of the United States. Also such countries as Ecuador, the Dominican Republic and Guatemala are left out, because they do not have a commercial wine industry of significance. On the other hand, since the book appeared in 1992, vineyards have been planted in Cuba and Cuban wine is now present in a small number of foreign markets. Cuba is included.

The range of countries profiled in the book is large. Some, like Chile and Argentina, are very important in the world of wine. If we are talking purely quantitatively, Argentina has been much more important, but production was seriously reduced in a bid to concentrate more on quality. Some, like Cuba and Bolivia, are very small; Venezuela is only just joining the wine club; Peru has been there for centuries. Some have a large domestic market, some have almost none. The contrasts between them are very apparent, but they all have one thing in common, their first roots were in the missionaries from Spain and Portugal. It is this that binds together the countries in this book.

Finally, what are my qualifications for writing the book? I first visited Latin America, or, at least, a part of it in July 1971, but my introduction to its wines was scarcely at the sharp end. On that occasion, when I was selling Scotch whisky, I can only remember tasting wines in Peru and Paraguay. More memorable was a rather louche Cuban I met in Panama, who produced a grubby handkerchief out of his trouser pocket, opened it up and invited me to take my pick from the selection of Brazilian diamonds it contained.

It was not for almost another 20 years that I first visited Chile. Since then I have been back regularly to South America and four trips have been made specifically for this book: the first to Mexico; the second to Brazil, Uruguay and Paraguay; the third to Venezuela, Peru, Bolivia, Argentina and Chile; and the last, by my assistant, Julie West, to Cuba.

One temptation that I have had in writing this book is that of turning it into a travelogue, as there has been any number of interesting and, occasionally, amusing experiences in the trips it has involved. However, I have done my best to keep it a wine book. It is, however, a book that reflects my own interests and one of those is history. I am fascinated by the three waves that have had a dramatic influence on wine production throughout Latin America. First of all came the missionaries, who planted vines to make wine for the mass from the first plantings in Isla la Española (Hispaniola or, nowadays, the Dominican Republic) in 1493, vines arrived in Nueva España (Mexico) in 1522 and in Peru in about 1548. From there it spread to Chile and Argentina. The last Mission to be built in California was that of Sonoma, as late as 1823.

As early as 1519, the Merchant Venturers of Seville were instructed to see that every ship leaving for the Indies should carry vine plants as part of its cargo. In the early years, this posed problems, as the vines would begin to shoot as they passed through the tropics and would give fruit irregularly. In order to minimise this problem plants were later loaded en route, either in the

Canaries or the Azores. Many of the early vineyards came to be planted from pips from raisins that formed part of the everyday diet of the Spanish military.

The Portuguese King John III sent Martin Alfonso de Sousa to colonise Brazil, where he arrived in January 1532. His cargo included bananas, oranges and, from the island of Madeira, sugar cane and vines. In parallel, then, the Spanish and Portuguese recognised the importance that the production of wine might play in the economies of their overseas possessions. Indeed the success of these wines can be judged by the fact that the Spanish king felt that, in 1699, in order to protect the domestic economy, he had to ban the production of all wine, except that destined for church use, in his American colonies. Indeed, 70 years earlier, the shipment of wines from Peru and Chile to Mexico or Spain itself had been restricted. There were similar bans imposed by the Portuguese crown on the production of wine in Brazil. The domestic wine-producers of both Spain and Portugal must have felt gravely threatened for such decrees to be made. As far as the Spanish were concerned, it is likely that such laws were imposed more strongly in Mexico, the seat of their colonial government, than in the more distant vice-royalty of Peru.

Whilst one can only speculate as to what varieties were planted in these early vineyards, it is likely that they were the ancestors of such current base-wine grapes as the Criolla and Cereza of Argentina, the País of Chile, the Mission of California and the Moscatels. These last are still widely planted for distillation into pisco in Peru and Chile and singani in Bolivia, as well as for wine in Argentina and Uruguay. Whilst the Criolla and the País are black grapes, the best wine that they are capable of producing, except in special circumstances, is a deep rosé. Such wines are still very popular throughout Latin America. Indeed, in Uruguay, for example, such rosés often contain a substantial proportion of Muscat d'Hambourg.

These early vineyards would have been planted close to the colonial cities that provided ready markets for the wine. The first plantings in Peru, for example, were around the capital city of Cuzco. Here the altitude and the harsh Andean climate were scarcely conducive to successful viticulture and it was not long before there were major vineyard plantings closer to the coast, particularly around the town of Ica. Similarly, the first vineyards in

Argentina were probably planted far to the north of Mendoza, the present viticultural capital.

I have spoken of the three waves in the wine history of Latin America. The second came with the vast emigration, largely of agricultural workers from Europe during the second half of the nineteenth and at the beginning of the twentieth century. Some were victims of the industrial revolution, some were victims of the revolutionary unrest that spared few European countries, and some were victims of war and a few of religious oppression. Just as the United States expanded rapidly at this time, drawing most of its immigrants from northern Europe, so Mexico and the new republics of South America attracted immigrants, for the most part, from southern Europe. These Italians, Portuguese and Spaniards had a long winemaking tradition. For them, wine was an everyday necessity. Whilst many may have worked in the expanding industries of the new countries, they planted small plots of vines to give them the wine they needed. One has only to look at the names of the largest wine companies of Latin America to see the enormous influence of the Italians, the Basques and the Catalans. Initially, again, wine was made for local consumption, but the coming of steamships and the railways opened up new markets. These, in their turn, demanded more, and better, wine.

The third wave has been the arrival of the multinationals. Often these have been major drinks companies, whose sales have been led by spirits. For the most part, the countries of Latin America have a history of protectionism and have tried to close their borders against the importation of foreign luxury products, such as spirits and Champagne. This has had two major results: first, certain economies in the area have based their existence on smuggling. One has only to look at the import figures for such sparsely inhabited countries as Paraguay, Belize and French Guiana, to understand how important this might be.

From my early days as a whisky salesman, I can remember arriving at Asunción, the capital of Paraguay, without any contacts. I found a very helpful commercial attaché at the British Embassy, who described graphically the local scenario: there was a legitimate market, which accounted for 10% of the business and a smuggling market, which accounted for the rest. Which did I want to attack? Taking pragmatism as my guide, I said that I was prepared to go for the bigger slice of the cake, as long as I could be certain that I would be paid. I was assured that in Paraguay, that was not a problem, however, to be a smuggler you had to have a smuggler's licence. To qualify for this, you had to have a turnover of, I think it was, US$250,000 a month. The only person who qualified for this was the brother-in-law of President Stroessner! A meeting was arranged for me with this man and he said that he was very happy to handle any goods that were already being legally sold in either Argentina or Brazil! That is how Old Bushmills first came to be sold in Paraguay!

The second approach to the market would be for the major companies to establish subsidiary companies in the various countries. They would invest locally in wineries, bottling-plants, or perhaps vineyards. By spending money on the ground, they hoped that this would make the way easier for the direct importation of their products. Naturally, this became more interesting, the larger the domestic market. It is not surprising that Brazil, Mexico and Argentina have proved to be more interesting targets for the multi-nationals than Chile, Bolivia and Peru.

In addition, such companies as Allied Domecq, for example, have tried to create as large a portfolio as possible for their sales-force. Thus wines have come to be added to the base range of spirits. Similar restrictions have led to the establishment of wineries in many countries by the leading Champagne houses.

More recent has been the arrival of the flying winemaker, and this is a concept about which I have certain qualms. Certainly, there is little doubt that they have improved the winemaking in every country covered by this book. However, the brief from their employers, ultimately, either directly or indirectly the major international supermarket chains, is to make wines that will appeal to the consumer. If one person is making wine in a number of countries, there is the danger that he will work to a standard formula and produce similar wine in all those countries. The dominance of the Big Four grape varieties – Cabernet Sauvignon, Merlot, Chardonnay and Sauvignon Blanc – is evidence of this. Whilst it might make better sense for a supermarket chain to sell Merlot, rather than Tannat from Uruguay, for example, it would be a great pity if the identity of the wines of individual countries were to become submerged into a basic style.

Whilst, as I have said earlier, I have tried to make this book as comprehensive as possible, the more that I have written, the more I have realised there is to write. I give notes on approximately 70 different wineries in Argentina, yet there are more than 1,400 that go unmentioned. Earlier in this chapter, I have said that there is no commercial wine production in Ecuador. However, since starting to write it, I have heard of a German producing sparkling wine there and a friend has given me a bottle of something called Castell Real, Tinto Seco, Vino de Cocina, 1988 Vintage, for which he paid, so a sticker tells me 75 c. The producer is the Unión Vinícola Internacional C. Ltda. at Guayaquíl. The label would suggest to me that it is a wine to be used for cooking, but in the small print it suggests rather that it is to be drunk, in moderation. The label also pictures such attractive dishes as chicken and chips, ham and eggs and a hamburger and relish; perhaps it is meant to be drunk with these. Is this wine made from grapes grown in Ecuador? Is it imported in bulk and bottled the country? Is it made from imported must concentrate? Should I extend my research and include a chapter on the wines of Ecuador?

I think not.

Argentina

═══════

Excellent secondary wines are made at Mendoza,
at the base of the Andes, which form an article of
considerable traffic with Buenos Ayres, a
thousand miles distant across the Pampas. They
are transported even during the summer heats,
and so far from spoiling, they prove all the better
from the journey. The wine is not carried in skins,
which so taint and disqualify the produce of some
districts in the mother-country, but is conveyed in
small barrels slung on each side of a mule and the
quantity thus sent is considerable.
James L. Denman, *The Vine and its Fruit*, 1875

Argentina is by far the most important wine country in Latin
America, both in terms of the area that it has under vines:
209,000 hectares as opposed to the next largest, 132,000 hectares
in Chile, and also in per capita consumption: 40.99 litres, as
opposed to 31 litres in Uruguay. Despite all this it is difficult to
comprehend that on all vinous sides, it is but a shadow of its former
self. In 1973, the production of wine in Argentina was 27 million
hectolitres; in 1997 it was exactly half this. In 1970 the annual
consumption per capita of wine in Argentina reached 91.79 litres,
now it is just 41. Like no other wine country in the world, the wine
industry in Argentina has been through a torrid time and is only
now just emerging from the ashes.

Geographically, there is no other country in the world that has a
broader spread of vineyards than those of Argentina. They stretch
in the lee of the Andes almost 1,600 km from Salta in the north to
Neuquén in the south. In altitude, the vineyards range from 450 m

above sea level in Río Negro to over 2,000 m in Salta Province. This means that there is a wide range of climatic conditions. As we shall also see the altitude of the vineyards plays perhaps a larger part than in any other wine country.

In many ways Argentina has much going for it as a wine-producing country. For a start, the family of the President, Dr Saúl Menem, has a background in the wine trade in the province of La Rioja. It has a good climate and no shortage of water for irrigation. It has no shortage of land available for the expansion of vineyards. Indeed, as has just been mentioned, the area under vines could increase by almost 50%, just by replanting the area that has been grubbed up since 1972. Land is cheap. There is also a healthy domestic market of approximately 35 million consumers, most of them of Italian or Spanish origin, with a tradition of wine drinking. All this makes the country an attractive proposition and the wine industry has attracted inward investment more than any other country in Latin America.

Are there clouds on the horizon? The main one must be the question of economic stability. Since 1991, the Argentine peso has been pegged to the US dollar in a bid to curb inflation and to give some solidity to the currency. Whilst there is no doubt that in the short term this has achieved the desired effect, as I write this, questions are being asked as to whether the economy is about to implode with dangerous results. A further problem is that of the wine that Argentina exports, three-quarters is just ordinary 'table wine'. This is no more than a commodity and, as a commodity, can easily be the victim of market circumstances beyond its control. For Argentina to be a truly major force in the world of wine, it must concentrate its efforts on the export of 'fine' wine. Here it is having some success, with sales in Britain, for example, rising fast. It is in this field that the future of the Argentine wine industry must lie.

HISTORY

The colonisation of Argentina took place in three different waves and from three different directions. The first colony in the country was established in 1536 at Buenos Aires, by the explorer Pedro de Mendoza, who arrived with a fleet of 16 ships and 1,600 men. However, largely due to the hostility of the local Querandí Indians, the settlement was abandoned and the Spaniards sailed up the Paraná River and built the city of Asunción, in what is now Paraguay. It was more than 40 years before the Spaniards established another bridgehead on the south bank of the River Plate.

The other two waves of exploration into what is now Argentina were financed by the wealth of the silver mines of Peru and Bolivia, and they came through the Andes. In 1553, Francisco de Aguirre, known as the 'Mother of Cities' for his role as a coloniser (and who has given his name to a major Chilean winery) established the first Spanish city in the country, Santiago del Estero. This became an important stage on the route between the food-supplying region of the Pampas and the colonial cities in the Andes. The third 'invasion' came from Chile through the Uspallata Pass and led to the foundation of the city of Mendoza in 1561, by Pedro de Castilla, and of San Juan, by Juan Jufré, the following year. There is little doubt that all these expeditions will have included priests, who most probably brought vine-shoots with them.

It is Juan Cidrón (or Cedrón), however, who is credited with being the father of the Argentine wine industry. In 1553, the citizens of Santiago del Estero complained that there was no priest in their community and asked that one should be sent from Chile. This was the man who was sent and he is recorded as having arrived with a crucifix in one hand and a bundle of vine-shoots and cottonseed in the other.

Early winemaking was almost totally in the hands of the Jesuits, who primarily made wine for their own needs. However, trade developed, mainly across the Andes, and, to a lesser extent, to Buenos Aires. Notwithstanding the transport difficulties of the seventeenth century, Antonio Vasquez de Espinosa could report that in Mendoza, 'there are very good vineyards from which they make quantities of wine which they export in carts via Córdoba to Buenos Aires'. This business must have been very risky, for apart from the natural hazards of a month's journey by ox-cart, entry and exit duties had to be paid to each province through which the wine travelled. In addition, the prices in Buenos Aires were fixed by the City Council. For example, in 1620, the price per *arroba* was 14 pesos for wine from Castilla, 12 pesos for wine from Paraguay and 10 pesos for wine from Chile (Mendoza and San Juan). In the same year the prices were reduced to 12, 10 and 6 pesos, respectively. By this time, there were officials deputed to check on the quality of any wine that was offered for sale in the city.

Morewood, writing in 1838, says, 'The genial warmth of the climate and soil in the valleys and plains under the Andes, are particularly favourable to the growth of the vine. Some of the vineyards, especially those in the vicinity of Mendoza, are said to contain 60,000 plants. The grapes are large, black, and highly flavoured, resembling the Hambro species more than any other. A duty of one dollar is imposed on every cask of brandy and four reals on every cask of wine. The wines and brandies of Mendoza, San Juan and Rioja, make their way to the Río de la Plata to the extent of 12,000 barrels annually, where they are bartered for English merchandise, besides which, large quantities are sent to Potosí, Santa Fé, and other places. In transporting these over the immense plains of the Pampas, oxen and mules are employed. The former to the number of six in a wagon, travelling about eight leagues in a day; and the latter laden with skins in pack-saddles, travel in troops together at the rate of ten or twelve leagues a day.'

In 1776, the Spanish government created the Viceroyalty of the River Plate and, for the first time, the provinces of the Cuyo (Mendoza and San Juan) owed allegiance to Buenos Aires rather than to Chile. This situation was comparatively short-lived, for in May 1810 came the revolution, in which the country gained independence. This led to a bitter internal struggle between the Federalists, who believed that each province should have autonomous powers, and the Unitarists, who demanded a centralised government, with the power being firmly held by Buenos Aires. Overall, the Unitarists continued to dominate the political life of the country. Naturally, in such circumstances, things were not easy for a provincial, rural industry, such as wine.

There were three important factors in the creation of a truly national wine industry. The first was the power of an ever-growing immigrant community used to consuming and, often, making wine. The first of these had arrived in San Juan as early as 1777. They were Portuguese prisoners, as a result of the war between Spain and Portugal, and they included a number of agronomists and viticulturalists. The real immigrant movement did not get under way, however, for almost another century. As Dr Emilio Maurín Navarro writes in his history of the Argentine wine trade, 'In 1874, the last year of the Sarmiento presidency, there arrived in Mendoza fifty-eight immigrants, who were received with enthusiasm by the city which organised a great celebration in their honour.' The following year there were 296 immigrants of whom 122 were Italian, 96 French, 30 Spanish, 18 German and 11 Swiss. It must be assumed that many of these came from wine-growing regions. (There were also eight Englishmen and two Americans.)

One has only to look at the histories of the major wine companies still in existence, to see that this was the time when many of their founding families first arrived in Argentina. Taking a random selection of brochures, I see that Juan Carlos Graffigna began producing wine in San Juan in 1869, Pascual Toso in 1880, Luis Tirasso established Santa Ana in 1891, Rodolfo Suter arrived in Argentina in 1897, Enrique Tittarelli in 1898 and the Pulenta family, of Peñaflor, in 1902. For every potential producer who arrived in Argentina, it must be realised that a host of potential consumers also arrived. These lived mainly in the big cities, for wine was an urban drink; on the farms, spirits were much more popular.

The second major influence was Domingo Faustino Sarmiento, a native of San Juan, who became Argentina's first President from the provinces. During his presidency (1868–74), he established wine schools in San Juan and in Mendoza. He also brought to the country three foreign experts: a Frenchman, Aimé Pouget, who is credited with introducing many of the noble French varietals; an Italian, Schieroni, who established an experimental vine nursery with more than 200 varieties; and a German, Röveder, who ran one of the wine schools.

The final influence was the arrival of the Buenos Aires al Pacífico railway in Mendoza in 1885, with a line to San Juan established the following year. This meant that delivery times to the major market, Buenos Aires, were reduced from a month to two or three days. This naturally had a beneficial effect on the quality of the wine and also opened up the possibility of wines being shipped to European markets.

These factors all led to an increase in the quality of the wine and a move away from total reliance on the Criolla grape, which had been the backbone of the industry since its introduction by priests in the sixteenth century. The use of European varietals was particularly recommended by Tiburcio Benegas, who might be described as the creator of the modern wine industry in Argentina. He recommended also that wines should be made in European styles and in one of his books that appeared in 1885, he gave recipes for producing 'Burdeos' and 'Borgoña'. He was also the founder of the wine company, Trapiche.

Tiburcio Benegas was also one of the driving forces behind the establishment of the Defensa Viti-Vinícola Nacional, which was created in 1904 as a vehicle to fight the sale of fraudulent or adulterated wines, on which taxes were rarely paid. This role is now the responsibility of the Instituto Nacional de Vitivinicultura.

In the early years of the twentieth century, the Argentine upper-classes still insisted on drinking French wines; it was the new wave of immigrants who kept the local wine industry in business. The first Argentinean 'Champagne', the brainchild of a German, Juan Von Toll, appeared on the market in 1905, and the writer Fernando Buzzi, puts its instant success to the proliferation of tango bars and brothels in Buenos Aires, providing solace to a predominantly male immigrant community.

During the middle of the twentieth century, there was a dramatic expansion in the vineyard area in Argentina. In 1936, there were 149,815 hectares of vines; in 1950 there were 175,013, but by 1977, at its peak, the figure had reached 350,680. Two other interesting peaks, were that in per capita consumption (1970 – 91.79 litres) and in overall production (1976 – 27 million hecto-litres). Interestingly, as a result of government policies, which resulted in the planting of low quality vineyards in Mendoza Province, a second peak in production was reached in 1987. Since then the decline has been rapid in all three fields. This has been brought about, as in many other traditional wine-producing countries, by a combination of factors. The first of these is the rapid rise in the consumption of beers, fruit juices and soft drinks, such as Coca-Cola. These are all very much brand dominated and have vast marketing budgets behind them. Also it might be said that, in hot climates, such as that of most of Argentina, they provide better 'refreshment'. Secondly, and this also comes with a growing market with higher aspirations, there is a move away from 'table' wine to 'fine' wine.

It is interesting that the first peak of production, in 1976, coincided with a dramatic leap in export sales which in that year shot up to 45 million litres from just 11 million litres the year before. However, this is accounted for very largely by sales in bulk to Chile, presumably because of a short harvest there. In the same year sales of 'fine' wine increased from 2.05 million litres to 2.78 million litres, two-thirds of this was sold in just three markets in South America: Brazil, Venezuela and Paraguay. The United States was the fourth biggest market.

Despite the fact that this increase was short-lived, it engendered certain optimism with regard to exporting. An article in the *Buenos Aires Herald* of 12 October 1977, was headed 'Argentine Wines Among World's Best'. Similarly, a month earlier a feature appeared in the *Financial Times* of London about Argentina and it included an article headed 'Wine Begins to Travel'. It finished up, 'If the export trade in wines grows – as is likely as a result of Government efforts to increase the exports of all Argentine manufacturers – this should lead naturally to more discipline in the industry. The discipline will come all the more quickly if special efforts are made to export bottled rather than bulk wines and the Argentine producers see the necessity of establishing and safeguarding the names of the wines and their constant quality.' Here two recurring problems in the Argentine wine trade were pointed out, the lack of constancy of quality and the pragmatism with which the wines were labelled. These are problems that are still present, though to a lesser degree than in the past.

For the first time eight of the largest producers jointly attacked the British market, until then just an importer of cheap wine, the equivalent of approximately 10,000 cases a year in bulk. These producers put on a tasting for the trade and the press at one of London's most exclusive clubs in October 1977. Overall the reactions were favourable and for the first time the capacity of Argentina as a potential source for good wine came to be recognised. A period of expansion in sales began. This good work was totally destroyed on 2 April 1982 when the Falkland Islands were invaded. It was more than 10 years before the ground that was lost on that day, was recovered.

The result of this gross over-production of 'table' wine was a collapse in prices, which fell below 10c a litre. An interesting comparison can be made in looking at the figures for new vineyard planting; from 1985 to 1990 an average of 2,000 hectares of new vineyards were planted each year, in the following five years, this fell to less than 100 hectares. It is important to note also that Argentina has only had an open economy since 1990. The hard currencies were not available for the wineries to invest in modern plant. As it was put to me by a leading figure in the industry, 'At the time, we did not have educated people who made wine for educated people.'

During the past few years, many of the traditional companies, specialising in low-price wines, have gone to the wall. Those that have survived are those who have also produced quality wine, particularly if they have been able to develop export markets. In the Argentine world of wine, big is no longer necessarily beautiful.

Today, the wine industry of Argentina lies at a crossroads. It can no longer rely on the domestic market; it must invest in exporting. The multinational companies seem to have confidence in its future; let us hope they are right!

THE WINE REGIONS

Whilst the vine is widely grown in Argentina, to all intents and purposes, wine is produced in the string of provinces that form the western border of the country, those that lie in the shadow of the Andes. As far as the Instituto Nacional de Vitivinicultura (I.N.V.) is concerned these are classified in four groups: the North-West; the Centre-West; the South; and Others. Of these the Centre-West, which comprises the Provinces of Mendoza and San Juan, accounts for more than 90% of production.

Argentina is the only country in South America to have a D.O.C. (Denominación de Origen Controlada) system. I would like to say that it has a well-developed D.O.C. system, but that is not the case. In fact the first wines to bear D.O.C. labels were Chardonnays from San Rafael in the 1992 vintage. At present there are just two D.O.C.s, both from the Province of Mendoza: San Rafael and Luján de Cuyo. Their relative unimportance in the Argentine wine scene suggests that their future is uncertain. Why should this be so? Perhaps most people think as did a spokesman for Bodegas Norton, when he said to me, 'We don't trust any control; the cuisine is not as it was twenty years ago. Look at the French and the Spanish, they have handcuffed themselves.'

Whilst it does not imply any qualitative controls, the growers of the Province of Río Negro have adopted as a regional statement of the origin for their wines, '*Los Vinos de la zona fría*' – 'Wines from the cold zone'.

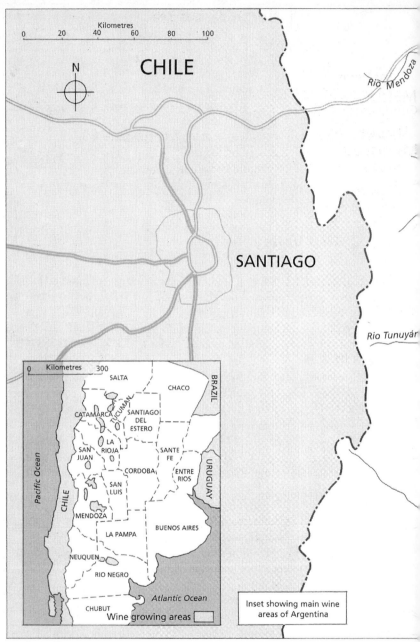

Argentina

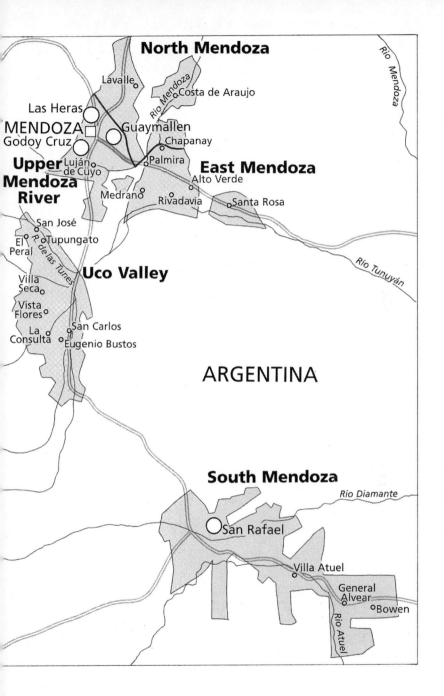

Generally speaking, the vineyard regions of Argentina have well-defined summers and winters. In summer the weather can be hot and there is little or no rainfall. The main climatic problem is hail, which can strike suddenly and devastatingly. Whilst rockets are still occasionally used to break up potential hail-clouds, the main protection is netting. Winters can be cold, but frost in spring is rarely a danger. Annual rainfall varies between 150 and 400 mm, but this is supplemented by unlimited water for irrigation, either from the rivers flowing down from the Andes, or from artesian wells drawing on subterranean aquifers.

In Argentina, more than in any other wine-producing country in the world, altitude of the vineyards is a powerful factor. Indeed it has been the marketing point behind the launch of the Terrazas range of wines from Chandon. Each grape variety has its ideal altitude. The vineyards in Argentina range from about 450 m above sea-level in Río Negro, to just over 2,000 m in Salta. The advantages of higher altitudes include better exposure to ultra-violet rays and higher contrasts between day and night temperatures. Similar results can be obtained by planting in the valleys leading down from the Andes. Here currents of air also make for greater differentials between day and night temperatures.

There are three dominant winds in the vineyard regions. Of these two, the southerly *Polar* and the south-easterly *Sudestada*, are generally moderate and rain bearing. The *Zonda*, which comes off the mountains to the north, can blow from August to November, is very hot, enervating and causes a dramatic drop in humidity levels. It is a particular problem in San Juan Province.

Because of the dryness of the climate, except in Río Negro Province, fungal diseases, such as mildew, oidium and botrytis are rare. Most vines are ungrafted, as *phylloxera* is not a common problem, though with the increase in drip-irrigation, nematodes might become a bigger concern. Certain viruses, such as leaf-roll, are also present.

For the most part, the soils are sandy and drain well. As you get closer to the Andes, and particularly in historic riverbeds, stones play a more important role in the composition. The vineyards are planted overwhelmingly on the plains; very rarely on slopes that exceed 2%. There are very few of the hillside vineyards, that one might find, for example, in Chile.

A wine label might well bear the name of a province, a department or a town – or any combination of the three. Alternatively, it might bear the name of a specific region. To give some examples of these:

Viña de Santa Isabel
Chardonnay
Mendoza

gives just the name of the province.

TRUMPETER
Merlot
Tupungato

gives just the name of a department, within the Uco Valley in the Province of Mendoza.

TERRAZAS
Cabernet Sauvignon
Perdriel, Mendoza

has the name of the town, Perdriel, and the name of the province, but no mention is made of the department, Luján de Cuyo.

Let us look at the various provinces and their vineyards, beginning in the north:

North-West

Salta Province (2000 grape crop, 24,151 tons, 1% of national total). For the most part the vineyards of Salta Province are centred round the pretty town of Cafayate, in the extreme south-west of the province, some three hours drive from the capital Salta. This is along the valley of the Río de Las Conchas, through an arid canyon of sandstone eroded into monstrous shapes.

Cafayate is an oasis town in a desert irrigated by the River Calchaquí. Where there is irrigation, it is very fertile. It is also a very important tourist centre and an airport is currently being built, which should bring it closer to the rest of Argentina. There is an interesting wine museum in the town.

The valley is about 200 km long and stretches into the adjoining provinces of Catamarca and Tucumán. The town of Cafayate lies 1,660 m above sea level, but there are vineyards in the region up to the 2,000-metre mark. Annual rainfall is between 100 mm and

200 mm, with November, January and February being the most important months. The claim is that it is sunny 350 days in the year, but the temperature is never excessive; in the summer it averages up to 25°C and in the winter 10–15°C. The mean annual temperature is 15°C.

Currently, there are approximately 1,500 hectares of vineyards in the province, mainly shared by Michel Torino, Etchart and Peñalba Frías, but vineyard areas are being extended. More than 80% of the production is of white wine, with the Torrontés grape dominating. Indeed Torrontés de Cafayate is a local speciality. Cabernet Sauvignon is the main red grape.

Catamarca Province (2000 grape crop, 17,889 tons, 1% of national total). This is the Cinderella Province of Argentina, which has long been the political, almost feudal, stronghold of the Saadi family. It has, until recently, been a backwater as far as wine is concerned. However, the government some years ago granted tax concessions for the establishment of vineyards and this has led to the planting of substantial areas of vines in the extension of the Calchaquí Valley, some 80 km from Cafayate. Here in the Chañar Punco Valley, some 400 hectares have been planted by a consortium of the Lavaque family and Peñaflor. The vineyard is 2,000 m above sea level and is planted in a 150-metre broad band along the hillside. Only red wines, particularly Pinot Noir, are being produced.

In preparing the ground for the planting, three Indian cemeteries were discovered and these are being preserved as a feature. These vineyards produced their first wine in 1999.

Tucumán Province. The western boundary of this province includes part of the Calchaquí Valley, though plantings are at present minimal and do not register on any national statistics.

La Rioja Province (2000 grape crop, 113,957 tons, 5% of national total). In terms of production, this is the third most important province. Within it, there are three ranges of hills running from the north-west to the south-east. The most westerly valley, that of the Río Vinchín, has vineyards and one of the subsidiary cellars of the La Riojana Co-operative at Villa Unión. It is the next valley to the east, the Famantina Valley, between the Sierra de Famantina and the Sierra de Velasco, that is the centre of production of quality wine in the province. The most important centre is Chilecito, which takes its name from the number of miners who came from Chile to work in the local gold mines in the nineteenth century. The sub-regions within the valley include Chilecito, Anguignán, Maligasta, Nonogasta (where the Nacarí cellar is based), Sañogasta and Vichigasta.

The town of Chilecito lies 935 m above sea level and has a mean annual temperature of 18.6°C. Rainfall is low at about 130 mm a year.

Within the province, there is something over 5,300 hectares of vines, of which 80% are white and 60% of the total are Torrontés Riojano. Almost 80% of the production of the province is vinified by the La Riojana group of co-operative cellars.

Grapes are not only grown for wine, but also for the table and for raisins. This is also an area of olive and walnut orchards. There is a wine festival at Villa Unión every March.

Centre-West (Cuyo)

San Juan Province (2000 grape crop, 642,672 tons, 31% of national total). In some ways San Juan is the industrial centre of grape production. Historically, it is here that products, such as vermouths, 'sherries' and 'ports', have been made. It is also the centre for the production of grape concentrates and the table-grape industry. Because of all this, there are still considerable plantings of traditional, high-yielding varieties, such as the Criolla and the Cereza. In all, there are about 21,000 hectares of 'fine' grapes planted, of which more than 18,000 are white, including in descending order of importance, the Moscatel de Alejandría, the Pedro Gimenez, the Torrontés Sanjuanino and the Torrontés Riojano. Among the red varietals, the Italian Bonarda, Barbera and Nebbiolo are all important, as are the Syrah, Cabernet Sauvignon and Malbec. However, during the past few years certain producers have made an effort to plant more 'modern' varieties to appeal to a broader market. Another aspect of the traditional nature of the vineyards is that here, more than anywhere else in Argentina, the *parral*, or pergola, system of training the vines is used. This gives the grapes a greater degree of protection against the sun.

Most of the historical vineyards lie around the city of San Juan at about 630 m above sea level. This region is called the Valle de

Tulum. Further down the San Juan River is another growing region round the town of 9 de Julio, some 580 m above sea level. Perhaps the most exciting viticultural development in the province is in the El Pedernal valley, in the south of the province, lying almost as close to the city of Mendoza, as to San Juan. Here the vineyards are 1,350 m above sea level and some are planted on the lower slopes of the valley sides, as well as in the valley bottom. As a region, this has the potential to produce great wines.

Mendoza Province (2000 grape crop, 1,283,474 tons, 61% of national total). This is the heartland of the production of fine wine in Argentina. All but a handful of the major wineries are based in this province. The city of Mendoza was founded in 1561, but has, throughout its history suffered from earthquakes, with perhaps the most serious being on 20 March 1861. As a contemporary report says, 'Such was the resistless power, of the volcanic forces, that not a house or church, or even a shed, was left standing more than six feet above the surface of the ground. Out of a population of 12,000 human beings, 10,000 were instantaneously engulfed beneath the yawning foundations; and of 2,000 rescued, at least 1,500 sustained grievous injuries from the ponderous materials everywhere falling about them.'

The city, with its suburbs, now has a population of over 600,000 and has been attractively rebuilt, with wide pedestrian streets. There are a number of wine bodegas within the city itself that can be visited. That of Escorihuela is also a museum and houses an exceptional restaurant, with an outstanding wine list. At the end of February, each year, there is an important wine festival, which lasts a week. At that time hotels tend to fill up. Five miles out of the city, there is a major airport, with regular flights to Buenos Aires and Santiago in Chile.

The province has something over 72,000 hectares of vineyards. Production is split almost equally between red and white wines. Despite the fact that this is the centre of fine winemaking, lesser varieties, such as the Bonarda for red wines and the Pedro Gimenez for white, are the most widely planted. The Italian, and Spanish, varieties brought in by the immigrants, are still more important than fashionable novelties, such as Cabernet Sauvignon, Merlot and Chardonnay.

In the Province of Mendoza there are 16 major wine-producing departments, centred on the valleys of four rivers: the Mendoza and the Tunuyán, in the north, and the Diamante and the Atuel in the centre. For purposes of classification these have been divided into five regions, each of which might contain a number of subdivisions. In the following table, I have only mentioned some of the more important subdivisions; ones that are likely to appear on labels:

Región del Norte Mendocino (North Mendoza)

Departments

Las Heras	Lavalle

Subdivisions

El Borbollón	Los Coralitos
El Plumerillo	Costa de Araujo
	Nueva California

Región Zona Alta del Río Mendoza (Upper Mendoza River)

Departments

Godoy Cruz	Guaymallén	Luján de Cuyo	Maipú

Subdivisions

		Agrelo	Coquimbito
		Carrodilla	Russell
		Drummond	Cruz de Piedra
		Las Compuertas	Lunlunta
		Perdriel	Las Barrancas
		Potrerillas	
		Ugarteche	
		Vistalba	

Región del Este Mendocino (East Mendoza)

Departments

San Martín	Junín	Rivadavia	Santa Rosa	La Paz

Subdivisions

	Medrano	Palmira	Las Catitas	Alto de Salvador
	Las Chimbas			

Región del Valle de Uco (Uco Valley)

Departments

Tupungato	Tunuyán	San Carlos

Subdivisions

La Arboleda	Villa Seca	El Cepillo
Aguas Amargas	Vista Flores	Chilecito
	Las Rosas	
	Los Sauces	

Región del Sur Mendocino (South Mendoza)

Departments

San Rafael   General Alvear

Subdivisions

Las Paredes   Carmensa
Cuadro Benegas
El Cerrito
La Llave
Goudge
Rama Caída
Cañada Seca
Las Malvinas
Villa Atuel
Jaime Prats

North Mendoza. This region is to the north and east of the city of Mendoza in the valley of the Mendoza River. The altitude of the vineyards varies between 760 m above sea level at Las Heras to 542 m at Lavalle. The average temperatures range from 7°C in the winter to 25°C in the summer, with a mean of 15°C. The soils tend to be poor and they can have a salinity problem.

This is an area for the production of soft red wines from such varieties as the Bonarda and Sangiovese and lesser white wines from the Chenin Blanc and Ugni Blanc. Low acidities mean that they have to be drunk young.

Upper Mendoza River. This region is often called the central zone, for it is the traditional core of the Mendoza vineyards. Of the four departments that make up this region, two of them, Godoy Cruz and Guaymallén, have largely been absorbed into the sprawl of suburban Mendoza city. The only vines that remain are a handful at Bermejo. However, many of the most important wineries are based here. Indeed, this region is the home of more than 350 wineries, out of a suggested total of about 400 in the whole country. The other two departments, Luján de Cuyo and Maipú, constitute what is considered the *primera zona*. Luján is one of the country's two D.O.C.s and there are plans for Maipú to follow in its footsteps.

In all there are about 30,000 hectares of vines here, with the vineyards ranging from 900 m above sea level up to 1200 m. The annual mean temperature is 15°C, with an average rainfall of 250 mm. In many of the vineyards the soils are stony.

This is the classic region of the Malbec and many of the vines are more than 40 years old. The best wines come from the higher vineyards in Agrelo, Perdriel and Vistalba. Fine Cabernet Sauvignon, Syrah and Sangiovese are also made. For white wines, Sémillon is the classic varietal, though recent plantings of Chardonnay and Sauvignon have also been very successful.

East Mendoza. Within the province of Mendoza, this is the bulk wine producing area. Its 60,000 hectares of vineyards stretch along both banks of the Tunuyán River as it flows away to the south-east. The best vineyards lie to the west of the region. Medrano, at 710 m above sea level is the highest village in the area and probably produces the best wine. La Paz, lower down the valley lies at 560 m. To the west the soils are mainly sandy, but to the east they become deeper and richer. Yields here can be high. The average rainfall is 152 mm and the mean temperature 14.2°C.

The Uco Valley. There are many mysteries for me about the wines of Latin America, but one of the most puzzling is the reason as to why this is called the Uco Valley. There are three rivers running through it: the Tunuyán, the De Las Tunas and the San Carlos, but not the Uco. I can also find no trace of a town or village with this name.

Historically, this is an area of fruit orchards and whilst one of the three main wineries in the region dates back to 1915, it has had the field to itself until the creation of Lurton and Salentein in the past three years. Whilst there may be few wineries, this is where many of the best companies source their grapes.

At present there are about 9,000 hectares of vines, but the figure is increasing rapidly at the expense of orchards. Wine is apparently now a more viable crop than apples. The vineyards rise up to 1400 m, the highest in Mendoza, at Tupungato, and the lowest ones are at 900 m. Whilst the mean temperature is 14.2°C, there can be severe frosts during the winter. These apparently pose more of a problem to the fruit trees than they do to the vines.

The wines here tend to be high in natural acidity and this gives them an ageing potential that is lacking in so many of the wines of Argentina. The traditionally successful vines here have been the Malbec and the Sémillon, but new plantings concentrate more on such varieties as Chardonnay, Cabernet Sauvignon and Merlot. There has also been some success with Pinot Noir.

This area has the potential to be a producer of great wines.

South Mendoza. The vineyards of this region are separated from the rest of the province by 100 km of barren scrubland. From this the driver descends to the oasis of San Rafael. The region has two important rivers flowing through it: the Diamante and the Atuel. The vineyards lie between 450 m above sea level and 800 m. The rainfall is 350 mm a year and the mean temperature is 15°C, there are approximately 30,000 hectares of vines.

This is an area where the overall acreage of vineyards has declined considerably over the past few years. It is a region particularly reputed for its wines made from the Chenin Blanc. San Rafael was the first D.O.C. to be created in Argentina.

PATAGONIA

Río Negro Province (2000 grape crop, 12,005 tons, <1% of national total). Until recently, the vineyards of the Río Negro were proud to describe themselves as the most southerly in the world, but that title has now been wrested from them by those of Central Otago in New Zealand. The plantings in the province total 5,400 hectares and these are mainly situated in the long valley of the Río Negro. They are composed of three separate parts, the Alto Valle, the Valle Medio and the Valle Inferior, with 85% of the production being concentrated around the town of General Roca in the Alto Valle. There are also vineyards in the valley of the Río Colorado, which runs parallel north of the Negro. This is also an important area for orchards of apples, pears and quinces and, historically, cider has been widely drunk locally.

These vineyards are the least affected by the influence of the Andes and they lie between 200 and 300 m above sea level. Despite their southerly location, rainfall is surprisingly low, from 200 to 400 mm a year. For the most part the vineyards are flood-irrigated, through a system constructed by British engineers. It is difficult to realise that, if it were not for this irrigation, this would be a desert. One has only to cross the river to its south bank, where until now vineyards have not been planted, to see how arid the country really is. (Nicolás Catena has, however, purchased land and is in the process of planting a large estate here.)

In some ways the climate resembles that of European vineyards, with the grapes having higher natural acidity than elsewhere in the country. In addition over 60% of the vines are more than 25 years old. These are two reasons why the Río Negro has the potential to produce the best quality wines in the country. The main factor mitigating against its success, is its distance from any important market.

This is predominantly red wine country, with the most widely planted varieties being the Malbec, the Merlot and the Syrah. Some Pinot Noir is also grown, primarily for base wine for sparkling wines.

THE GRAPES

When considering the grape varieties grown in Argentina, there is almost the feeling that you are entering into a world of anarchy. It must also be taken into consideration that wine making is just one of the uses for grapes; there are considerable industries for table grapes, raisins and grape concentrate. These each have their own favoured varieties.

In the official government wine statistics for 1974, there are 30 different varieties listed for the production of red wine, 18 for the production of white and eight for rosé. In addition, grouped globally there are 3,200 hectares of vines listed as 'other varieties'. One cannot imagine what additional number is included here! To complicate things further a number of varieties are quoted together. Thus we have the Malbec (Verdot), the Pinot Blanco (Chenin) and the Sirah (Balsamina). In Argentina, things are not always what they seem to be.

Since then, there appears to have been an effort to tidy things up somewhat. The latest list that I have has cut down the numbers to 14 for red wines, 11 for white wines and one for rosé. Interestingly, the variety that accounted for almost 30% of the total area in 1974, the Criolla Grande, has now totally disappeared! Given the lowly reputation that this variety has, it may well be that there has been some sanitising of the lists for foreign enquirers.

It is clear, however, that whilst Chile, for example, has concentrated its efforts, historically, for export markets, on just four grape varieties, Argentina has had a much more pragmatic approach and has made a very broad variety of wines. In addition, whilst in Chile the varieties have primarily been French, as result of the bourgeois international aspirations of those who established the major wine estates in the nineteenth century, in Argentina the grape varieties have been influenced more by the nationality of the immigrants, primarily Italian and Spanish. It can be said that the Argentine wine industry has its roots much closer to the soil.

For international selling, countries now seem to try to concentrate their efforts on 'signature' grape varieties, thus California has its Zinfandel, South Africa its Pinotage and Uruguay the Tannat. Argentina is richly endowed with possibilities, but seems to have chosen the Malbec for red wines and the Torrontés for white wines.

Of the approximately 100,000 hectares of vines in Argentina planted in 'fine' vines, about 48% are for white wines, 43% for red wines and 9% for rosé wines.

Red varieties

Bonarda (12,423 hectares). Despite the fact that this is the most widely planted quality red grape in Argentina, there is surprisingly little information about it. One of the reasons for this is that many of the vines are very old and there is some confusion as to what they really are. There is no doubt that there has been some inter-mingling with the Barbera, which gives a higher class of wine.

The Bonarda originally comes from Piedmont in Italy and gives light fruity wines, which are often best served chilled. One can therefore see the appeal that it might have in Argentina.

Malbec, Malbeck (10,314 hectares). This varietal, which in Argentina is often spelt with an additional k at the end, has a long history. It was the basis of the wines of the *Haut Pays* that were brought down-river in the middle ages to add substance to the wines of Bordeaux. Under the name of Cot, or Auxerrois, it is the base grape for the wines of Cahors.

Whilst in France it has now become something of a marginal variety, in Argentina it has been selected as the choice variety to front the image of red wines. How has this come about? There is little doubt that in Argentina, the grapes obtain a degree of ripeness that is just not possible in France. This means that they do not have the harsh tannins that they regularly have in their home country. Fully ripe Malbec is a very versatile grape; it blends well with other varieties, such as the Cabernet Sauvignon, but also can stand alone either with oak treatment or without.

Malbec existed in Argentina as long ago as 1861, for there are vines going back to that date, still existing in a vineyard at Las Heras just north of the city of Mendoza. How did they get there? It is known that the Chilean government imported a broad range of French vines in 1850, at a time when the trade links between Mendoza and Santiago were very close. Alternatively, they may have come straight to Mendoza, when the provincial governor ordered the French viticulturalist Pouget to import a selection of 'interesting' vines.

In Argentina, this variety is probably at its most successful in Mendoza Province in Luján de Cuyo, Cruz de Piedra and Vistalba. It has also been successfully planted in Bolivia, Peru, Uruguay and Chile.

There are also about 5,000 hectares of Fer in Argentina, which is a clone of the Malbec.

Tempranilla, Tempranillo (5,009 hectares). Whilst this is the great red variety of Spain, in Argentina it rarely plays a quality role. This may be because, as a variety, it is relatively low in acidity. In the challenging climate of the Rioja, in Spain, this may not pose problems, particularly when it is blended with other varieties, such as Mazuelo and Graciano, but in the heat of Argentina, it may lose whatever character it has.

Cabernet Sauvignon (4,942 hectares). As in many countries, this is considered to be the top red variety for quality red wines and is widely grown, particularly in Mendoza and Salta. Again in Argentina it benefits from an extra ripeness which it often does not achieve in its native Bordeaux. It particularly benefits from barrel ageing and is a useful constituent in blends, especially with Malbec.

Sangiovese (2,867 hectares). This is the variety behind many of Italy's top wines, including Chianti. Sadly, in Argentina, it rarely has a quality image – indeed, for long, it was confused with the Lambrusco. One of the problems is that it can give large yields with little effort and, as a result, appears disguised as such products as 'Beaujolais'.

Syrah, Sirah (2,571 hectares). Until comparatively recently this variety was confused in Argentina with the Balsamina and the two names were used indiscriminately. However, the true Balsamina is a synonym for the Bonarda. Nothing is simple in the world of ampelography! Better clones of Syrah have now been introduced into Argentina and it produces, particularly in Mendoza Province, a number of fine straight varietal wines.

Merlot (2,482 hectares). The international popularity of the wines from this grape has led to increased planting in Argentina. Often it is blended with the Cabernet Sauvignon and/or Malbec. Perhaps the finest straight varietal wines come from cooler regions, such as Tupungato or the Río Negro Valley.

Barbera (d'Asti) (1,125 hectares). This is yet another variety that has been confused with the Bonarda. Whilst it is true that they both originally come from Piedmont, the Barbera produces superior wines there. In Argentina, it is generally blended and is grown mainly in San Rafael, in the south of Mendoza Province.

Pinot Negro (668 hectares). The Pinot Noir is a comparative newcomer to Argentina as, generally speaking, the climate is too hot for it to show its maximum complexity. However, with the development of cooler areas, such as Tupungato and Río Negro, it is becoming more widely appreciated.

Nebbiolo (176 hectares). This variety was brought to Argentina by immigrants from its native Piedmont. Sadly, it rarely produces wines of top quality and is generally used for blending purposes.

Cabernet Franc (128 hectares). Used again largely as a blending agent, this grape reaches degrees of ripeness in Argentina that it does not often achieve in its native France. As a straight varietal, therefore, it lacks some of the herbaceousness that one might expect.

Amongst the red grape varieties grown in lesser proportions are the

Tannat, the Verdot and the Cinsaut. The first two were historically planted together with the Malbec and were often sold as such. The grape known as Lambrusco in Argentina is, in fact, another Italian grape variety, the Refosco.

Three of the most widely planted varieties in Argentina, the Criolla Grande, the Criolla Chica and the Cereza, have not been mentioned at all. These are all used for the production of ordinary table wine and provide the raw material for the concentrated must business.

White varieties

Pedro Gimenez (19,684 hectares). The experts finally seem to have come to the conclusion that whatever the grape variety is, it is not the Pedro Jiménez, as grown in Andalucía in Spain. Interestingly, though, it, and not the Palomino, is used for the production of Argentine 'sherries'!

Widely planted, and boring, it tends to oxidise easily and is mainly used for everyday 'table' wines and turning into concentrate.

Torrontés (9,482 hectares). There are three members of this family grown in Argentina: the Torrontés Riojano, the Torrontés Mendocino and the Torrontés Sanjuanino. Whilst they are all closely related, it is thought that, at best, they are distant cousins of the variety of the same name grown in Galicia in Spain. Of the three the Riojano is the most widely planted and is responsible for giving what is generally considered to be the best wine under this label, from Cafayate in Salta Province. It is possible that it is a South American adaptation of the Spanish Malvasía grape.

It gives wines with a distinctive flavour, marrying Muscat-style flavours to dryness. At its best, it has very floral characteristics. One of the problems with this variety is that it tends to over-crop, so pruning has to be severe and irrigation ungenerous.

The Argentines have decided that this gives 'the' distinctive white wine from their country and are seeking to promote it as such. Because of its very pronounced flavours, however, it is difficult to match with food other than some oriental dishes.

Moscatel de Alejandría (9,154 hectares). It is interesting that in a number of countries in South America, the white wines drunk locally have a solid base of Moscatel wine. Such is the case in Argentina. With the possible exception of one or two 'Late Harvest' wines, the grape rarely is found in a quality wine.

Ugni Blanc (3,930 hectares). In Europe this is considered to be a supremely boring grape, largely good for little else than distillation. However, its outstanding characteristic, its acidity, stands it in good stead in Argentina where, in blends, it can counteract the inherent flabbiness of most white wines. This acidity also gives it a role to play as a base wine for sparkling wine.

Chenin Blanc (acreage uncertain). Whilst this is considered to be the most widely planted quality white wine grape in Argentina, it is one about which there is a great deal of confusion. For many years it was sold as Pinot Blanc and now much is sold as Pinot (sic.) de la Loire. The best wines probably come from around San Rafael in South Mendoza. They tend to be dry, fragrant and fruity.

Chardonnay (2,649 hectares). As in every New World wine-producing country, the Chardonnay has come into its own during the past decade. Interestingly though, there is less than half the acreage that there is in Chile. It is, however, to be considered the most 'noble' variety and is mainly sold as a straight varietal wine and as a base for sparkling wines. Tupungato is perceived to be the area where the best wines are made.

Sémillon (1,280 hectares). It is only recently that this grape has come into its own in Argentina. For long its name was synonymous with cheap, low quality wines. Now some excellent wines are being produced in the Río Negro and Luján de Cuyo.

Tocai Friuliano (1,032 hectares). This variety is considered by some leading ampelographers to be the same as the Sauvignonasse, for so long confused with Sauvignon Blanc in Chile. It would be interesting to know if the variety came from Argentina to Chile or vice versa. Perhaps neither is the case! It is a native of north-east Italy and may well have arrived in Argentina with immigrants from there. Generally speaking, it is used for white-wine blends, though it is occasionally made as a straight varietal.

Sauvignon Blanc (699 hectares). Though this is not very widely planted, it is perceived in Argentina to be a premium varietal. Generally it is harvested before peak ripeness so as to maintain sufficient acidity in the wine.

Riesling (158 hectares). Riesling as a grape name is probably the most abused in the world. In Argentina, where there is a great deal of confusion about many grape names, it is scarcely surprising that Riesling is one of them. Somewhere amongst what passes under that name, there is some genuine Rhineriesling, but the proportion is probably small.

Amongst the other grape varieties that are grown, the Gewürztraminer is considered as raw blending material for rosé wine, though there are some straight varietal wines made, notably from fruit grown in Tupungato. Amongst the more interesting recent arrivals is the Viognier, which appears to be capable of producing great wines in the favourable climate of Argentina.

THE WINES

The first thing that must be said about the wines of Argentina is that, whilst more white wine might be produced than red, the red wines tend to be more interesting than the whites. This may be because, with strict currency controls in the decade up to 1990, it was very difficult to buy modern winery equipment. In a hot country, such as Argentina, it is also much easier to make fine red wine than it is to make fine white wine. Similarly, the historical white grape varieties of the country, Pedro Gimenez and Ugni Blanc, produce very boring wines. Yes, there is plenty of Torrontés and Moscatel de Alejandría, but unblended they produce such powerfully flavoured wines that it is difficult to drink any quantity of them.

We must also not forget that the history of the wine trade in Argentina for the past 30 years has been a roller-coaster ride. It was able to rely on a thriving domestic market, with one of the highest per capita consumption figures in the world. It could also rely on export markets, such as Eastern Europe, which would absorb vast quantities of basic bulk wine. Japan, too, needed such wines for stretching out its own domestic product. The area under vines grew to keep pace with demand from markets that were undemanding as far as quality was concerned. In 1976, for example, the country exported 42 million litres of table wine in bulk at an average price of 10.9c per litre; the previous year, the average price had been 16.2c. On the internal market, the wholesale price of a litre of wine in 1982 was, in real terms, a seventh of what it had been 10 years earlier. The whole wine industry was in a catastrophic state.

Given these circumstances, it is not surprising that there was a dramatic decrease in the area under vines, from a peak of 350,680 hectares in 1977 to 209,102 hectares in 1989. Since then the figure has not changed much. The result is that a leaner wine trade is having to work harder to make a living. However, by arriving late as a 'New-World' producer, Argentina has been able to learn from other people's mistakes. It has been able to move smoothly to the latest techniques. One example of this is the use of inner-stave treatment for the 'oaking' of wines. This is widespread in Argentina, whereas the use of oak chips seems to be much less general than it is in Chile, for example.

Argentina suffers from one major problem that is current throughout South America. The wines that the locals drink are, for the most part, not acceptable in international markets. Both during my latest visit to Argentina and the subsequent Argentine generic tasting in London, I was offered wines that may have been highly regarded in Argentina, but were undrinkable in Europe. It does not need a great deal of research to find out what markets are looking for. As the Australian writer Alan Young says in his *Wine Routes of Argentina* (1998), 'It has been heartening to observe this industry during this last decade when it moved from the darkest night to the dawning of a new tomorrow. Although a number of traditional bodegas produce a different style of wine, more than 95% of the 1,485 professional wineries registered with the National Institute of Vitiviniculture (I.N.V.), still produce what could rightly be called *old-fashioned* style wines. Some could be classified as 18th century wines.'

What role does the vintage play in the wines of Argentina? This is a subject that I have deliberately avoided throughout this book. Some years ago, I was asked by a publisher to research a book on the question of vintages around the world. (This is one of a number of projects that I have been involved in, which has not come to fruition.) As a result, I wrote to a number of worldwide official bodies. By chance, I have just discovered the reply I received in September 1977 from Mario Rodriguez, then Director of the I.N.V. in Mendoza: 'With regard to your question as to the variations in quality between the different vintages, I can tell you that given the climatic conditions we have in the wine regions of Argentina, the quality does not differ fundamentally from one crop to another as happens in some European countries. Because of this it is not usual to mention the vintage on the label.'

Since then, international demand has meant that the vintage is generally mentioned on the labels of all wines for export. It is still probably true to say that, in most cases there is little difference between the vintages, either from year to year, or from region to region. There are, however, notable exceptions. Once of these was 1998, the year of El Niño. In Cafayate, in the north of Argentina, it was an outstanding year; in Mendoza, on the other hand, Las Terrazas were so disappointed with the quality that it sold no wine under its label bearing that vintage.

A number of forward-looking producers are now making one style for the domestic and South American markets, and a more appealing, international style, for the export markets of Asia, Europe, North America and the Pacific countries. A smaller group has switched to only one style for all markets but these wines may come in different labels for different countries.

Where the country has been wise, or perhaps just lucky, is that it has been able to select two varieties, the Malbec and the Torrontés, with which it can attack the world markets and offer something distinctive. Furthermore, in such grapes as the Bonarda, the Sangiovese, the Tempranillo and the Nebbiolo, it can draw on its European roots to offer a broad range of New-World wines that are distinctly different from the Big Four French varietals that everyone else seems to be offering.

Argentina has happily embraced the teachings of a succession of foreign experts, such as the Frenchman Michel Rolland in the field of winemaking and Richard Smart in vineyard techniques. They have been eager to learn. However, I foresee one potential problem. So many flying winemakers are now being sent out to Argentina that they may well make standard wines in which the Argentine character is subsumed. In the long run, this could do the country much harm, if a new source turns up which can provide such wines cheaper. Fortunately, though, there is little evidence that Argentine wineries are being forced to compete in price with the wines of Chile, for example.

What then is different about the wines of Argentina? As far as the red wines are concerned, many of the varieties could be described as being rustic. This means that they often have natural tannins which give them the ability to last. One gets the impression that all Chilean wines are made for immediate consumption as soon as they are released. On the other hand in Argentina, there are many Malbecs and Malbec blends that will benefit from further bottle ageing.

I am the fortunate possessor of a quadruple magnum of Trapiche Milenium 1955, as far as I am aware, a one-off 70% Cabernet Sauvignon/30% Merlot blend, aged for 14 months in new French oak before bottling. If ever there was a wine destined for a long life, I imagined that it was this. However, when I visited the winery in August 2000, they expressed surprise when I said that I had not yet opened it. I hope that it is not over the top when I do finally take the expensive decision to draw the cork!

In Argentina, I do not think that I tasted any wines more than five years old, but traditional companies, such as Lopez and Weinert, still offer on their price lists older wines than that. The excellent Mendoza restaurant, 1884, still offers a Cabernet Sauvignon 1992 from Goyenechea at $16 a bottle and a 1991 from Cicchitti at $22. Malbecs of a similar age are also available at a similar price. This would suggest that older wines are appreciated and that a high price does not necessarily come with age.

Are there the same icon wines in Argentina that are receiving so much hype in Chile? The answer is that super-premium wines do exist and that newcomers, such as Salentein, are trying to raise the stakes with wines, such as Primus. Other wineries, which appear to have high-flying prices include Finca La Anita and Luigi Bosca with their Finca Los Nobles range. In the same restaurant the most expensive wine is Catena Zapata 1990, a Cabernet/Malbec/Merlot blend. It may be that this is a wine released from personal reserves, as the restaurant is in cellars belonging to the Catena Group! (An interesting footnote at the beginning of 1884's wine list says, 'Wines whose price is above $40 a bottle will be served from a Riedel decanter into Riedel glasses. Otherwise this will cost $3 per person'.)

Perhaps as a generalisation, it might be said that the best red wines of Chile are well-honed and smooth, whilst those of Argentina tend to have a more individual personality, but there is some truth in it. In the end, it depends what appeals to you!

I have already suggested that I have reservations about the Torrontés as much more than a novelty grape variety. Whilst it has a fresh, fruity appeal to the novice wine drinker, it is difficult to take it too seriously. Can a Torrontés be a great wine? I doubt it.

As in Chile, even the best white wines do not seem to be as highly valued, or as highly priced as the reds. There are now some excellent Chardonnays coming out of cooler regions, such as Tupungato and Río Negro. There is no doubt that the availability of French barrels and grapes with sufficient acidity, is helping growers, such as Salentein to make great wines.

However, the white grape that appears to me to have the greatest potential is the Viognier. Whilst plantings are at the moment limited, those wines that I have tasted have shown intense varietal characteristics. This may be a future winner for Argentine wine-makers.

Like most New-World wines, those of Argentina can be relied on to be sound. They have the climate to see that the grapes are sufficiently ripe and enough new equipment has been bought in the past decade to ensure that the wines are well made. What is more, most of the wines are not in the common mould; they are different. Why select a Cabernet Sauvignon, when a Malbec has just as much character? In many ways, at the moment, Argentina is the most exciting wine country in Latin America.

THE WINERIES

Adunka S.A., Mendoza. This was founded by Guillermo and Juan Adunka some 50 years ago. Their estate consists of vineyards in Maipú where they grow a broad range of varietals including Chenin Blanc, Torrontés and Riesling for white wines and Bonarda, Tempranillo and Cabernet Sauvignon for red wines.

La Agrícola, Mendoza. In 1963 Alberto Zuccardi obtained the rights in Argentina for a new form of irrigation that had recently been introduced in California. In order to demonstrate this effectively, he bought an estate at Fray Luis Beltrán in Maipú and planted a vineyard. Now under the guidance of his son José Alberto, the company has been built up into one of the most dynamic in the Argentine wine trade, now claiming, for example to be the top-selling winery in Britain, having only begun to export as late as 1991.

José Alberto believes that good wine is made in the vineyard and here his ideas are at variance with many of his competitors. For example, he is a proponent of the traditional pergola system of training the vines, rather than on low wires. When I say that he is a proponent of the pergola system, he has a modified *parral* system, which lets more light get through to the leaves and gives better ventilation. Whilst machine harvesting is impossible, he believes that the extra cost is outweighed by better quality. His vines are also netted as a protection against hail damage. This, he believes, delays the harvest date by no more than four days.

Fifty hectares of his estate are being grown organically and he will be offering organic wines from six different varietals with the 2001 vintage.

Whilst Argentina must have one of the broadest range of grape varieties in the world, at La Agrícola, they are not frightened of extending the range and have trial plantings of Grenache, Mourvèdre, Tannat, Aglianico and Zinfandel.

The winery, is also ultra-modern, having been rebuilt in 1998. Equipment includes rotary fermenters, micro-oxygenation is used for red wines and skin maceration for the whites, while a number of wines are made with carbonic maceration.

Total production is now running at over 700,000 cases a year with two-thirds being sold on export markets.

As well as the home estate of 170 hectares at Fray Luis Beltrán, in 1973 the Zuccardi family bought another estate to the east at Santa Rosa. Here, in the middle of the desert, they have a further 400 hectares planted out of the thousand available. This vineyard has its own crushing facility. On certain markets, the Santa Rosa wines are sold under their own label of **Santa Rosa Estate**. Another label of this vineyard is **Santa Julia Vineyards**.

Wines I have particularly enjoyed: Malbec/Cabernet Sauvignon 1999.
Other brands: Santa Julia, Santa Rosa Estate, Q-Familia Zuccardi.

Viñas del Alto Salvador SAVAIC, Morón, Lavalle. This impeccably clean winery, just north of Mendoza City, has 20 hectares of vines and has set out to achieve full organic status for its wines. Only red wines are produced. This should be achieved for the 2002 vintage.

Wines I have particularly enjoyed: Sangiovese 2000.

Finca la Altura, Catamarca, see **Bodegas Lavaque.**

Bodega Finca la Anita, Alta Agrelo, Luján de Cuyo, Mendoza. This small winery has for long provided grapes, particularly Syrah to other wineries, but recently the brothers Antonio and Manuel Mas took the decision to create their own wines and brands. The vineyards are managed ecologically and the intention is to have recognition as organic winemakers. Production is small, amongst their first releases are two wines under a private label for the Argentine Quarter-Horse Association.

Anubis, see **Vintage S.A.**

Viña Amalia, Mendoza. In some ways this is as close as one comes to a boutique winery in Argentina. In 1996 the Basso family sold its interests in the large Santa Ana winery to Santa Carolina in Chile and bought a small winery, which had fallen into disrepair, at Carrodilla, just outside Mendoza city. This has been totally restored and now has all the latest equipment with storage capacity of 60,000 litres in stainless steel and 180 oak barrels. Production is anticipated to be about 30,000 cases a year.

As well as buying in grapes, the company owns two estates. Finca La Amalia lies 120 km south of Mendoza at Altamira, some 1,050 m above sea level, on light sandy soil. Here there are 52 hectares of Cabernet Sauvignon, planted in 1970 and 17 hectares of recently planted Malbec. The Finca Los Montes Negros is at Tunuyán in the Uco Valley, at some 1,150 m above sea level. The soil is alluvial with stones. Here there are 200 hectares planted and just coming into production. The varieties are, for red wines: Cabernet Sauvignon, Malbec, Syrah, Merlot, Pinot Noir and Petit Verdot and for white wines: Chardonnay, Sauvignon Blanc and Viognier.

Wines I have particularly enjoyed: Chardonnay, Maipú, 1999, Malbec Luján de Cuyo 1999, Finca La Amalia Cabernet Sauvignon 1998.

Allied Domecq Argentina S.A., see Bodegas Balbi.

Alta Vista, Luján de Cuyo, Mendoza. Jean-Michel Arcaute, the owner of Château Clinet, in Pomerol, has broad horizons. He was one of the first foreigners to invest in Hungary's Tokay region and in 1997 he purchased some old Malbec vineyards in Agrelo, Luján de Cuyo and a winery dating back to the last century in Chacras de Coria. He now has an estate of approximately 60 hectares of old Malbec and Cabernet Sauvignon vines.

Monsieur Arcaute is deliberately making wines to last and his opening wines, from the 1998 vintage, reflect this. He has a range of three red wines, a Malbec, which is partly aged in new oak, a Cosecha, which receives no barrel treatment and the Alto, which retails at about £25. This last is a Malbec 80%/Cabernet Sauvignon 20% blend aged in new French oak for 18 months.

Wines I have particularly enjoyed: Alta Vista Alto 1998.

Antic Vinos, Mendoza. This company is based at Dorrego and has a very modern winery. It has just launched a range of easy-to-drink varietal wines on the British market, under the brand Enough Z.

Leoncio Arizu S.A., Mayor Drummond, Luján de Cuyo, Mendoza. This is one of the great family wineries of Argentina. In 1890, Leoncio Arizu arrived in Mendoza from Navarra in Spain and established a winery in the city in 1906. Another branch of the family owned vineyards at Villa Atuel in the south of the province and, for a time, owned what was the largest single vineyard in the world. Now only the ruins of the winery remain.

Leoncio Arizu now owns 650 hectares of vineyards, spread between six different sites in Luján de Cuyo and Maipú. Annual sales are approximately 150,000 cases, with two-thirds being on the domestic market. The winemaker is Alberto Arizu.

One reason for unfamiliarity of the company name is the fact that its wines are largely sold under the brand name Luigi Bosca. One wine of which it is proud is the Finca Los Nobles Cabernet Bouchet, which is aged on Tronçais oak for 24 months.

Other brands: Luigi Bosca, Señor del Robledal, Finca la Linda, Finca Los Nobles, Viña Paraíso.

Arriero, see **Resero S.A.**

Bodegas Balbi, San Rafael, Mendoza. This winery at Las Paredes, some 5 km from the pleasant country town of San Rafael, was established in 1930 by Juan Balbi. In 1992 it was taken over by the British multinational Allied-Domecq, which has invested considerable sums in new equipment. The winery has a dual image, for in Argentina the wines are sold under a French image as Calvet and Maison Calvet, whilst in export markets they are sold with the Argentine name Balbi. Effective exporting started as recently as 1995, with sales in the first year totalling 8,000 cases.

The name Calvet has a long history on the Argentine market. Originally, it had a bodega in Mendoza and used to send its wines in bulk to Buenos Aires for bottling. The bodega was then sold and the brand franchised out to a distributor, Hudson Ciovini y Cía., who used to purchase the wine in bottle from a number of producers. Now the brand is firmly back in the hands of the company, with Bordeaux winemaker, Jean-Louis Brun, coming over at vintage time.

The company has approximately 100 hectares of its own vineyards, many of them directly around the winery and also buys in grapes locally and from Tupungato in the Uco Valley. Capacity of the winery has now been built up to 5.6 million litres and there is a cask hall with 400 barrels of French and American oak. Annual sales are now running at approximately 400,000 cases, of which 45% are to export markets.

Basically the Calvet line runs in parallel with that of Balbi. However, on the domestic market there is an additional range under the name of Petigny, which includes a tank-fermented sparkling wine. At present this is produced elsewhere, but the intention is to eventually make it in house. A premium red wine is now being sold under the name of Barbaro. This is basically a Bordeauxish style blend, with the constituents varying from year to year. The 1997 vintage consisted of Cabernet Sauvignon 70%, Malbec 13% and the balance Shiraz and Merlot; in the 1999 vintage, the blend was Cabernet Sauvignon 50%, Merlot 20%, Malbec 20% and Shiraz 10%. Half of the wine is fermented in barrel and half in stainless steel, but it is aged 100% in new French oak.

Wines I have particularly enjoyed: Chardonnay, San Rafael 2000,

Bonarda Luján de Cuyo 1999, Malbec 1999, Shiraz Tupungato/San Rafael 1999 (in the USA and Canada, this is sold as Syrah), Shiraz Barrel Reserve 1999, Barbaro 1999.

Other brands: Calvet, Maison Calvet, Petigny.

Jorge Luis Balbo S.A., Los Alamos, Maipú, Mendoza Senor Balbo has 100 hectares of vines and has historically sold most of his wine to a major supermarket chain. When this was taken over by the Carrefour group, he lost the business and therefore he decided to sell his entire 2000 crop, as grapes to the Medrano Co-op (q.v.).

Cavas Banyuls S.A., Luján de Cuyo, Mendoza. This company has the 30-hectare estate of Finca Don Joaquín at Russell in Maipú and has recently planted 10 hectares of Chenin Blanc at Barrancas. In addition it buys in grapes. At the moment very little of its production is exported and it specialises in making soft, easy-to-drink wines.

Other brands: Pontigny.

Valentín Bianchi S.A.C.I.F., San Rafael, Mendoza. As you drive into San Rafael from Mendoza, on the left-hand side of the road, at Alto de Las Paredes, you see the magnificent fountains and winery of the new Valentín Bianchi premises, built in 1996. Here are the reception facilities and stainless-steel storage, as well as a production centre for *méthode traditionelle* sparkling wines. (By law in Argentina, sparkling wine production, has to be in a separate building from still wine production.) This is a company that goes out of its way to welcome tourists and they receive 15,000 a year. In the centre of the town there is another bodega; for wood ageing. The total capacity of the two bodegas is 16 million litres.

Valentín Bianchi arrived in Argentina from his native Puglia in 1910 and appears to have had a broad range of entrepreneurial careers before he founded the wine company in 1928. He worked on the railways and in a bank, he was a builder and a pioneer in the timber business. He even established the local bus company. His first bodega was called El Chiche and his first wine labelled Super Médoc. The company is still run by his children and his grand-children.

The company has three separate vineyards around the town of

San Rafael, all between 700 and 750 m above sea level. Finca Alto Las Paredes and Finca Asti are on one side of the town and Finca Doña Elsa is at Rama Caída on the other side. There is a total of 230 hectares in production, with a broad range of varieties, including such novelties as the Caladoc, a Grenache × Malbec. The vineyards are now netted as a protection against hail, but, on the 'belt and braces' principle, there are still some hail-cannons among the vines!

On export markets, there are three levels of wine offered: Elsa, followed by Valentín Bianchi and at the summit, the Familia Bianchi Cabernet Sauvignon. Whilst all are sold as straight varietal wines, this last does, in fact, contain small percentages of Merlot and Malbec. In total the sales are 60% red wine and Malbec dominates its export sales. One enormously successful product that has been launched on the domestic market is New Age, a lightly carbonated Malvasia wine with 35 g residual sugar.

Annual sales of the company total about 650,000 cases, of which 20,000 cases are sparkling. This product was only launched about four years ago. Exports, mainly to Britain, the United States and Paraguay, account for no more than 10% of turnover. Whilst the wineries and the brands belong to the Bianchi family, distribution in Argentina, and certain other markets, is carried out by the Canadian multinational spirits company, Seagram

Wines I have particularly enjoyed: Valentín Bianchi Chardonnay 1999, Elsa Barbera 1998, Elsa Barbera 1999. Elsa Malbec 1998, Familia Bianchi Cabernet Sauvignon 1995, Familia Bianchi Cabernet Sauvignon 1997.

Bodegas y Viñedos Cabrini, Perdriel, Luján de Cuyo, Mendoza. This is quite a small company specialising in red wines. It has 36 hectares of its own vineyards and also buys in grapes from local growers.

Establecimiento Humberto Canale S.A., General Roca, Río Negro. The ways that companies arrive in the wine trade are many and diverse, but that of the Canale family is stranger than most. At the beginning of the century it owned one of the biggest biscuit and cake manufacturing companies in Argentina and one of its best-selling lines was *pannetoni*. In order to make sure of supplies of fruit, it took the decision to plant orchards and vineyards in northern Patagonia, in the valley of the Río Negro. Now the biscuit company is part of the Philip Morris empire, but the company owns 270 hectares of orchards (apples, pears and quinces) and 172 hectares of vineyards. There are two estates, on the main one, at General Roca, are the orchards and 150 hectares of vines; the other 22 hectares of vines lie lower down the river at Isabel.

This company is the pioneer of vineyards in Patagonia, for this is more traditionally an area of cider production, and consumption. It has now been joined by Catena and the French-owned Infinitus estate. The Canale estate is a community in the traditional Argentine manner, with full facilities supplied for the workers. There is also a museum of historic wine equipment.

The vineyards are run with IPM (integrated pest management) and the only non-organic treatment is with herbicide. The company has its own vine nursery and is experimenting with new material from France and Italy. Recent plantings include Viognier, Riesling, Sauvignon Gris and Tintorera Italiana; presumably destined for a broad range of uses! All the classic main varietals are also planted. Rather peculiarly, there is a plot of Merlot and Pinot Noir planted together. About a fifth of its requirements are bought in from local growers.

For winemaking, Humberto Canale is advised by Raúl de la Mota, the country's leading traditional winemaker, and, specifically for the British market, by Hans Vinding-Diers. Whether it is because of the coolest climate in Argentina or not, this company turns out some of the most exciting wines in the country. In the past it produced much more wine; its cellars have a storage capacity of 5 million litres, but less than half of this is currently being used. It has 250 barrels, mainly of American oak. Its top barrel-aged Cabernet Sauvignon is sold under the name Intimo.

Production is about 85,000 cases a year of which a quarter is exported, to Denmark, Britain, the United States, Canada and Switzerland. On the domestic market, sales are oriented to the off-trade, particularly through supermarket chains.

Wines I have particularly enjoyed: Sauvignon Blanc 2000, Merlot/Pinot Noir 1999, Merlot/Pinot Noir 2000, Merlot 1998, Malbec 1996.
Other brands: Marcus, Diego Murillo, Black River.

Familia Cassone, Mendoza. The Cassone family are now in its fourth generation in Argentina and have just made the change from being nothing more than grape-growers, to making and selling its own wines in bottle. It has 32 hectares of very old vines split between two vineyards in Mayor Drummond (Luján de Cuyo) and Lunlunta (Maipú). Its first wines, launched in 2000, were an oaked and an unoaked Malbec. It also has plantings of Cabernet Sauvignon and Chardonnay. The wines are sold under the labels Finca La Florencia and Obra Prima.

Bodegas Catena, Agrelo, Mendoza. The wine empire of Nicolás Catena in Argentina has three main wineries. This one, which used to be known as Bodegas Esmeralda, Escorihuela (q.v.) in Godoy Cruz and Bodega la Rural (Felipe Rutini) (q.v.) at Junín. The new winery is modelled on a Mayan pyramid and it rises out magnificently from the vineyards.

Nicolás is the third generation of his family in the wine trade. He studied oenology in California and was the first in Argentina to develop drip irrigation and is a big partisan of clonal selection. For example, for the Malbec, he has planted 130 different clones and made a short-list of 17, from which five or six will finally be used. He also works closely with Paul Hobbs, from Simi Winery in California. The resident winemaker is the inspired Pedro Marchevski, who is married to the equally inspired consultant winemaker, Susana Balbo.

This winery has holdings of 280 hectares in Mendoza, whilst, in all, the family controls 2,000 hectares. This winery produces wines solely for export markets under the brand names, in increasing order of quality, Argento, Alamos and Catena.

The Esmeralda name is still used widely on the domestic market, where it markets such wines as Valerrobles. It also has the single vineyard, old-vine Malbec, Finca Los Quiroga.

Wines I have particularly enjoyed: Argento Chardonnay 2000, Argento Malbec 2000, Catena Malbec 1997.

Alfredo V.A. Catena Luján de Cuyo. The Catena family is famous in the world of Argentine wine; Alfredo is a cousin of the better-known Nicolás. The company has 500 hectares of vines, split between the vineyards of La Misión and La Argentina, where the winery is situated. The winemaker is a Chilean, who was recruited from Chandon in Brazil!

Its wines have only been sold on the domestic market since 1995 and current production is about 100,000 cases a year using only its own grapes, sold under the brand name Alto Verde.

Wines I have particularly enjoyed: Sauvignon Blanc 1999.

Bodegas Chandon S.A., Agrelo, Mendoza This company is the dominant player in the Argentine sparkling wine business with, according to one of its competitors, between 70% and 80% of the business. It is also a major shareholder in the sister company in Brazil. A recent venture in Argentina is the premium winery **Las Terrazas** (q.v.).

Moët & Chandon came to study the Argentine market as early as 1958 and must have liked what it saw, for it built a winery at Agrelo the following year and began to buy vineyards. Now its domain extends to almost 500 hectares, with holdings south of the river Mendoza in Luján de Cuyo, in Maipú and Cruz de Piedra and, perhaps most importantly in the cooler climate areas of Tupungato and Vistalba.

The company makes both tank-fermented and bottle-fermented wines. The former is sold under the label Chandon and the latter as Baron B, presumably in honour of their first director in Argentina, Baron Betrand de Ladoucette.

How is the wine described on wine lists in Argentina, given that it is made by a subsidiary of one of the largest companies in Champagne, France? I quote from *Los Buenos Vinos Argentinos*, written by Enrique Queyrat in 1974. 'Although I do not like the word *champaña*, I am going to use it when speaking of M. Chandon, given that the company, ever respectful of laws justifiably imposed by the producers of Champagne, insist that one uses the word *champaña* and not *champagne*.'

As well as the sparkling wines the company makes a broad range of still wines, both straight varietals and blends.

Other brands: Renaud Poirier, Paul Galard, Comte de Valmont, Clos de Moulin, Castel Chandon.

Bodega J.A. Cicchitti, Rodeo de la Cruz, Mendoza. This is a small bodega whose speciality appears to be small batch production of individual wines, including bottle-fermented sparkling wines. Grapes are sourced from a number of producers around Mendoza.

Bodega J. Edmundo Navarro Correas S.A., Russell, Mendoza. Juan de Díos Correas planted vines in Mendoza as long ago as 1798. He subsequently became a governor of the province and was a close collaborator of General San Martín, a hero of independence in Chile as well as in Argentina. Various branches of the family are still involved in the production of wine, though the company is now part of the Diageo Group.

Navarro Correas began to sell wine under its own label less than 20 years ago. It has three estates: Don Javier (30 hectares) in Russell, Maipú; La Meme (100 hectares) in Las Barrancas; and, at Tupungato in the Uco Valley, Los Arboles (15 hectares). This last is 1,250 m above sea level and has Chardonnay, Sauvignon Blanc and Pinot Noir vines.

Rather strangely, the company also has three wineries and three winemakers; one each for red wines, white wines and sparkling wines. These last are all bottle-fermented.

Wines I have particularly enjoyed: Malbec Reserva Privada 1999.

Domaine Luis Segundo Correas, Medrano, Mendoza. This estate was founded in 1860 and has more than 300 hectares of vines in the prime locations of Medrano, Maipú and Luján de Cuyo. The winery has a capacity of 2.5 million litres and is well equipped with stainless-steel tanks and French and American oak barrels. There are two levels of wines; the higher is sold under the brand Luis Correas and the lower as Don Luis.

Bodegas y Viñedos Crotta, Palmira, Mendoza. This winery is in the Eastern Region, some 40 km south-east of the city of Mendoza and is one of those companies moving over from traditional products, such as fortified wines and *mistelas* for the domestic market, to more sophisticated wines for export markets. It has an estate of 300 hectares at Ramblon and this provides something over half of its needs. The winery has a capacity of 18 million litres.

Wines I have particularly enjoyed: Torrontés 1999, Tempranillo 1999.

Raul Davalos, Molinos, Salta. A small producer of an old vine

Malbec-Cabernet blend in what is claimed to be Argentina's highest, and remotest, winery.

Bodegas Escorihuela, Godoy Cruz, Mendoza. This company, established in 1884, is described by one Argentine wine writer as 'a complete tradition in wine'. Certainly the names of wines it sells have something traditional about them! Their names include San Julián (tipo Sauternes), Carcassonne and Pont l'Evèque. These have been long time leaders on the domestic market. The reds are aged in large oak vats. The company was bought some years ago by Nicolás Catena, who has transformed the winemaking but kept the old brand names.

The cellars are amongst the most beautiful in Argentina with more than 7 million litres capacity in oak vats, the largest of which was specially commissioned in France, in 1910. This holds 63,000 litres and is decorated with a carving of Dionysius and his court. The cellars are a major tourist attraction. They also house what is perhaps the best restaurant in Mendoza, Francis Mallman's 1884.

Bodegas Esmeralda, see **Bodegas Catena.**

Bodegas Etchart, Cafayate, Salta and **Perdriel, Luján de Cuyo, Mendoza.** This company, which is part of the French Pernod Ricard Group, has wineries and vineyards in two very distinct regions. In the northern province of Salta, it has a winery and 300 hectares of vines at Cafayate, on the La Florida ranch. These vineyards are some 1,700 m above sea level. Here 60% of the production is of Torrontés, with the balance being made up of Chardonnay, Malbec, Cabernet Sauvignon, Merlot, Chenin Blanc, Sauvignon and Pinot Blanc. This winery is very much on the tourist route, and it receives about 30,000 visitors a year.

The vineyards are laid out to support the local fauna with pots of water among the vines for the foxes (this also deters them from chewing the irrigation pipes) and spent *marc* spread out for the birds. The yields here are 20 tonnes to the hectare for the Torrontés and no more than 12 for the other varieties. The wines are made under the supervision of the ubiquitous Michel Rolland. This winery has a capacity of 11 million litres and 800 French oak barrels.

The Santa Teresa ranch in Perdriel, Mendoza, is altogether on a smaller scale. It has just 50 hectares of vines in production at the moment, mostly Malbec, though there is also some Tempranillo, Merlot, Cabernet Sauvignon, Chardonnay and Chenin. They lie between 800 and 1000 m above sea level. The winery has a capacity of 5 million litres, all in bulk. No casks are used here.

Total annual sales are about 700,000 cases on the domestic market and 300,000 cases on export markets. Its top wine, a 50% Malbec/50% Cabernet Sauvignon blend aged in new French oak for 18 months, is sold under the name Arnaldo B. Etchart.

Wines I have particularly enjoyed: Oak aged Chardonnay 1999, Torrontés 2000, Arnaldo B. Etchart 1997.
Other brands: Río de Plata.

Fabre Montmayou/Domaine Vistalba, Vistalba, Luján de Cuyo, Mendoza. This winery, just north of the Mendoza River in Vistalba, was established by Hervé Joyaux Fabre, from Bordeaux in 1992. Here he has 80 hectares of vines, some of them more than 50 years old. Whilst the wines were initially aimed at export markets, they can now also be found in Argentina.

They sell a range of varietal wines, Chardonnay, Merlot, Malbec and Cabernet Sauvignon and a premium barrel-aged blend Grand Vin, which is based on Malbec, with some Merlot and Cabernet.

The company also has 110 hectares of vineyards, based around Allen, in the Río Negro Province in Patagonia. From here mainly dual varietals are sold: Chardonnay/Sémillon, Cabernet/Merlot and Malbec/Syrah, under the brand **Infinitus.**

Wines I have particularly enjoyed: Fabre Montmayou Merlot 1997, Infinitus Malbec/Syrah 1997.

Jesus Carlos Fantelli e Hijos, San Martín, Mendoza. This company has an estate of 150 hectares on the plain to the south-east of the city of Mendoza. It also buys in grapes, to produce a range of sound low-priced varietal, and dual-varietal, wines. Guest winemakers have included Englishman David Cowderoy and Australian Ross Whiteford.

FeCoVita, Maipú, Mendoza. Whilst co-operative cellars in Europe have largely managed to slough off their image of old-fashioned equipment and uninteresting wines, for the most part this is not the case in Argentina. This organisation is the Argentine co-op of co-ops and, as such claims to be the largest winery in the country and the fifth largest in the world. The wines that I have tasted, I have noted as being old-fashioned. In Britain they are sold under the brand name Valdéz.

Finca Flichman S.A., Barrancas, Maipú, Mendoza. This is a winery with a complex history. It was originally founded in 1893, but was bought in 1910 by Sami Flichman, a Jew with interests in the clothing industry in Buenos Aires. He and his son Isaac, who went to France to study oenology, literally built up the vineyards, by bringing ox-cart loads of soil to lay over what had been the bed of a river. They also built up the image of the winery by creating the brand Caballero de la Cepa.

In 1983, Flichman was taken over by the Wertheim Group, with interests in banking and general commerce. In 1998, it sold the company to the Sogrape Group, with wide wine interests in Portugal, including Mateus Rosé. The Bacardi Group has also come in as minority shareholders. The new owners have immediately put in place a five-year investment programme, which will total approximately US$12 million. One of the first results of this is a new state-of-the-art winery at Barrancas. There has also been investment in the planting of new vineyards.

In all the company has an estate of almost 850 hectares, but of these, 300 are planted in vines. There are two vineyards: the larger one in Barrancas and the second in the cooler climate zone of Tupungato.

Sales, at the moment are running at about 850,000 cases a year, with a quarter of the production being exported to more than 20 different markets. It is one of the top five exporters of Argentine wines. It has a broad range of brands including Aberdeen Angus, made under licence from the cattle society of that breed. (This was previously made by Goyenechea.)

Wines I have particularly enjoyed: Reserva Chardonnay 1999.
Other brands: Caballero de la Cepa, Claire, Jubilé.

Goyenechea y Cía., Villa Atuel, Mendoza. This family company was established in Buenos Aires by the brothers Santiago and Narciso Goyenechea, who had emigrated to Argentina from the Basque region of Spain. The estate that they established at Villa Atuel, south of San Rafael, in the south of Mendoza Province, was named La Vasconia, in honour of their roots. It now has fourth and fifth generations of the family working in the company.

La Vasconia is a very traditional estate with most of the workers having lived there for generations. There are currently about 100 hectares of vines planted on mainly sandy, alluvial soil. Historically the vineyards were more than four times this size, but production is now concentrated on quality rather than quantity.

The Goyenechea family is a fierce supporter of the D.O.C. status for wines and San Rafael is one of the two areas currently to have it. One of the very first wines to receive this qualification was its 1992 Chardonnay.

Wines I have particularly enjoyed: Cabernet Sauvignon Reserva 1997, Chardonnay 2000, Merlot Rosé 2000.

S.A. Bodegas y Viñedos Santiago Graffigna Ltda., San Juan. This is one of Argentina's historical wineries, for Juan Carlos Graffigna began making wine in San Juan as long ago as 1869. It is also a company trying to convert itself from its historical image on the domestic market, where it is very successful, to one that can offer modern wines to the markets of the world. Interestingly, it claims to have been the first Argentine wine company to have exported.

In the former class, its wines have been described by one local writer as being as traditionally Argentinean as the tangos of Gardel and Razzano. (Though, in the interest of veracity, I should point out that Gardel was born in Uruguay!) One speciality is the 'sherry' Tío Paco, which ages in the courtyard in second-hand Bourbon barrels – as opposed to the best Scotch whiskies, which age in second-hand sherry casks! It also has a stock of 'port' more than 60 years old, which ages in poplar-wood casks. The company has passed through the hands of Spanish sherry mogul, and MEP, José Ruíz Mateos, but now is financed by American banks.

Graffigna has 125 hectares of vines in the Tulum Valley in San Juan and, in 1995, bought the **Santa Silvia** winery in San Rafael in the south of Mendoza Province. This winery currently has 35 hectares in production, but has planted a further 425.

Annual sales at the moment are running at just under a million cases a year, of which about a tenth is exported, with Britain being the leading export market. Overall sales in 1999–2000 increased by more than 30%, with exports more than doubling.

Its premium varietal wines, Cabernet Sauvignon and Chardonnay from its own vineyards, are sold under the name Centenario.

Wines I have particularly enjoyed: Shiraz Reserve 1999, Oak-aged Malbec 1999.

Bodegas Hispano-Argentinas, Mendoza. This is the name under which the Spanish winemaker, the Marqués de Griñon, Carlos Falco, is commercialising his Argentine wines, in conjunction with the Rioja-based company, Berberana. Whilst he has bought a property, the Dominio de Agrelo, he has made his wines until now at Bodegas Norton.

He is producing three levels of wine: Duarte red is a Malbec/Tempranillo blend and the white is Torrontés/Chenin. Vino de Autor Crianza is a straight Tempranillo, with six months ageing in new American oak and Dominio de Agrelo is old-vine Malbec, again aged in new American oak.

Lagarde S.A., Mayor Drummond Luján de Cuyo, Mendoza. This company has approximately 220 hectares of vineyards, of which all but 27 are in Luján de Cuyo; the balance is in Tupungato. Approximately half of the area is planted in either Malbec or Cabernet Sauvignon, though Lagarde has the distinction of having been the first in Argentina to plant Viognier. Also, the company offers a Sémillon 1942, bottled in 1997, which it claims, and who would doubt it, to be the oldest domestic wine on the market!

Although this winery has the most modern equipment, it specialises in making what it describes as 'artesanal' wines. These include a traditional-method bottle-fermented sparkling wine. Annual sales are about 40,000 cases on the domestic market and 15,000 cases on export markets.

Wines I have particularly enjoyed: Malbec 1996, Syrah 1997.
Other Brands: Río Mendoza, Letra de Tango.

Bodegas Lavaque, Cañada Seca, San Rafael, Mendoza. The wine trade in Argentina appears to be singularly entrepreneurial at the moment, with several examples of people selling one winery and buying another immediately. This might be said to be true of Rodolfo Lavaque and his partner Alfredo Mattei, the owners of Bodegas Lavaque. They were the owners of the large Cafayate winery Michel Torino, which they sold to Peñaflor, after a time under joint ownership. They then established another winery in Cafayate, Peñalba Frías (q.v.) and have developed, again as a joint venture with Peñaflor, a 400-hectare vineyard, 2,000 m above sea level, in Chañar Punco Valley, in Catamarca Province. Organic wine is also being produced at the Nanni winery (q.v.).

The 'home' winery is just south of San Rafael. It was established as the result of the father of Rodolfo Lavaque marrying the daughter of a vineyard owner in San Rafael. Here there is an estate of 280 hectares, split between four different vineyards. The bodega has a capacity of 5.3 million litres and it was one of the earlier ones in Argentina to invest in new French barrels for its prestige Félix Lavaque range. The wines from Catamarca are being marketed under a Lavaque label as Finca la Altura.

Until recently, the winery has concentrated most of its marketing methods on the domestic market, but with its expanded range of products is now seeking to establish itself internationally.

Wines I have particularly enjoyed: Félix Lavaque Cabernet Sauvignon 1996, Finca La Altura Pinot Noir 1999, Finca la Altura Malbec 1999.

Bodegas y Viñedos López S.A.I.C., General Gutiérrez, Mendoza. In the middle of the nineteenth century the López family was driven from its olive groves and vineyards of its native Andalucía by *phylloxera*. It came to seek a new life in Argentina and, after 30 years in Buenos Aires, arrived in Mendoza. Here it established vineyards and olive groves and built a winery. Now it claims to be the most important company on the Argentine domestic wine market, with brands Château Montchenot, Château Vieux and Rincón Famoso in every shopping basket.

Recently it has decided to move into export markets and has had some initial success. However, the wines that I have tasted have appeared to be too traditional for the British market, the red wines particularly resembling historical Riojas, with their long ageing in oak vats. One of their specialities is to offer a range of old vintages. As one Argentine wine writer says, 'It has the best-conserved old oak vats in the world . . . but it has the fastest bottling-machine in Argentina.'

Jacques & François Lurton S.A., Tunayan, Uco Valley, Mendoza.
The ubiquitous Lurton brothers had been making wine in Argentina
for 10 years before they built their winery in a remote fruit-growing
area in the foothills of the Andes, just a few kilometres from one of
the country's most famous sources, Eco de Los Andes, which now
belongs to the Nestlé group. Even though this winery has been built
at Tunuyan, it is only producing red wines. The white wines are still
being made at Escorihuela.

The company has two vineyards; one of 62 hectares on stony soil
around the vineyard. Here the closeness of the mountains means
exceptionally cold nights and the day/night temperature difference
can be as much as 25°C. This concentrates the fruit flavours in the
grapes. The other vineyard, of 64 hectares at Medrano, was planted
in 1999.

Its top wine, Gran Lurton, is billed as a Cabernet Sauvignon,
though it contains 20% Malbec. It is aged for 18 months in equal
proportions of French and American oak.

Wines I have particularly enjoyed: Pinot Gris 2000, Malbec 2000,
Cabernet Sauvignon 1999, Gran Lurton 1998.

Viña Maipú, Maipú, Mendoza. This is one of those wineries that
promises little until you taste its wines, which came under the
influence of David Cowderoy three years ago. The current winemaker is Ramón Salvatierra. The winery has a large capacity and
most of its efforts are turned towards making ordinary table wine
for the local market, but have some outstanding wines at higher
levels.

Wines I have particularly enjoyed: Malbec 1999, Malbec Sublimis
1999.

Bodegas y Viñedos Amadeo Maranon, Guaymallen, Mendoza. This
winery is a joint venture between the Maranon family and the
German wine company from the Mosel Valley, Zimmermann-
Graeff & Muller, and is aimed almost exclusively at export markets.
The wines are produced under the guidance of Swiss winemaker,
Thierry Fontannaz, and then shipped in bulk to Germany for
bottling.

The company has 400 hectares of vines, split between four different vineyards. Reserva wines receive French oak stave treatment.

Wines I have particularly enjoyed: Shiraz 2000, Malbec Reserva 2000.

Mariposa, see **Viñas de Tupungato.**

Bodegas Martins S.A., Cruz de Piedra, Mendoza. This company has a somewhat different history; in 1948, two Portuguese, José Martins Domingos and his son Rui, established a cork company in Argentina. In due course this came to specialise in wine corks. In 1969, the son decided to transfer his interest to what was in the bottles and he bought a 39-hectare wine estate in Cruz de Piedra and built a winery.

Martins is noteworthy in that it was one of the first Argentine wine companies to concentrate its efforts on selling varietal wines – long before they became fashionable.

Two important developments are that in 1996, the company entrusted its worldwide distribution to the Spanish Berberana group and, in the same year, appointed Susana Balbo, one of the country's leading winemakers, as consultant.

Other brands: Don Rui.

Viñas de Medrano, Medrano, Mendoza. With one or two honourable exceptions, the co-operative movement in the Argentine wine industry does not have an important role to play as far as quality is concerned. The co-operative cellar at Medrano is, however, one of those exceptions. Founded in 1988, its mission-statement includes such noble objectives as 'introducing a new way of doing business, improving the quality of life of the winegrowers, especially supporting education, research work and the social and economic growth of the region.'

Grouping together 36 wine growers from around the town of Medrano, it controls more than 200 hectares of vineyards. Sensibly, the members took the decision to employ a French winemaker, Jean Yves Deyras, and to produce quality wines. Whilst they make no effort to hide the fact that they are a co-operative cellar, they have managed to create for themselves a distinct, quality, brand image.

Wines I have particularly enjoyed: Filos Oaked Syrah/Malbec 1999, Syrah/Tempranillo 2000.

Mostomat S.A., San Juan. I am sure that there are many who will say that there is no place for a company like this in this book, for it produces no wine. However, it is the largest producer of rectified grape concentrate in Argentina and a very important consumer of lesser grape varieties, particularly Criolla and Cereza. Whilst its plant is not at all glamorous, it is fascinating to see truck-loads of grapes arrive at one end and sticky, colourless juice come out the other.

Argentina is one of the largest producers of concentrate in the world and it has two distinct uses in the wine world. In certain countries, it is permitted to increase the strength of wine by using concentrate; more generally it is used to sweeten wine. In the wider food industry, it is valued as a sweetener, for it has a lower calorific count and a higher sweetness level than sucrose.

Bodega Nacarí, Chilecito, Famatina Valley, La Rioja. This bodega first came to the notice of the wider wine world when its Torrontés won a major award at the Vinexpo wine fair in Bordeaux.

This is a small winery, managed by the La Riojana Co-operative, producing small lots of interesting wines, including such rarities as Alicante Bouschet and Favorita Díaz.

Bodegas Nanni, Cafayate, Salta. This is a joint venture between the Lavaque family (q.v.) and José Nanni, with vineyards in the Chimpa Valley at Cafayate. This project is devoted to producing organic wines and by the 2004 vintage, it is forecasting production of 350,000 litres a year of five varietals. Over half the total production will be of Torrontés.

Wines I have particularly enjoyed: Torrontés 2000, Cabernet Sauvignon 1999.

Bodegas y Viñedos Horacio Nesman S.A., San Juan. The Nesman family arrived from Udine in Italy at the end of the First World War and established a winery in San Juan. It now has an estate of 300 hectares of vines in production, split between seven different vineyards. Its winery has a capacity of 6.4 million litres.

Historically, the company has sold wine in bulk to other wineries and has grown Cereza grapes for turning into juice and concentrate. The family has realised, however, that it must develop its own brand

and it now sells 15,000 cases a year of bottled wine. A quarter of this is exported to the United States and Canada.

Wines I have particularly enjoyed: Torrontés 2000.

Casa Vinícola Nieto y Senetiner, Luján de Cuyo, Mendoza. This company was established in 1969 by Nicanor Nieto and Adriano Senetiner and has something of a split personality, having two wineries and two product ranges, Nieto y Senetiner and Viña de Santa Isabel. The cellar, at Vistalba, was bought from Perez Cuesta (q.v.) and has a capacity of 2 million litres, whilst that of Santa Isabel, at Carrodilla, is much larger, with a capacity of 6.2 million litres. The company has recently been sold to a steel company by the original controlling families, who have, in their turn, established Viniterra (q.v.) at Luján de Cuyo.

The vineyard estates total 118 hectares, with 70 hectares in the prime location of Tupungato. This is yet another company, where Alberto Antonini, formerly of Antinori, acts as a consultant wine-maker.

Currently sales total approximately 125,000 cases a year of which a fifth is exported to 20 markets. It is particularly proud of the ranges of Malbecs, of which it sells five different styles. Its top-of-the-range wines are marketed under the brand Cadus. These wines have been aged in French oak barriques.

Wines I have particularly enjoyed: Cadus Malbec 1999.
Other brands: Valle de Vistalba, Finca Las Marias.

Bodega Norton S.A., Perdriel, Luján de Cuyo, Mendoza. One subject that is, as far as I know, unexplored is the influence of the railways on the world of wine. When it comes to be written, I hope that there will be some mention of Edmond James Palmer Norton, who gave his name to this winery. This Englishman was working the Buenos Aires al Pacífico Railway as an engineer, when he fell in love with a local girl. Together with a partner, Grant Dalton, he bought an estate at Perdriel and became the first person to establish a winery south of the Mendoza River, on land that soon turned out to be ideal for the production of wine. From this small beginning has sprung one of the country's premium quality wineries, with an estate totalling 680 hectares of vines in production, in a variety of locations between 800 and 1,200 m above sea level. Included in these are 50 hectares of organic Malbec. Each year, a further 50 hectares or so of vines are planted.

The vineyards are under the control of Carlos Tizio-Mayer and Horacio Bazán and they have an intense belief that it here that the quality of a wine is created. Yields are controlled more by irrigation than by pruning; after fruit-set, berry size is controlled by deficit irrigation; leaf removal and green harvesting, at the time of *véraison,* are additional tools to improve fruit quality. Goat dung and pumice are used as fertilisers. Sadly viruses, particularly leaf-roll, are a problem – they were imported with rootstock in the 1950s.

The head winemaker is Jorge Riccitelli and he has at his disposal 10 million litres of stainless-steel capacity and 5,000 barrels of which 95% are French.

The company was taken over in 1989 by Gernot Langes Svarovski, of the Austrian crystal company, and his stepson, Michael Halstrick, is in day-to-day control as General Manager. (Interestingly the company has also invested in a winery, with 160 hectares of vines, north-east of Beijing.) As a small gesture to the company's Austrian ownership, one hectare of Gruner Veltliner has been planted; perhaps the only planting of this variety in all Latin America!

The annual production is currently about 600,000 cases a year, of which 35% is exported to more than 25 different countries. This makes Norton the largest export brand of Argentine wine and the third largest exporter of wine in dollar terms. Seventy per cent of sales are in red wine, where the top of the range is Privada, a Malbec/Cabernet/Merlot blend. Tank-fermented sparkling wine is also made.

Wines I have particularly enjoyed: Syrah 1999, Malbec 2000, Unwooded Merlot 1997, Cabernet Sauvignon 1997, Privada 1998.

S.A. Viñedos y Bodegas José Orfila Ltda., Junín, Mendoza. This is one of the historic wine companies of Argentina. Not only does it have a history going back to 1905, but also the winery is built on the site of a property that once belonged to the hero of independence General José de San Martín.

The company has more than 300 hectares of vines in Junín. About 40% of these have only recently come into production and represent a considerable investment on the part of the company. The winery has a capacity of 7 million litres. One of their specialities is a Cabernet Sauvignon de Las Reinas.

Orfila have also bought the Thomas Jaeger Winery in California.

Viña Patagonia, Maipú, Mendoza. The first question that many people ask when they visit this winery, is 'Why is it called Patagonia, when it is nowhere near Patagonia?' The answer is that its owners, the Chilean company, Concha y Toro, when they established it in 1996, wanted a name that sounded typically Argentinean. Somehow, I have the feeling that they are beginning to regret their choice and that a name change is a possibility!

The arrival of Concha y Toro's sales clout in Argentina has been little short of remarkable. Within 18 months of starting, Viña Patagonia was among the 12 largest exporters of bottled wine from Argentina. In order to support such a rapid growth, the company has planted 448 hectares of vines on three different sites, one by the winery in Maipú, the second in the cool climate area of Tupungato and the third in the rather hotter area of Rivadavia. Whilst these are still coming into production, they provide about half of the company's grape requirements.

In conjunction with this, the company totally rebuilt an old winery, formally called Premier. Under its old guise it had a capacity of 2.5 million litres, now it can stock 4.5 million litres. The total investment has represented US$12 million.

The wines are sold under the brand name Trivento, this is to honour the three winds that affect winemaking in Argentina. These are the mild Polar and Sudestada and the enervating Zonda, north-northwesterly. In the Trivento range, the ordinary varietal wines have no oak treatment and the Reserve wines have been aged, for a greater or lesser period, in French oak.

Wines I have particularly enjoyed: Malbec 1999, Malbec Reserve 1999 (70-year-old vines), Syrah Reserve 1999, Syrah/Malbec Reserve 1999, Cabernet/Malbec Reserve 1999, Late Harvest Malbec 2000.
Other brands: Concha y Toro (USA).

Bodegas y Viñedos Peñaflor, Coquimbito, Maipú, Mendoza. This is the largest wine company in Argentina, but it must also be one of the most reclusive, apparently not seeking to present its own face but rather that of one of its more glamorous subsidiaries Trapiche (q.v.), Santa Ana (q.v.) or Michel Torino (q.v.).

The company is reputed to be the third largest in the world, but after whom it is not quite clear. No one would dispute Gallo's claim to be number one, but there is competition between Castel Frères in Bordeaux and K.W.V. in South Africa for second place. (Interestingly I have a hand-out from Peñaflor, dating back to the 1970s. This places them then at number three after Gallo and United Vintners.)

Peñaflor belongs 80% to Luis Alfredo Pulenta and 20% to an American investment bank. In 1902, Antonio Pulenta arrived in Argentina from Italy and in 1913 he established a small vineyard and a winery with a capacity of 30,000 litres in San Juan. In 1924 he died, leaving the nascent company to his nine sons. The turning point in the company's history came in 1930, when the decision was taken to ship the wines by tank-train to Buenos Aires and bottle and sell them there.

The company controls 1,500 hectares of vineyards on its own account and has wineries in both Mendoza and San Juan, with a capacity of 90 million litres in each. One of the focal points of the Mendoza winery is La Pileta Central, the largest vat in the world, with a capacity of 5.25 million litres. This was used for blending table wines, which would then be shipped away in bulk on the direct line to Buenos Aires.

One of the surprising facets of this winery, is the fact that one can gain no impression of its size from the outside, because it goes down many levels into the ground.

In order to strengthen its position on the home market, Peñaflor has been buying up brands. Most of its business, it appears, is in selling wine for other people's labels. For example, on the British market, its wines are sold under the Bright Brothers label, with Peter Bright as guest peripatetic winemaker, and Australian, Steve McEwen, resident on the spot.

Wines I have particularly enjoyed: (All under Bright Brothers label) Viognier 2000, Shiraz Barrica 1999, Cabernet Sauvignon Barrica 1999, Cabernet Franc Barrica 1999, Malbec Barrica 1999.

Bodegas Peñalba Frías, Cafayate, Salta. Historically, this bodega under the name of El Recreo, belonged to the same family as that of Michel Torino, the most important in Cafayate, however, it became separated in a family inheritance. It is interesting that it should now belong to the Lavaque family, which has only recently sold Michel Torino to Peñaflor. At present they have approximately 200 hectares of vines in production, with another 100 already planted. Much of the emphasis is on Torrontés, though there are also Chardonnay and Cabernet Sauvignon vines. The wines will be sold under the brand Río Seco. The historic winery is also being totally re-equipped with the most modern plant.

Wines I have particularly enjoyed: Río Seco Torrontés 1999, Río Seco Chardonnay 1998.
Other brands: Dos Estribos, Gaucho Viejo.

Bodega y Viñas de Perez Cuesta, Mendoza. This company, founded in 1920, sold its winery at Vistalba to Nieto y Senetiner (q.v.). However, it continues to offer a range of red wines of which the Syrah regularly wins prizes in international competitions. It specialises in wines aged in French oak. Its wines sell at premium prices.

Bodega y Viñedos Quattrocchi, Lavalle, Mendoza. A company with a good estate of 300 hectares mainly in red varieties. Sadly, however, both the winery and the wines need some attention.

Viña Quintana, Las Heras, Mendoza. This 400-hectare estate lies just to the north of the city of Mendoza. The wines labelled as Viña Quintana, a range of four varietal wines, have received some barrel ageing, whilst those sold under the name Château Trivier have not seen oak. Tank-fermented sparkling wines are also produced.

Wines I have particularly enjoyed: Château Trivier Malbec 1999.

Resero S.A., Lavalle, Mendoza. This company was founded in 1936 and now forms part of one of Argentina's largest agro-industrial holdings groups, Cartellone, which is particularly strong in dairy products. Until recently the company specialised in selling bulk wine, but is now using a separate company name, Arriero, for selling bottled wine, mainly in the lower price levels.

The company has an estate of 800 hectares and sells single

varietal wines under the label Alto Agrelo and dual-varietals as Andes Sur.

Wines I have particularly enjoyed: Andes Sur Ugni Blanc/Sémillon 2000, Alto Agelo Malbec 1999.

Finca El Retiro, see **Pacífico Tittarelli S.A.**

Bodega La Rioja, Nonogasta, La Rioja. This company is not to be confused with its provincial neighbours, La Riojana (q.v.). It is a privately held company, belonging since 1968 to the Waidatt family. Its vineyards extend to 562 hectares and produce a full range of varietal wines. These sell under the Waidatt label, with the higher quality wines selling as Waidatt Privé. Of special interest are the Torrontés and the Barbera. The United States is the company's most important export market.

Bodega La Riojana, La Rioja. This is one of the few really successful wine co-operatives in Argentina and it claims to be the largest single co-operative cellar in Latin America. It was founded in 1940 and now has five wineries of its own, rents another complete one and has space at two others. The company controls almost 65 million litres of storage capacity. In all it groups together 640 growers, controlling more than 3,000 hectares of vines. Fifty-five per cent of the area under production is in Torrontés Riojano, 15% Cabernet Sauvignon, and 10% Barbera.

Naturally, much of the production appears on the domestic market in tetrabriks, but Australian winemaker Steve Hagan has been brought in to produce more export-friendly wines, these include two organic wines, a Torrontés and a Barbera under the label La Nature. These claim to be the first such wines made in Argentina. Sparkling wines are also made, both by the tank and the traditional method.

Perhaps the best wines are the local specialities, Torrontés de Nonogasta and those based on Barbera and Bonarda.

Other brands: El Montonero, La Masia, Caballo de Plata, Santa Florentína, Viñas Riojanas, Cepas Riojanos Selecto.

Bodega Jean Rivier, San Rafael, Mendoza. This small bodega was founded 40 years ago by the Swiss man, whose name it bears. It is now run by two of his sons, Carlos and Marcelo. The former is the winemaker and the latter looks after the commercial side of the business. They own 48 hectares of vines and concentrate on making small quantities of top-quality wines, using the finest French oak when needed.

Amongst their best wines is a 'Bordeaux blend' Becquinol.

Bodegas y Viñedos Robino y Cía., Luján de Cuyo, Mendoza. Dante Robino was a young Italian, who, in the 1920s, left his native country and set up a restaurant in Buenos Aires. He used to import wines in bulk from his family vineyards at home and bottle them for sale in his restaurant. Their appeal spread and he began to supply a number of his competitors.

About 1950, he took the decision to buy an estate in Mendoza and produce his own wines in Argentina. Perhaps not surprisingly, these are sold under such names as Nebiolo (sic.), Chianti, Marsala and Santo. The only wine to be sold as a straight varietal is the Malbeck. The finest wine is considered to be the Chianti, a blend of Sangiovese and Lambrusco.

The company now belongs to the Squassini family.

Roca S.A., San Rafael, Mendoza. A family firm with 114 hectares of vines, making predominantly red wines. Its total annual production is about 800 hectolitres.

Bodegas Rodas, San Rafael, Mendoza. The Cinzano group took over this old-established company in 1974 and have invested considerably in the plant. Both still and sparkling wines are made; amongst the former the highest reputed is the red, Rodas Escondido. The Rodas du Vallé *champaña* is produced from 100% Chardonnay.

Bodegas La Rural S.A., Coquimbito, Maipú, Mendoza. After qualifying from wine school in his native Italy, in 1885, Felipe Rutini was hired by the provincial government of Mendoza to come to Argentina and advise them on the nascent quality wine industry. He established his own bodega at Coquimbito. The company's estates now amount to something over 200 hectares, with a quarter just coming into production.

This is one bodega that has managed to marry together progress and tradition. The latter is marked by many of their labels and a museum of wine artefacts at the winery; the former has been encouraged by its relationship with Nicolás Catena, which dates from 1994, though the President of the company is a member of the Rutini family.

On the domestic market sales are led by Pequeña Vasija in a dump bottle and San Felipe in a *bocksbeutel,* however, the main brand is Felipe Rutini. On export markets, which have expanded rapidly since 1996, the main brands are Trumpeter, La Rural, Libertad and Mesa.

Wines I have particularly enjoyed: Rutini Merlot 1996, Rutini Traminer 1998.
Other brands: Cepa Tradicional.

Viñedos y Bodegas Sainte Sylvie S.A./Santa Silvia, San Rafael, see **Santiago Graffigna.**

Bodegas Salentein, Tupungato, Mendoza. It is hard to envisage the reaction of the wine trade in Argentina in 1998, when Carlos Pulenta, who has recently been appointed the honorary British consul in Mendoza, sold his shares in Peñaflor and left to become general manager of a new venture in the upper Uco Valley, Salentein. The finance for this has come from the owner of the Dutch dealership rights for BMW, who had already invested considerably in Argentina in a substantial cattle-ranch in Entre Ríos Province.

The vision behind Salentein is considerable. To provide vineyards, three neighbouring estates, El Portillo, La Pampa and San Pablo, totalling 2,000 hectares were bought. These provided 300 hectares of existing vineyards, situated between 1,050 and 1,500 m above sea level. Some of the vines are more than 30 years old. In addition, Señor Pulenta brought with him 700 hectares of his own vineyards.

The winery alone represents an investment of US$8 million. It takes the form of a cross, with each of the arms representing a separate winemaking facility, with stainless-steel tanks on the ground floor and oak barrels in the basement. There is a common bottling line. The whole building has controlled humidity and temperature. There are already more than 1,300 new casks, 90% of them French. The interior looks like the nave of some futuristic cathedral; from the outside on the cold winter day that I visited it, the winery had the look of some high-security prison. The cellar and bottling-line workers have to be bussed in more than 20 km.

With 1999 being the first vintage from this winery, it is early to comment much on quality, but no corners are being cut in the search to create some of Argentina's finest wines. The highest level is Primus. Each vintage selection will be made of the best grapes to make limited parcels of wine. In 1999, these were Pinot Noir and Chardonnay, with just 200 cases of the former being made. Potentially, this should become one of the great wineries of Latin America.

Wines I have particularly enjoyed: Primus Pinot Noir 1999, Primus Chardonnay 1999, Merlot 2000, Tempranillo 2000.
Other brands: La Pampa.

San Pedro de Yacochuya, Salta. This may well claim to be the highest commercial winery in Argentina. At 2,035 m above sea level it has a distinct advantage over most other claimants. It is the particular interest of Arnaldo Etchart Jnr, who has called in French oenologist Michel Rolland to help him handcraft wines from this boutique operation. The results are perhaps the most complex Torrontés in the world and a full-bodied red wine based firmly on Malbec, but with a proportion of Cabernet Sauvignon, harmonised in new oak barrels.

Bodegas Santa Ana, Guaymallén, Mendoza. This company is one of the largest in the Argentinean wine industry, though it has passed through a number of hands since its foundation in 1891. It was founded by Luis Tirasso and remained in his family's hands until 1935, when it was sold to Bass, Tonnelier y Cía. In turn it was sold to the Chilean winery Santa Carolina, who, at the beginning of 2000, sold it to Bodegas y Viñedos Andina S.A., a subsidiary of Peñaflor. It is rumoured that the reason for the purchase was primarily to strengthen the group's position on export markets, for Santa Ana is the country's fourth largest exporter.

The company has four wineries, three in Mendoza Province and one in San Juan. Its estates total almost 2,000 hectares, but at present there are no more than 251 in production, with a further 1,200 having been planted.

Sales on the domestic market are approaching 3.5 million cases a year and on abroad, they are the market leaders in the United States. It also exports vast quantities of wine in bulk. Among its best wines are those labelled Cepas Privadas and Special Reserve. It also produces sparkling wines and cider.

Wines I have particularly enjoyed: Special Reserve Malbec 1999. *Other brands:* Moulin Rouge, Villeneuve, Casa de Campo.

Santa Elena S.A., Luján de Cuyo, Mendoza. This company has belonged to the Bertona family for three generations and has 300 hectares of vines of which just under half are for table grapes. It exports quite extensively, with half the quantity being Malbec. One of its specialities is an aged Moscatel.

Santa Julia, see **La Agrícola.**

Santa Rosa Estate, see **La Agrícola.**

Bodega San Telmo, Cruz de Piedra, Maipú, Mendoza. This winery takes its name from a quarter of Buenos Aires renowned for its tango bars. It was created by Sigifredo Alonso and is very much California inspired. The winery building itself, just north of the River Mendoza, has been described as 'that white elephant of Mediterranean-Californian design'. Greg Fowler and Paul Hobbs, from California, have advised on winemaking.

The company has vineyards in San Martín, Junín and Cruz de Piedra.

With just one exception, the blended Cuesta de Madero, all the wines are single varietals aimed very much at the modern young drinker. Both French and American oak barrels are used.

Worldwide distribution of the wines is currently carried out by the Canadian multinational drinks group, Seagram.

Bodegas y Viñedos Simonassi-Lyon S.A., Rama Caída, San Rafael, Mendoza. This winery appears to believe in name changing. Originally, and it would be interesting to know why, it was known as El Alamein and the wines were sold under the brand Grand Bourg. Now both the company and the wines appear as Simonassi-

Lyon. The Simonassi comes from the owner's name, Jorge Simonassi; where the Lyon comes from I do not know.

The family originally comes from Canelli, in the Asti region of Italy, and Jorge has been making wines since 1975. He has 36 hectares of vines in Rama Caída and a further 14 in Los Claveles. If anything, his speciality is white wines, particularly Chenin Blanc. He is not a believer in the use of wood, except for his premium red wine, a Cabernet Sauvignon.

Bodega y Viñedos Suter S.A, San Rafael, Mendoza. At the beginning of the nineteenth century San Rafael was no more than a frontier town, protected against Indian raids by a fort. It was here that a young Swiss, Rodolpho Suter arrived with his wife Ana, to create one of the earliest vineyards in the region. His first vines were Pinot Blanc and his first crop 17 barrels. In 1910, he brought in from his home country some Riesling vines and these provided the base wine for his most successful blends.

Until very recently Suter has aimed its wines at the domestic market, successfully selling such wines as Fritzwein, Grand Vintage and its premium red wine, a Cabernet Sauvignon called Rojo.

The company owns 300 hectares of vines and has land available for planting a further 1,800. The cellar has a capacity of 10 million litres, of which almost 3 million litres can be stored in Nancy oak vats.

The company has recently been taken over by a local bulk wine supplier Covisan.

Other brands: Diamond River.

Bodega Terrazas, Perdriel, Luján de Cuyo, Mendoza. Terrazas de Los Andes is a range of varietal wines created by the Moët & Chandon Group. The basis of its presentation to the world is that every varietal is grown at an ideal height above sea level (in Argentina, this relates directly to the mean temperature). The launch advertisement contained such phrases as 'Ode to the Heights' and 'We are seeking absolute perfection, therefore we look upwards'. Essentially, it claims that the best height for Cabernet Sauvignon is 980 m, for Malbec, 1,067 m and for Chardonnay 1,200 m. Coincidentally, it controls vineyards at these specific altitudes!

The initial investment in this project, including the cost of 300 hectares of vines, is US$20 million. The vineyards are at Perdriel for Cabernet Sauvignon, Vistalba for Malbec, and Tupungato for Chardonnay. A 100-year-old, red brick, winery, La Perla, which originally belonged to the Arizu family and since was used by Domecq, has been totally remodelled to become one of the showplaces of Argentina. This has a capacity of 1.8 million litres in stainless steel and also holds 2,500 barrels, of which 80% are made of French oak and the balance American.

The manager of the winery is Roberto de la Mota, who comes from what is, perhaps, the most famous winemaking family in the country. Tony Jordan has acted as a consultant. Hervé Birnie-Scott, the head winemaker at Chandon, acts as director of winemaking. This is a powerful team of professionals.

There are many simple things about the winery. At present, wines are made from only three grape varieties: Cabernet Sauvignon, Malbec and Chardonnay, though when they find Syrah of a good enough quality, this will also be used. They only make three qualities of wine: the Alto, the Reserva and the Gran Reserva. All three varietals are made in the two lower qualities, only the Cabernet Sauvignon and Malbec in the highest. The Gran Reservas are also vineyard designated.

Wines are not necessarily made every year if the vintage is not considered to be good enough. For example, no wine was made in 1998. Total production runs at about a million litres a year, of which 90% is red.

Wines I have particularly enjoyed: Terrazas Chardonnay 1999, Terrazas Cabernet Sauvignon 1999, Terrazas Gran Malbec Finca Las Compuertas 1997, Terrazas Gran Cabernet Sauvignon Finca Los Alamos 1997.

Pacífico Tittarelli S.A., Rivadavia, Mendoza. In 1904, Enrique Tittarelli started in the wine trade by working for two of the great historical names in the Argentine wine industry, Juan Giol and Bautista Gargantini. Eleven years later, he established his own company at Rivadavia, south-east of the city of Mendoza. Here he planted vines and olive trees; these remain the backbone of the company to this day.

The Tittarelli family owns estates totalling more than

650 hectares in the provinces of Mendoza and San Juan. Of these, 372 hectares in Mendoza are planted in vines. It also owns three wineries with a capacity of 22 million litres. As consulting winemaker, it has Alberto Antonini, formerly technical director of the Italian company Antinori.

On the domestic market the company is particularly, and predictably, known for its Italian-style wines, such as 'Asti', Lambrusco and Sangiovese. It premium red wine is the traditional Bodega del Novecientos, a Cabernet Sauvignon/Syrah blend aged in large oak vats and then given further bottle ageing. For export markets, the brand Finca El Retiro was created in 1998. This comprises a range of mid-priced varietal wines.

Wines I have particularly enjoyed: Finca El Retiro Sangiovese 2000, Finca El Retiro Bonarda 2000.

Michel Torino, Bodega La Rosa, Cafayate, Salta. I never cease to be amazed by the amount of money that is being poured into wineries in South America. In 1993, the Lavaque (q.v.) family bought this somewhat run-down bodega and in the following five years spent US$80 million in modernising it and its vineyards. In 1999, it was sold to Bodegas y Viñedos Andina S.A., a subsidiary of the Peñaflor group, which, reputedly, wished to strengthen its position in branded wines on the domestic market. Since this take-over, the investment has continued, with, in 1999, US$1.5 million dollars being spent on the grape reception facilities alone.

Cafayate is a tourist town and the winery receives up to 50,000 visitors a year. The manor house, which adjoins the winery is being converted into a luxury hotel and the company has donated some scrubland to the provincial government so that an airport can be built, thus cutting out the long, but picturesque, drive from the nearest city, Salta.

Money is also being spent on the vineyards, where the Australian, Dr Richard Smart, has been called in to advise. Canopy management is being adapted to maximise the benefits of the 350 days of sunshine with which the region is blessed. Scott-Henry trellising is being used for the Chardonnay vineyards and many of the historical vineyards planted in the *parral,* or pergola system are now being trained in the Geneva Double Curtain. Currently the company has 350 hectares of vines in production, with another 100 coming on stream. Included in the latter are 24 hectares of Tannat. This is Torrontés country and historically 80% of the production has been white wine. In the future this is set to change dramatically, as export markets are opened up. Given the nature of the wines that are currently being sold, barrel ageing is not widely used, though there are 500 French and American barrels in the cellars.

Sales are running at approximately a million cases a year, predominantly on the home market.

Wines I have particularly enjoyed: Don David Chardonnay 2000, Don David Sauvignon Blanc 2000, Don David Torrontés 1999, Don David Malbec 2000, Merlot Colección 1999, Malbec Colección 2000.

Bodegas y Viñedos Pascual Toso S.A., Guaymallén, Mendoza. Fewer wine companies in Argentina can claim to have more in the way of tradition than Pascual Toso. On his father's side, the president of the company is descended directly from Pascual Toso, the creator of the company, who emigrated from Piedmont in 1880; on his mother's from one of the first Spanish settlers, who founded the city of Mendoza in the middle of the sixteenth century.

The company has a very traditional estate of 320 hectares at Las Barrancas, with 260 hectares planted with vines. Here the proportion of old vines is high, some going back 85 years, and many, both Malbec and Cabernet Sauvignon, going back 60. Most of the vineyard workers live in company houses and there are two state schools on the estate. Until quite recently, much of the vineyard work was carried out by a team of 200 horses, who also contributed to the organic fertilisation!

There are two wineries: one in the middle of the vineyards at Las Barrancas and one at San José, in the city of Mendoza, where much of the wine is stored and where all the bottling takes place. The city-centre winery is maintained largely because of ease of access to the labour market. Between them the wineries have a capacity of 10 million litres.

Sparkling wines are an important part of the Toso production. Approximately 10,000 cases of bottle-fermented wine are sold each year and 750,000 cases of tank-fermented. In addition, still wine production runs at 750,000 cases a year, of which a quarter is exported to 24 different countries.

Wines I have particularly enjoyed: Chardonnay 1999, Torrontés 1999, Malbec 1997, Malbec/Bonarda 1999, Merlot 1999, Malbec 1999, Cabernet Sauvignon Reserva 1997.

Bodegas Trapiche S.A., Coquimbito, Maipú, Mendoza. For many consumers Trapiche is the image of quality wine from Argentina, for it had a presence of foreign markets long before most other companies. It started exporting in earnest in the 1970s. Founded in 1883, it now bears the standard for fine wines within the Peñaflor (q.v.) empire, sharing a site, but not cellars, with them at Coquimbito. The name, Trapiche, means press and comes from the name of the original property bought by the founder, Tiburcio Benegas, which had on it a mill for corn and olives.

Its cellars have recently been totally renovated and have a capacity of 5 million litres in stainless steel and 3,500 small oak barrels, a quarter of which are renewed every year.

The company owns 400 hectares of vineyards in production and has a further 500 hectares under long-term contract. Richard Smart is the adviser on vineyard management. All the grapes are brought into the winery in baskets, to ensure minimum damage.

On the domestic market, it is known for such brands as Fond de Cave and Broquel. Its top market range, Trapiche Medalla, is also sold on export markets. Michel Rolland has worked with wine-maker Angel Mendoza on designing two special wines. The first of these is Iscay (the Quechuan word for 'two') a straight Merlot/Malbec blend from a single vineyard, Las Palmas, in Maipú. The second is Milenium, reputedly the most expensive wine ever made in Argentina, where it retailed at US$1,000 a bottle. I say a bottle, but it is a limited edition of just 2,000 Mathusalem (6 litre) bottles of the finest Cabernet Sauvignon (70%) and Malbec (30%) grapes of the 1995 vintage. The wine was aged in new Nevers oak barrels before bottling.

Wines I have particularly enjoyed: Sauvignon Blanc 1998, Malbec Oak Cask 1997, Cabernet Sauvignon Oak Cask 1995, Medalla Merlot 1997, Medalla Cabernet Sauvignon 1996, Iscay 1997, Iscay 1998.
Other brands: Falling Star.

Bodega Valderrobles, see **Bodegas Catena.**

Villa Atuel S.A., San Rafael, Mendoza. This is an entrepreneurial company, with a managing director based in Madrid. At present it has planted 400 hectares of vines, but has several more thousand hectares available. Its wines are made by Susana Balbo at the Roca winery (q.v.)

Le Vignoble S.A., Rivadavia, Mendoza. This company is primarily a producer of Henri Piper sparkling wines, which are made with the technical assistance of Piper Heidsieck in Reims. The base wines come from Pinot Noir, Chardonnay and Pinot Blanc, mainly grown in Tupungato. In descending order of quality, the three wines made are Extreme Cuvée Spéciale, Brut de Brut and Brut. Some still wines are also made.

Other brands: Paul Rigaud.

Bodega y Viñedos Vila, Cruz de Piedra, Maipú, Mendoza. This is a small company specialising in red wines, particularly in Bonarda. It has 150 hectares of vineyards in General Martín and Junín. The wines that I have tasted have been traditional in style with rustic flavours. The company exports in bulk and bottle to a small number of international markets.

Casa Vinícola Viniterra, Luján de Cuyo. This company was established as recently as 1997 by Flavio Senetiner and Walter Bressia, after the sale of their previous company, Nieto y Senetiner (q.v.) to a steel company. Viniterra has been established primarily with export markets in mind; the objective is to export up to 80% of its production. Currently, it is making 100,000 cases of wine a year, with half being exported. Capacity, in its functional winery, by the side of the main road south out of the city of Mendoza, is 3 million litres.

The policy is to pursue quality. All grapes for its top-quality wines are hand-harvested and brought into the winery in small plastic cases, Only French oak is used, and 70% is new. The coopers include Vicard and François Frères.

Whilst in Britain it sells entry-price wines under the brand Parral, generally it markets its wines under three distinct names: Viniterra – top varietals; Terra – dual varietals; and Omnium – Chardonnay, Malbec and Cabernet standard wines. In addition there is a premium blended red wine, Jubileus. Something of a novelty, but an agreeable one is Malbec Espumante, fermented in bottle with eight months on lees.

At present the company owns 40 hectares of vines and these provide a fifth of its needs. The plan is to expand its vineyard holdings.

Wines I have particularly enjoyed: Omnium Malbec 1999, Viniterra Malbec 1997, Jubileus 1999.

Viñas de Tupungato, Ugarteche, Luján de Cuyo, Mendoza. This is the name of the venture by Californians Kendall-Jackson into Argentina. In all the company has purchased 1,400 hectares of land on three different sites. There are 400 hectares south of the Mendoza River in Luján de Cuyo and a further 1,000 hectares split between two different sites near Tupungato in the Uco Valley. Whilst there are also plantings of Cabernet Sauvignon and Chardonnay, Malbec is going to be the main grape variety featured. The wines, under the brand Mariposa (butterfly) will be aimed mainly at the American market.

Vintage S.A., Mendoza. This is a joint venture between Susana Balbo, winemaker at Martins (q.v.) and elsewhere and Italian consultant Alberto Antonini, to produce wines under the brand Anubis. Grapes are sourced from a variety of locations in Mendoza Province and a variety of oak treatments are used.

Bodega y Cavas de Weinert S.A., Luján de Cuyo, Mendoza. I do not think that there is a wine company in Argentina that inspires more emotion than Weinert. Founded by Brazilian entrepreneur Bernardo Weinert it has cocked a snook as its competitors and, more than once, flirted with insolvency and one is never quite sure whether it has managed to maintain its independence.

As well as the company, the wines too have been controversial. Raúl de la Mota, perhaps the country's most classic winemaker, has been responsible for the production of many of these and they have often been made in a very traditional style with long ageing in large oak vats, sometimes for five years or more. The extreme example of this is the Malbec Star 1977, which was aged in oak vats for up to 20 years before bottling. As another example of the independence of thought, take its wine Miscelánea; this is produced from up to

17 different grape varieties ranging from Malbec and Cabernet Sauvignon to Moscatel de Alejandría and Pedro Ximenez. Robert Parker believes that Weinert makes the best wines in South America. Certainly they are to his taste, full-bodied and packed with fruit and oak.

The total production is about 100,000 cases a year.

Bolivia

===

Minor wine-producing country of South America.
Some of the vineyards of Bolivia are the highest
in the world. More or less ordinary table wines.
André Simon, *Gazetteer of Wines*, 1972

The first thing that any writer says about Bolivia as a wine-producing country, is that it has the highest vineyards in the world. This claim is now being challenged by some of the vineyards of the Calchaquí Valley in northern Argentina, but what I found most striking about the vineyards of Bolivia, was their remoteness. They mostly lie in the Province of Tarija, in the extreme south-east of the country, which borders both Paraguay and Argentina. The vineyards lie on the eastern flanks of the Andes, mainly to the south of the city of Tarija.

To get to Tarija you fly from either the cities of Santa Cruz de la Sierra or Cochabamba in Bolivia or from Salta in northern Argentina. The longest of any of these flights is 90 minutes; by road it is 32 hours to Santa Cruz and 16 hours to Salta. My guide book says of this latter drive, 'The views are spectacular (sit on right).' I would add, 'Unless you are of a nervous disposition,' as the road in many places seems to be falling away into the river and is no wider than the bus itself.

Bolivia is not a major wine-producing country; it has some 4,000 hectares of vineyards and produces less wine than England. However, this last figure is rather deceptive as vast quantities of the local wine-brandy *singani* are also produced. As opposed to *pisco*, this is twice-distilled, mainly from Moscatel wines. Consumption of wine in Bolivia is also on a small scale, averaging approximately one litre per person per year. About half of this is imported, much of it smuggled in from Chile. The local wine producers accuse the government of taking no steps to control this smuggling and protect local industry. They say that a bottle of Concha y Toro Cabernet Sauvignon is cheaper in La Paz than in Santiago! Basically, two types of wine are produced in the country, ordinary table wine which retails at about US$2 a bottle and 'fine wine', which sells at about US$6 the bottle. Of the domestic production, 70% is red wine, the rest white.

Whilst wine legislation in the country is still in a rudimentary stage, the Spanish expert Isabel Mijares, is helping to draw up a code. Initial laws will be more to create recognised regions of production than to restrict yields. A semi-official appellation of *Vino de Altura Boliviano* is now beginning to appear on labels.

The earliest vineyards in Bolivia were probably planted in Mizque, near Cochabamba. This was one of just a handful of archiepiscopal sees of the Spanish Empire in the Americas and wines were needed for the mass. It was in 1574 that the Viceroy Francisco de Toledo, concerned by the attacks being made by the native Chiriguanos, instructed Luis de Fuentes to construct in what was then frontier country, the city of Villa San Bernardo de la Frontera de Tarija on the banks of the Guadalquivír River.

Tarija is a very pleasant provincial city and I can recommend the newly constructed Parra Hotel, built on a bluff overlooking the river. However, as I have already said Tarija is remote from central government and has little in the way of industry to support employment. However, salvation is on the way. The Province of Tarija consists of six *departmentos*. The biggest and most remote of these is Gran Chaco, where oil has been discovered. Untold riches have been promised!

Whilst there are vineyards in four of the provinces of Bolivia: La Paz, Cochabamba, Chuquisaca and Tarija, it is only in the last two that anything other than singani is made on a commercial scale.

When Luis de Fuentes arrived at Tarija he soon realised that the climate and land were suitable for the production of olives and vines. Jesuits planted vines locally in the Concepción Valley as early as the seventeenth century. One peculiarity of these early plantings was that vines were encouraged to grow up the local *molle* or 'pepper' trees. Indeed, in some of the more traditional vineyards, this form of viticulture continues to this day, with both the trees and the vines being pruned every year.

The first wine *négociant* company in Peru, **Bodega San Pedro**, was established in Camargo in 1925, and this company still exists, being, currently, the only producer of sparkling wine in Bolivia. The importance of Camargo, however, as a wine-producing centre has diminished, following the investments made by a number of Tarija businessmen in local vineyards and wineries in the 1960s.

Nowadays, most of the vineyards lie to the south of the city of Tarija in the arid valleys of the rivers Guadalquivír and Camacho. The dried-up creeks are a good hunting ground for fossils of prehistoric reptiles. The vineyards are at an altitude of between 1,800 and 2,600 m above sea level (elsewhere they are planted up to 3,000 m). In Bolivia land reform took place successfully in 1952. (Interestingly, Che Guevara was rejected by the local agricultural workers when he came to stir them up; they were satisfied with their lot. Perhaps he might have been more successful if he had targeted the miners of Potosí.) Now there are 900 smallholders in the area with between a quarter of a hectare and three hectares of vines. It is considered that just one hectare of vines will give a *campesino* family a reasonable standard of living. In all there are 10 companies in the association of wine producers and a further three who will probably join in the near future.

The great advantage that Tarija has for the production of wine is its climate. Because of its altitude, the grapes receive very high exposure to ultra-violet rays and the mean difference between day and night temperatures throughout the year is about 20°C. Annual rainfall is in the region of 450 mm, and, whilst there is some rainfall in the run-up to the harvest, this is normally minimal and the steady winds coming through the nearby mountain passes (one local village is called La Ventolera, or 'gust of wind') means that rot cannot develop. Any water shortfall can be met by irrigation from the local rivers, where there are unlimited supplies available. All this creates concentrated fruit flavours in the grapes. One winemaker from another South American country told me that he believes that Bolivia has the best wine grapes in the world. What it lacks is experience and equipment.

The lead in responding to this very problem is being taken by the **Centro Nacional Vitivinícola**, or CENAVIT, under its director,

Oscar Daroca. The cellar is at Pampa Colorada in the Camacho Valley and the finance to establish this came not just from the local provincial government, but also from Spain. Here trials are being carried out on 20 different grape varieties, of which 14 are classic European wine varieties and six different lesser varieties for the production of cheap wine. These latter are mainly members of the Mission/Criolla family, with such local names as Vischoqueña and Mollar. There are no hybrid vines in Bolivia. Tests are also being carried out to find the best rootstock for the area.

The Centre has nine hectares of its own vines and sells a certain amount of wine locally under the label Pampa Colorada. The Spanish influence upon the Centre is apparent in the choice of grape varieties planted, amongst which can be found in reds, Tempranillo, Cariñena and Garnacha, and amongst the whites, Xarel-lo, Parellada and Viura. These last three may well be used in the experimental vinifications being carried out of the country's first tank-fermented sparkling wines.

The first wine company to establish itself in Tarija was **Kohlberg** and its foundation came about in a rather strange way. The grandfather of the current owners, Don Julio Kohlberg, lived in Buenos Aires and was recommended wine for health reasons. For advice he consulted Father Pedro Pacciardi, a Franciscan monk. Don Julio's children went on to study oenology in Argentina and business management at Michigan University. The result is the 300-hectare La Cabaña estate, 15 km south of Tarija. Here the family has more than 100 hectares of vines in production and is clearing terraces for further plantings.

The vineyards are run on a system of devolved management, with individual families being given the responsibility for maintaining a certain area throughout the year. One person is in charge of pruning between 8,000 and 10,000 plants. In all, the estate supports almost 500 people.

Fourteen different varieties of grapes are planted, beginning with Moscatel de Alejandría for basic wines for the domestic market and ranging up to Syrah, Cabernet Sauvignon, Chardonnay and Barbera. Out of an extensive tasting the wines here that I preferred were the Syrah, the Malbec, the Cabernet Sauvignon and a Grenache/Alicante Bouschet blend in the reds, and the Pinot Blanc in the whites.

Bodegas y Viñedos de la Concepción S.A. is based on one of the oldest estates in Bolivia, La Angostura just outside the attractive small town of La Concepción. Vines were first planted on this property by the Jesuits as early as the seventeenth century. It still has some Criolla and Moscatel vines more than 200 years old, which are trained up *molle* trees.

In many ways this is the most outward-looking of the Bolivian wine companies. Work first began on modernising the vineyards in 1968 and in 1978 a new winery was built.

The company belongs to the Pinedo and Prudencio families and they are proud that both family signatures are on the document that finally secured the full independence of the Bolivian republic. The company is now quoted on the La Paz stock exchange and there is some foreign investment from a Swedish trust. In a different international direction, Sergio Prudencia trained at UC Davis.

The company has 90 hectares of vines, split between three farms and uses only its own grapes to produce its range of wines under the La Concepción label. It produces almost 30,000 cases of these a year. Its singanis sell almost 60,000 cases a year under the name Rujero. The products are exported to North America, Europe and the Far East.

This is the best-equipped cellar in Bolivia with a capacity of 2 million litres, much of it in temperature-controlled stainless steel. It is also beginning to age some of its wines in 400 litre oak casks from the Radoux cooperage. As well as using these for some of the Merlot and Cabernet Sauvignon wines, it has, on an experimental basis begun to age some singani in new oak. This is now six years old and rates with top-quality cognacs.

Most of the wines are sold as straight varietals; amongst those I most enjoyed were a Pinot Blanc, an unoaked Merlot and a range of Cabernet Sauvignons in different styles. This is one of the few companies in South America to have stocks of bottle-aged wine. I tasted Cabernet Sauvignon Reservas going back to 1993. The new premium barrel-aged Cabernet bears the label Cepas de Altura.

The cellars of **Bodegas Milcast Corp.** lie close to the centre of the city of Tarija. Here they produce two distinct brands, Aranjuez and Campos de Solano. The latter will be having its own separate winery, built with the help of French advice. This will hopefully be in production in time for the 2001 vintage and will be treated as a domain using grapes solely from their own vineyards. At present these consist of 20 hectares, with a similar area again shortly to come into production. However, the singani company of Casa Real is part of the same group and its vineyards are an additional source of supply. It is envisaged that, in due course, it will be producing 20,000 cases a year of Cabernet Sauvignon, Malbec and a red blend. At present the joint sales of the two labels are in the region of 100,000 cases a year of which 60% is lesser-quality wine.

Concentrated varietal flavours are again apparent with the wines of this bodega. Amongst the whites, the French Colombard and the Gran Vino Blanco, a spicy blend of Moscatel and Torrontés, were outstanding. In addition, it produces a good range of reds based on the Malbec and Cabernet Sauvignon. The unoaked Malbec is one of the best young wines of South America.

The **Casa Real (Sociedad Agroindustrial del Valle Ltda.)** winery and distillery lies out of the city close to the Kohlberg premises. As well as having 150 hectares of its own vineyards, it also buys in from a number of local growers. The estate produces not only Moscatel grapes for distillation, but also Riesling, Chenin Blanc and Cabernet Sauvignon, for its associated company. Its five gas-fired pot stills are active for over seven months in the year, with the spirit coming off after the second distillation at an average strength of 72%alc. This is reduced before bottling to 40%alc.

Annual sales of singani are approximately 2 million bottles a year under four different qualities. The top one, Aniversario, is distilled solely from wine made from Moscatel grapes from its own vineyards; Gran Singani uses some bought-in Moscatel grapes, Primera Clase is still pure Moscatel, whilst the lowest quality Mezclador is made from what the label describes as *uva negra* or Criolla.

A more exotic speciality product is *Ginsen Gani Elixir*, which is singani with a ginseng root in the bottle, which was originally aimed at the large Korean community in Bolivia, but which is also now exported to Korea itself. I can give no guarantees as to some of the claims that are made on the back-label!

Another company to produce just singani, and no wine, is **Bodegas y Viñedos Kuhlmann & Cía. Ltda.** The founder of this company was Franz Kuhlmann, who left Hamburg at the age of 15 and stowed away on board a boat bound for New York. Having spent some time there working as a pastry cook, he joined the merchant marine. In due course he jumped ship and made his way to Chile, travelling around South America, finding work where he could. At the age of 35 he became a distiller in Camargo in Bolivia and used for his first product * * * Cognac labels. The company's main brand is still called Tres Estrellas.

In 1973 the distillery was definitively established at Tarija and it has 20 hectares of its own vineyards and also buys in grapes, for its singanis which are sold throughout Bolivia. The business must be profitable, as Carlos Molina, Herr Kuhlmann's son, has invested heavily in a luxury resort hotel just outside the city!

Even though Bolivia is no more than a minor player in the world of wine production, I feel that it has great potential. The climate is ideal, land is not expensive (a hectare of fully planted and irrigated vineyard would cost a maximum of US$18,000) and labour is cheap. Despite all this almost no foreign capital has been attracted. Perhaps the financiers have been put off by the remoteness, the small size of the domestic market and a past history of inflation and political instability. This is a pity, for I am sure that Bolivia is capable of producing wines the equal of any in South America.

Brazil

Brazilian wine is improving but vile.
Lonely Planet Guide – Brazil, 1998

It is not easy to understand just how vast, and how varied, Brazil is.
In size it is almost as large as China, stretching from its border with
Venezuela and Guyana, five degrees north of the equator, to that
with Uruguay, more than 33 degrees south. One could expect
that within such a range of latitudes there must be some ideal spot
for the production of wine. When one also thinks of the European
roots, Portuguese, Italian and German, of many of its immigrants,
one could imagine that there would be considerable knowledge of,
and demand for, wine. However, as Professor Harm Jan de Blij
has pointed out, 'Brazil's relative location on the South American
landmass suggests some of the environmental obstacles facing
the country's grapegrowers. There is no Mediterranean zone in
the country, nor is there a dry climatic regime comparable to
Argentina's Andean rainshadow.' Even in the south of the country,
'Summers are moist and warm, winters are cool, and there is no
pronounced dry season to favour the ripening of grapes. Such a
regime, propitious for the cultivation of many other crops, is not the
best for viticulture. First the missionary settlers, then the Portuguese
immigrants, and later the Italian winegrowers discovered this in
turn.' Despite all this, Brazil is the third most important wine-
producing country in South America, with some 57,000 hectares of
vines and is rated as the seventeenth most important producer in the
world, just after Greece and Moldova, but just above Bulgaria. To
put things in perspective, this means that it produces about four
times as much wine as New Zealand.

The first plantings of vines, brought from Madeira, in Brazil were made at Santos in 1532. Not surprisingly, because of the climate, these were not successful and the city's founder, Bras Cubas, then planted a vineyard inland in the hills of Piratininga. Wines that he produced are mentioned in an inventory of his possessions made when he died; this inventory is dated 1551. At about the same time vineyards were planted on the island of Itamarca, off Pernambuco. Specific varieties of grapes mentioned as being planted include the *Ferral*, the *Moscatel* and the *Dedo de Dama*. Shortly afterwards, Spanish missionaries from Buenos Aires, sailed up the Uruguay and Paraná rivers and established colonies inland, where they planted vines, sugar-cane, bananas and maize.

During the eighteenth century considerable efforts were made by the Portuguese to encourage emigration to Brazil and large numbers of immigrants arrived and settled in the south of the country in Rio Grande do Sul. It was here that winemaking came to establish itself most firmly. The majority of the early settlers were from Madeira and the Azores and they brought with them their traditions of wine production and their own vines of Malvasia, Bastardo and Alvaralhao. Despite an effort by Queen Maria I in 1785 to protect home industries by banning wine production in the colonies, the Brazilian wine industry seems to have flourished, even if only in a small way.

The nineteenth century saw two major developments for Brazilian wines. First was the introduction of American and hybrid vines, which proved to be better suited to the humid climate. The *Isabella* was first planted on the Morumbi estate near São Paolo in the late 1830s; it arrived in Rio Grande do Sul very shortly afterwards. It is American vines that still dominate viticulture in Brazil.

The second move of importance, was a series of waves of immigration from European countries other than Portugal. First to arrive were Germans, from 1824 onwards. They settled in the coastal plains around Porto Alegre, founding towns, such as Novo Hamburgo. Further north in 1865 a number of French families arrived from Algeria; they settled around Curitiba. As far as wine-making is concerned, however, the most important nationality to arrive was the Italians. Small groups established themselves in São Paolo as early as 1820, but in the 1880s larger numbers came to settle in Rio Grande do Sul. Finding the Germans well established in the plains, they moved further inland to the hillier country of the Serra Gaucha, which reminded them of the homes that they had left

Brazil and Uruguay

in Piemonte and elsewhere. The names of towns in the region bear witness to their roots: Nova Roma and Nova Padua, not forgetting Garibaldi.

It was at the turn of the century, that the families of many current producers began to produce wine, mainly for their own family needs. Soon, however, major merchant companies were established, some of which, such as Salton, are still in existence today. In 1913, Emanuelle Peterlongo Jnr was the first to produce locally 'Asti' sparkling wine from Moscato de Canelli grapes, a style of wine that is still very popular. In 1931, the two largest co-operative cellars, Aurora and Garibaldi, were founded, and finally the 1970s saw the arrival of the multinationals attracted by the burgeoning economy and the size of the domestic market. These included National Distillers from the United States, Seagram from Canada, Domecq from Spain, Martini & Rossi from Italy and, just a few years later, Suntory from Japan.

What is the current situation of the Brazilian wine industry? It appears to be happy, but I see little reason for its happiness. As the government has failed to ratify the Uruguay Round agreement of the World Trade Organisation, it is unable to sell anything other than basic red and white wine to the markets of the European Union. There were, for example, major customers for varietal wines; these have now gone. In addition, the United States, which used to be by far the most important export market, has all but closed its doors. The story behind this will be revealed later. In 1997, Brazil exported 9,760,686 litres of quality wine; in 1999, it exported just 197,379 litres.

The reason for the apparent contentment of the trade is that it sees its future in an expanding domestic market. At present wine consumption represents just 1.52 litres per person per year, and with a population of over 150 million people, this adds up to an important quantity of wine. If everybody in Brazil were to drink just one more glass of wine a year, the wine producers would be under serious pressure. However, this figure for consumption has fallen steadily over the last decade and whilst there appears to be some evidence of increasing interest in wine from the middle classes, it may well be that this will be reflected first in increased consumption of wines from fellow members of Mercosur, such as Argentina, Chile and Uruguay. Indeed, in 1999 there was a shortage of available red wine and at least two Brazilian wine brands appeared with Uruguayan wine in the bottle. What is interesting is that even in the major wine-producing state of Rio Grande do Sul, the average consumption is still less than five litres per person per year and in five of the 27 states, it amounts to less than a single glass of wine a year.

There are two other major problems that the wine industry has to face. First, the price of cane spirit is remarkably low, with a bottle of the ever-popular *cachaça* costing as little as one dollar. This spirit accounts for 85.6% of the market, with one brand, '51', selling over 80 million cases a year. Against this, wine is taxed at a rate of 42%.

The second problem is one of quality. Whilst, I disagree totally with the quotation from the *Lonely Planet Guide* at the beginning of this chapter, Brazilian wines are not vile, little effort seems to be made to make wines of outstanding character. As I see it, there are two major reasons for this. The first being that producers are still happy to use European names, such as Champagne, Asti and Cognac (or Conhaque, as it is generally called in Brazil). This means that they are cut off from access to many export markets and they can cloak their products under convenient aliases. Secondly, and more importantly, the production of *vinifera* grapes is still very much in the minority. Almost six times as much wine is made from American grapes and hybrids as from European varieties and, if anything, this proportion has increased over the past decade. Uruguay, which has very similar climatic problems, has taken a positive decision to uproot its hybrids and replace them with *vinifera* grapes in an effort to improve quality at all levels of wine. On the other hand, the Brazilians can make good, and, in a few cases as we shall see, outstanding wines, but, for the most part they do not seem bothered. This situation is exacerbated by the high yields that are regularly obtained (and this is a problem it shares with Uruguay). Of the 34 most widely planted grape varieties, *vinifera* and others, only three, Pinot Noir, Pinotage and Gewürztraminer, have an *average* yield of less than 10 tonnes to the hectare, and four have one of over 20 tonnes.

At the moment, the producers appear to have been caught unprepared by an increasing demand particularly for red wine. This means that for grape-growers it is a sellers' market and there are ready buyers for grapes of any quality. The government fixes prices, and these are taken as a minimum, without sanctions being imposed for low potential degrees of alcohol or rot. As one oenologist said to me, 'The biggest problem I have to face is the grapes.' Similarly, the chairman of a co-operative cellar remarked, 'As far as grapes are concerned it is a sellers' market. We have to dance to the tune the growers play.'

The wine industry has been slow to organise itself with the Instituto Brasileira do Vinho (IBRAVI) only being formed in 1999. This has 47 members, representing all sectors of the trade, and is a conduit for discussions with the government.

Wine legislation is limited. There are three categories of table wine allowed on the market. These are defined in a law of 1988 as being:

- *Vinhos finos* or *Vinhos nobres*: these are produced from *vitis vinifera* grapes.
- *Vinhos especiais* must taste predominantly of *vinifera* grapes, but may also contain American and/or hybrid grapes.
- *Vinhos comuns* are made from American and/or hybrid grapes.

There are also three official classifications of sparkling wine:

- *Champanha* (or *Champagne*) is a sparkling wine in which the carbon dioxide is solely the result of secondary fermentation either in a bottle or in a larger vessel, with a strength of 10–13% and a minimum pressure of three atmospheres.
- *Vinho Moscatel Espumante* (or *Asti*) is a sparkling wine made from the Moscato grape, with a strength of 7–10%. The carbon dioxide must be the result of a single fermentation in a bottle or a larger recipient and a minimum pressure of three atmospheres.
- *Vinho Gaseificado,* generally locally known as *Frisante*, is a wine into which carbon dioxide has been introduced by any method, with a strength of 10–13% and a minimum pressure of two atmospheres and a maximum of three.

Chaptalisation is permitted but not always used.

A varietal wine must be made from a minimum of 60% of the specified grape variety, though this figure is due to rise to 75% under Mercosur legislation.

At present there are 12 regions in Brazil, recognised by the national government for the growing of grapes. Of these, six are in the state of Rio Grande do Sul (Serra Gaucha, Campanha, Pinheiro

Machado, Rolante, Jaguari and Sao José do Ouro), two are in Santa Catarina (the Upper Valley of the Rio do Peixe and Urussanga) and two are in São Paolo (São Roque and Capão Bonito). The last two are situated in the region of Andradas in Minas Gerais and the Middle Valley of the Rio São Francisco, which is the border between the states of Bahias and Pernambuco.

By far the most important state for both grape growing and for wine production is Rio Grande do Sul in the south of the country. This accounts for 90% of the national wine production and within the state the region of Caxias do Sul, or the Serra Gaucha (Cowboy Hills), gives 96% of the production of wine and grape-must in the state.

The vineyards of the region are, for the most part, smallholdings with more than 16,000 individual growers, of whom more than 80% own their vineyards, and 90% rely just on members of their families to work them.

The wine capital of Brazil must be the town of Bento Gonçalves, where IBRAVI, the wine research station (EMBRAPA) and a number of the major wine companies are based. Not very long ago, wine accounted for 80% of the town's economy, but the arrival of a number of furniture factories has lessened its dependence on just one industry. Nevertheless, wine is still king and the entry into the town, if you are coming from Porto Alegre, the state capital, is through a stylised concrete wine-vat!

The first Italian immigrants in the area arrived shortly after 1875 and the town itself was formally incorporated in 1890. Most of the newcomers came from northern Italy and each family was granted a parcel of land of about 25 hectares. This was a region of poly-culture and wine did not dominate for some time. In the early days, most of the produce was sold through German merchants who used to transport the goods to the coast by ox-cart for shipment to the major cities. It was not until the arrival of the railways that the major wine companies established themselves in Bento Gonçalves and neighbouring towns, such as Garibaldi, Farroupilha and Caixas do Sul.

The wine research station, EMBRAPA, is an offshoot of the Brazilian Ministry of Agriculture. The Bento Gonçalves branch deals not just with viticulture, but also with fruit trees, particularly apples and peaches. With regard to vineyards it is looking at developing resistant rootstocks and controlling chemical treatments. It sees that there is an enormous amount of work still to be done in such fields as clonal selection.

Together with the University of Caxias do Sul, EMBRAPA has carried out extensive research aimed towards the creation of Brazil's first true *appellation contrôlée*. If it comes to fruition, this will be for the aptly named Vale dos Vinhedos (Vineyard Valley), which lies south-west of Bento Gonçalves and north-west of Garibaldi. It consists of the valley created by a number of streams that join together and flow north-west into the Das Antas River. The valley has its own microclimate and already produces some of the country's best wines. At this moment the authorities are only considering the creation of a geographical appellation – such ideas as selection of the most suitable grape varieties and restricting yields are in the unseeable future.

For the tourist, or wine lover, the Vale dos Vinhedos makes an enjoyable drive and a day's challenging wine tasting. If you set out in a clockwork direction from Bento Gonçalves, the first cellar that you come to is more of a tourist trap than anything else. This goes under the name of **Vinícola Cordelier,** with the wines sold under the Granja União and Cordelier labels. Granja União is a historical label in Brazil, established by a group of producers as long ago as 1929. Cordelier says it has no vineyards of its own and produces something over 3,000 cases of wine a year, which it sells at the cellar door. It seems much prouder of the Brazilian whisky and Conhaque that are also produced. Just beyond its cellars, a dirt track leads off to the left to the village of Garibaldini. It is only when you arrive there that you notice a well-tarmaced road that leads to the main road from Bento Gonçalves to Garibaldi. In Garibaldini there are two producers **Courmayeur** and **Brandelli.** The previous day, someone had recommended that I should visit the Brandelli's, without specifying which; there are three separate Brandelli wineries in the valley, all descended from the same family, with six sons, which arrived in the valley from Verona in 1887.

Brandelli appears to be the least sophisticated of the three, with a simple cellar and nine hectares of vines. He also buys in some grapes from local growers. The wine of which he is proudest is a Cabernet Sauvignon/Cannaiolo/Seibel 10.096 blend, of which he makes about 5,000 bottles a year. I think I can best describe it as having a feral charm.

His distant cousin **Julio Brandelli – Casa Graciema** has an estate of 30 hectares, which he supplements with grape purchases. In all he makes about a million litres of wine and a further 200,000 litres of grape juice. The latter is as important a product in the valley as wine and there are a number of producers who make no wine at all, but just concentrate on juice. Much of Senhor Brandelli's sales are in demi-johns, where his range includes a Cabernet, a Merlot and a Sauvignon Blanc. He does have 20 barrels for his best wines, but most is aged in vats of the local *grapia* wood. Being right on the main road, he attracts much passing custom and he has constructed a minute restaurant in one of his old vats. Those he cannot tempt with food, he tries to seduce with his home-distilled grappa. Next time I will settle for the food!

The third branch of the family, selling under the name of **Don Laurindo**, has an estate of 30 hectares, with 10 planted in vines. All their wines are made from their own grapes and they make 70% of their sales at the cellar door. They go out of their way to attract visitors and have a most attractive cellar. Personally, I preferred their white wines to their reds, especially enjoying the Malvasia de Candia and a blend made from Riesling Italico, Flora and Prosecco. Of their reds, my preferred wine was their Tannat. They also make a bottle-fermented sparkling Malvasia.

There was much that depressed me about my visit to Brazil, but, as is usual, there are rays of sunshine and one of these was **Miolo**. This is another family to have emigrated from Italy at the end of the nineteenth century and to have settled in the valley. For almost a century they were just grape-growers, but after two of them had studied oenology, one locally at Bento Gonçalves and the other at the wine school in Mendoza in Argentina, they built a winery in 1989. This is now expanding and in the right directions, including temperature-controlled stainless-steel vats and new American oak barrels, which they have made up in Brazil from imported staves. Their estate in the Vale dos Vinhedos is of 30 hectares and they also truck down grapes from the sub-tropical São Francisco Valley way to the north.

Here, I found three outstanding wines: a barrel-fermented Chardonnay 1999, which had spent six months on its lees in new oak; a delicate Sauvignon Blanc 1999 and a soft Merlot 1997. They also make a carbonic maceration Gamay. Whilst these were the best wines, they were not the most interesting. This was the Terra Nova Shiraz 1999 made from the bought-in grapes. In the São Francisco

Valley, the vineyards lie in an irrigated desert and, because they are so close to the equator they can be harvested five times every two years. With grapes from these vineyards, Miolo currently makes this Shiraz and an 'Asti Spumante'.

Whilst the one side of the valley appears to be dominated by members of the Brandelli family, the other seems to be under the sway of the Valdugas, who originated in the Italian Tirol. **Casa Valduga** has two facilities on the road, offering the tourists not just wines, but also juices, jams, vinegar, grappa and brandy. I liked both its Gewürztraminer and Cabernet Franc.

Adega de Vinos Finos Dom Candido appears to be run independently by a separate branch of the family, though it is literally next door. The company produces about 60,000 cases of wine each year and its 12-hectare estate gives them about 40% of the fruit that they need. Among its award-winning wines are a Cabernet Sauvignon 1998 (Gold Medal in Argentina) and, more interestingly, a Chardonnay 1998, which in 1999 won a bronze medal in the 'World Chardonnay Championship'. This wine is part barrel-fermented. Another award winner, this time in Budapest, is its Riesling Italico 1999. Like the best racehorse trainers, Senhor Valduga seems to have matched his runners well to the races!

In the heart of the town of Bento Gonçalves is the largest of all Brazil's wine companies; this is **Cooperativa Vinícola Aurora** and its cellars attract more than 120,000 tourists a year. This keeps eight guides in employment. The company was founded in 1931 and now groups together more than 1,300 growers, controlling more than 1,350 hectares of vineyards, and selling the equivalent of over 4 million cases of wine each year. It provides its members with a full technical back-up service and has created its own viticultural research station.

Over the past few years, times have not been easy for Aurora. It had as its importers in the United States the second biggest wine group, Canandaigua, which had a runaway success with its Marcus James Aurora Valley Brazilian White Zinfandel. When sales approached a million cases a year, competitors began to ask questions. This is scarcely surprising, given the limited plantings of the Zinfandel in Brazil, and the limited extent of the Aurora Valley vineyards. Rumour has it that when the California Wine Institute, after a visit of inspection, wanted to take matters further, they were warned off by the State Department in Washington, who wanted to avoid an international incident with a fellow American country.

I was told at Aurora that the pressure was always on from Canadaigua, who thought that it would be a good marketing idea to label the wine as coming from the Aurora Valley when it knew that most of it did not. As for the grapes used for the wine, in the end it used whatever was available in order to satisfy demand. As they say, it always showed well in competitive tastings! In any event, Aurora's relationship with Canandaigua came to an end, nominally because the Brazilians were not able to supply enough red wine. The brand, Marcus James, now belongs to Aurora in Brazil and to the Americans in the rest of the world.

On top of this, the fact that Brazil has not signed the Uruguay Round Agreement has meant that very important customers within the European Union have been lost. Aurora used to supply over a 100,000 cases a year to the British supermarket chain Tesco; now they supply nothing. Whilst Aurora has traditionally been responsible for more than 80% of the country's wine exports, now these do not account for a very big proportion of the company's sales. These problems have come together to put Aurora under severe financial pressure and it has had to be supported by the Banco do Brasil. Now, it claims, these difficulties are over and is seeking to consolidate its position as market leader in Brazil.

With such enormous sales, the company has a broad range of brands, including Terra Nostra, named after a television soap opera, featuring a family of Italian immigrants. They also sell wine coolers, and this is a category which has more than doubled in the past five years, with over 6 million litres being sold each year.

The top quality brand is Aurora, a range of 100% varietal wines including a range of Reserva wines. The Gewürztraminer Reserva 1999 I found to have excellent typicity and it was very long on the palate. This won a silver medal in the Vinalies international wine competition. The Chardonnay Reserva 1999 I also enjoyed. This had finished its first fermentation and also its malolactic in cask. The red wines I tasted, I found to be sound, but less exciting. Other brands that they produce include Clos des Nobles, Conde de Foucault and, of course, Marcus James. In these the varietal content is generally not more than 80% of what is stated on the label – well above the 60% permitted by the legislation.

With Aurora dominating the national industry to such a large extent, and being its major representative on export markets, it is essential that it recovers from the difficult times that it has been passing through. Of course, matters are not totally in its hands. If, because of government policy, or incompetence, its exports are largely restricted to selling bulk wine to Japan, as happens at present, with a predominantly stagnant domestic market, and a shortage of red wine, its expansion must be limited. It is, however, moving in the right direction. It has invested in stainless steel and in 1,300 oak barrels to replace partly the local wood vats that it has used since its foundation. For Brazilian wines to have a worldwide reputation for quality, Aurora has to succeed.

Of the other merchants based in Bento Gonçalves, mention should be made of the sparkling wine specialists **Vinhos Salton** who were founded in 1910. They are the third largest producers of sparkling wine, after Moët & Chandon and Georges Aubert, and they make wines from both the Charmat (tank fermentation) and the Asti method from a broad variety of grape varieties. Their top-of-the-range Champagne, Salton Brut, comes from Chardonnay, the Demi-Sec from Riesling Italico and the Meio Doce from Ugni Blanc and Sémillon. All these are largely grown in their 50-hectare estate at Tuiuti.

Whilst Bento Gonçalves claims to be the wine capital of Brazil, the neighbouring town of Garibaldi claims proudly to be the Champagne Capital of the country and it has a number of very important cellars, not just for sparkling wine. These include the second most important co-operative cellar, **Garibaldi**. The year of co-operation in Brazil must have been 1931, for not only was Aurora founded then, but also Garibaldi, Linha Jacinta and a number of other co-operative cellars. With an annual production of 30 million litres of wine and some 400 members, this cellar comes close to rivalling Aurora in size, though it seems to lack much of its competitor's commercial acumen. (Perhaps playing it safe may have been a better solution.) It, too, makes a big play for the tourists and welcomes over 100,000 a year. Certainly the promotional video that it shows its visitors verges on soft porn, as it recommends Garibaldi wines to lovers as an aid to seduction – and to authors for inspiration!

As with its competitors, it tries to cater for all tastes with wines and grape juices. Leichtwein Suave and Precioso are no more than they claim, but towards the top end of the range, I enjoyed the

Acqua Santiera Riesling 1999 and Chalet de Clermont Reserva Especial 1996, a barrel-aged blend of 80% Cabernet Sauvignon and 20% Merlot.

De Lantier is part of the Bacardi/Martini & Rossi empire, and it proudly describes its products as 'Vinho Brasileiro Mais Premiado No Exterior', which I suppose can be loosely translated as 'No Brazilian wine wins more prizes abroad'. To me the reasons for this were not immediately apparent. The company first began producing its vermouths in Brazil in 1950 and it was not until 1968 that it began to produce table wines. In 1974, it launched a range of *cuve close* sparkling wines under the brand De Gréville. It is difficult for me to give a clear opinion of the wines, as all the bottles I tasted had been opened the previous day and had spent the night, red and white, still and sparkling, in a refrigerator. Nevertheless, they lead the medal table by a distance!

The second most important producer of sparkling wine is a company called **Georges Aubert,** which has its origins at Die in the Rhône Valley. History does not relate why Monsieur Aubert should have left France in 1951 to settle in Brazil, but his arrival was greeted in the press as an event of major importance – the first French 'Champagne' company to establish itself in the country. In the event, he soon became the largest producer of sparkling wines in Brazil, a position he has since lost to Moët & Chandon – the first Champagne company (without inverted commas) to establish itself in the country.

Notwithstanding this, Aubert is still very important, producing one and a half million litres of sparkling wine a year as well as a range of still wines, *conhaques*, and arak. (This last drink is currently the fashion in São Paolo!) The sparkling wines, made by the Charmat method include Formidable Champagne Extra Brut, Fétiche Brut red and Asti Inamorare.

The company does not have its own vineyards but has contracts with a number of local growers. For its sparkling wines it uses yeast imported directly from Champagne. It also believes in putting on a good show for the tourists; in the tasting-room, the *sabrage* method of opening bottles is regularly performed and as well as the traditional sights there is a cultural centre and museum and *estufas* for vermouth production. There must be few wineries with so much to offer!

Sparkling wine is an important and rapidly growing market in

Brazil, between 1996 and 1998, sales increased by more than a half. When Moët & Chandon first set up a winery in 1973, it was a joint venture with the Italian vermouth company Cinzano and a Brazilian company called Monteiro Aranha. Now **Chandon do Brasil** forms part of Domaine Chandon Estates, which also has interests in California, Australia, Spain and Argentina. In fact Champagne Moët et Chandon S.A. of France owns 72% of the capital of the Brazilian company and Bodega Chandon S.A of Argentina owns the remaining 28%. As both presumably belong to LVMH, I am unclear as to the full meaning of this; what is clear is that more than 7 million dollars have so far been invested in the project.

The company owns 40 hectares of vineyards, which supply them with approximately one-fifth of its grape needs. The rest it buys from contract growers, whose vineyards it closely supervises. Four per cent of what it produces is still wine, the balance all being sparkling wine made by the tank method. It produces approximately 2 million bottles of wine a year and have 2.8 million litres of wine in stock, meaning that, for its better quality products, the base wine is at least two years old.

The grapes are all pressed in a range of Bucher presses, with only 40% of the resultant juice being used. After ageing and blending, the wine spends six months developing its bubbles in a Charmat tank.

Tom Stevenson in the *New Sotheby's Wine Encyclopaedia*, criticises Moët & Chandon and Piper Heidsieck for using the words *Champaña* and *Champanha* to describe their sparkling wines in South America. Certainly, as far as Brazil is concerned, Chandon do Brasil use neither term about their local produce and use the word *Champagne* only to describe wines from its French parent company. It says in their promotional material, 'The establishment of the company in Brazil is due to the developments in grape growing in the south of the country and the climate which favour the production of sparkling (*espumantes*) wines.' Later the same Portuguese word is again used to describe the production of the wines. Mr Stevenson also doubts that the laws of Argentina and Brazil oblige users to use such terms. As far as Brazil is concerned he is technically right. Article 11 of Law no. 7678 of the 8 November begins '*Champanha (Champagne) é o vinho espumante,*' so whilst it is not obligatory, it does seem to be the preferred option of the Brazilian authorities!

Basically, the company produces three classes of sparkling wine. At the top is *Excellence*, a Chardonnay/Pinot Noir blend, which is an outstanding sparkling wine by any standards. Then come *Chandon Brasil Brut* and *Demi-Sec*, made from what is described as 'the classic Serra Gaucha' blend of Chardonnay, Pinot Noir and Riesling Italico. Finally, Chandon Passion from the 'original' blend of Malvasia Bianca, Moscato Canelli and Pinot Noir with a faintly pink colour and distinct Muscat flavour.

What these wines say to me is that a good tank-fermented wine, made with a good base product, is better than many bottled-fermented wines, indeed, better than some genuine Champagnes.

Chandon do Brasil also produces two still red wines, from grapes from its own vineyards. Grand Philippe 1997 is a 100% Cabernet Sauvignon, which has clean varietal characteristics, with soft easy tannins. The Grand Philippe Reserva is altogether a more serious wine. Whilst it is sold as non-vintage, it can be recognised by its bottling letter; the current bottling of almost 60,000 bottles has the reference 'I', and is a blend of 49% Cabernet Sauvignon, 32% Merlot and 19% Cabernet Franc. This is one of the few outstanding red wines from Brazil that I tasted.

Whilst the heartland of local wine production is in Bento Gonçalves and Garibaldi, there are a number of other wine towns. The co-operative cellar of **Linha Jacinto** has split its operations, with the winery being in the village of the same name, and a new bottling cellar on the main road outside Farroupilha, on the way to Caxias do Sul, by far the largest town in the Serra Gaucha and the scene of a wine fair at the beginning of March each year.

This cellar has just over 100 members and controls over 600 hectares of vineyards. From these, and the grapes that it buys in, it will produce approximately 2 million litres of wine each harvest. Of this just a quarter is made from noble varietals. It bottles little of its wine under its own labels, but mainly under those of multiples. It also exports a substantial quantity in bulk to Japan.

The **Cooperativa Vinícola São João, Vinos Castelamare & San Diego** is based at Vila Jansen, in the hills north of Bento Gonçalves, though it has two subsidiary vinification plants, just for hybrid grapes, at Nueva Roma and Pinto Bandheira. Each year it vinifies 100,000 tonnes of grapes and it has stockage capacity for 10 million litres of wine. Ninety per cent of its production is sold in bulk for bottling elsewhere. Interestingly, here it manages to achieve something that appears to be rare in Brazilian wine co-operatives, it pays for its grapes not just on the weight and the variety, but also on the potential degree of alcohol, thus introducing quality more into the equation.

The establishment of vineyards in the region of the Serra Gaucha at the end of the last century came about not because of ideal soils and climate, but because coastal plains had been settled by German immigrants and because the hilly countryside reminded the Italians of their homeland. Neither of these reasons can guarantee quality wine production. However, beginning in 1973, there was considerable investment, made principally by the American group National Distillers, through its Californian wine subsidiary Almaden, in researching the ideal location for vineyards in the state of Rio Grande do Sul. With professors from Davis and the Carrau family from Uruguay, they looked at a number of sites on the border between Brazil and Uruguay. They finally settled on Bagé on the River Jaguarão near Pinheiro Machado where, in a three-year project, they planted an initial 20 hectares, later extended to 60. Here they carried out trials of 52 different grape varieties flown in direct from California on a chartered Boeing 707. A friend has described to me the stir that this caused when it arrived at the local airport!

The vineyards in Bagé, however, did not prove to be a success and they no longer exist. However, in 1976, National Distillers bought 1,200 hectares of grazing land at Palomas, some 10 km to the north-east of the border city of Santana do Livramento, 'the corned-beef capital of the world'. At its maximum, there were as many as 720 hectares of vines on this site, but, because of over-production, this fell as low as 410 hectares and currently stands at 530, with 470 in production, and a vine nursery of a further 30 hectares. In 1980 a functional modern winery was constructed on the site with a large stainless-steel tank farm. In 1983, after 10 years, and an investment of $60 million, the first Brazilian **Almaden** wines appeared on the market. In one of those classic about-turns so common in the world of multinational spirit companies, National Distillers decided to call it a day as far as Brazilian wines were concerned and sold the winery and vineyards to its Canadian competitors Seagram for just $14 million dollars. Seagram was already well represented on the market with its brand **Maison Forestier**, which was established in Garibaldi in 1974.

Since its absorption of Almaden, Seagram has recently sold its plant in Garibaldi, with part of the price being paid for in wine-making on its behalf by the new owners. No wines are bottled for it in either Palomas or Bento Gonçalves; everything is shipped in bulk to São Paulo, a distance, as far as the former is concerned of more than 1,600 km. This leads to the rather bizarre situation that you are able to taste at Palomas nothing but tank samples, they have no bottled wine available, or, on the one occasion that I insisted, only those of historical, and oxidised, nature.

Out of the original 52 varieties planted, now just 11 remain commercially. Of these, there are Cabernet Sauvignon, Cabernet Franc, Merlot and Tannat for red wines; Chardonnay, Riesling Italico, Riesling Renano, Sauvignon Blanc, Trebbiano, Sémillon and Gewürztraminer for white wines. At present 60% of the production is of white wine, and this is so out of balance with market demands that red wines have been imported from Uruguay to make up the shortfall. Interestingly, the winemaker says that it has far too important an acreage of Chardonnay and Riesling Renano.

In the 2000 vintage, expectations from its own vineyards in Palomas were of over 7,000 tonnes of grapes, with half as much again also being bought from growers in the Serra Gaucha. All its wines are chaptalised as a matter of course and are made in a very easy-drinking commercial style. The rather controversial quotation, with which I have begun this chapter, reads more fully, 'Brazilian wine is improving but vile. Forrestier (sic) is at the top of a very low heap of vintages.' I am not sure that I agree with at least two statements in these two short sentences!

In the region of Santana do Livramento, there are two other wineries. The more important of these is the Japanese-owned **Livramento Vinícola Industria Ltda.**, which sells under the brand name Santa Colina. Here attempts are being made to produce top quality wines, including Cabernet Sauvignon and Chardonnay, using new oak. Initial tasting suggested that it has yet to get the balance right, though it is encouraging to see what it is trying to achieve. The wines are sold locally and exported to Japan. In all it has 88 hectares of vineyards, though yields are being affected by regular problems with downy mildew. This is a brand to look out for.

The third of the wineries in the area is the most recent (having only come into effect for the 2000 vintage), the smallest and has the most interesting history. As has already been said, the Uruguayan Carrau family was involved in the first research with National Distillers into the potential for vineyards in the area. Juan Luis Carrau was, at that time, involved in a project with Dubonnet for production of its apéritif in South America for local distribution. In addition he had created a Brazilian winery in 1968 which featured 'the sole Brazilian wine château' complete with crenellations and wine cellar with Nancy oak vats. This was called **Château Lacave**. In 1977, with National Distillers as minority shareholders, the family bought just over 300 hectares of land for potential vineyards on the Uruguayan side of the border and 72 hectares on the Brazilian side.

In 1979 the relationship with Dubonnet collapsed and, in 1983, Rémy Martin, bought the minority shareholding of National Distillers. Subsequently, it obtained control of a further block of shares and control of Château Lacave passed from the hands of the Carrau family into those of Rémy Martin. Notwithstanding this, Juan Luis Carrau still owns the 18 hectares of vineyard that came to be planted on the Brazilian side of the border. In addition, he has created a new wine company **Vinícola Cave Velho Museu Ltda.**, based at Caxias do Sul. Now the labels, instead of featuring a castle, picture a Surrey stockbroker belt manor house.

Senhor Carrau specialises in producing wines in limited quantities, which he sells at high prices. These are principally bottled into a distinctive *bocksbeutel* and carry a hanging neck tag instead of a label. His specialities are a Cabernet/Merlot blend, aged in bulk for three years before bottling, and a Gewürztraminer. Whilst the wines are distinctly better than most of his competitors, those that I have tasted have gained little by having been aged for as long as they have – and are distinctly expensive!

Is Brazil the Sleeping Beauty of the wine world, just waiting for a handsome prince to come and bring it back to life? Or is it better left to itself, producing the style of wine that is wanted just by Brazilians and relying on a burgeoning birth-rate to create a regular increase in demand? The most important thing that it has against it is its climate. It is sad that in such an enormous country, there is not somewhere ideal for the production of wine – but that is the case. However, on a smaller scale, Uruguay faces the same problem and is seeking to overcome it. If Brazil's wines are to have any international success, the first thing that must happen is that the dominance of hybrids and American varieties must cease. This will demand much more rigorous controls both in the vineyards and in the cellars, but, given the will, this is achievable. *Vinifera* grapes now grow with success in many regions that 20 years ago would have been considered impossible.

Secondly, Brazil will have to adapt to international norms for the labelling of wines and spirits. Its reluctance to abandon such terms as *Asti*, *Champagne*, and *Cognac*, means that it is already cutting itself off from such important potential markets as the European Union. It would also seem dangerous to rely just on an expanding domestic market, for, with the country's entrance into Mercosur, there are alternative wine-producing countries eager to profit from any demand. Uruguay has already eagerly helped out with red wine. Argentina has vast quantities of wine available at low production cost. Are the Brazilians strong enough to protect their domestic market? I have my doubts.

Brazil is capable of producing good commercial wines for export markets. In the past it has succeeded in both Britain and the United States. It has a currency sufficiently weak to attract foreign buyers; it needs to be strong enough, however, to sell abroad on its own terms and not be dictated totally by the customer. Aurora has paid a very heavy price for the substantial sales it once achieved.

Brazil's wine industry can have a global future, but it needs to adapt radically, and quickly.

Chile

———

Travelling up from the Falkland Islands through the wonderful Strait of Magellan, with its fine glaciers and snow-clad mountains, the first port of call one makes in Chile is Punta Arenas – 'Sandy Point' – the southernmost town in the world. Ensconced gratefully in the English Club at tiffin, I tasted for the first time the wines of Chile. They are excellent wines, many of them quite good enough for export, were there any wine-drinking market within reasonable distance. As it is, they are mainly consumed, like those of the Argentine, in the country of their origin as *vin ordinaire*, red and white. All the big liners sailing on that coast produce a full wine list of Chilean wines, with the names of the different growers and vineyards attached.

Chile has about 170,000 acres under the grape and her vintage is about a thousand million gallons of wine. In the 200 mile passage from Coronel (36° S.), where the naval battle was fought in 1914, to Valparaiso 'The Pearl of the Pacific' and the principal port of Chile, one sees the vineyards and fruit-trees of all kinds stretching back to the Andes.

From the ship at her moorings the snow-capped peaks of the towering *cordillera* present a majestic panorama, while at night the Southern Cross gleams overhead and the city is ablaze with myriads of lights. Viña del Mar, the residential

suburb of Valparaiso, with its race-course and
sports ground, is a great society gathering-place
in the summer season, and visitors come to it
from Santiago, the capital of Chile, and even
across the continent and over the mountains from
Buenos Ayres.
Few wines are grown north of Coquimbo
(30° S. lat.), or south of Valdivia (40° S. lat.). The
summer begins in December and lasts until
March.
Frank Hedges Butler, *Wine and the Wine Lands
of the World*, 1926

These farmers have, in the growing of vines, a
source for prosperity which they will certainly
not neglect.
Raymond Sempé, *Etude sur les Vins Exotiques*, 1882

For many wine consumers, Chile will be the only South American country whose wines they will have tasted. They have come into their own with the comparatively new uncomplicated fashion of drinking varietal wines. The wines of Chile are nearly always sold under the names of the grape varieties from which they are made. To simplify things even more, generally there have only been four available, and those all-long familiar through contact with French wines: Cabernet Sauvignon and Merlot for red wines and Chardonnay and Sauvignon Blanc for white.

Whilst these are the wines that have been appearing on the shelves of wine-merchants around the world, these are not the wines that the Chileans themselves have been drinking. Indeed, the Chileans have never really been the wine-drinkers that their neighbours across the Andes, the Argentines have been. The average consumption of the Chilean is approximately a third that of the Argentine. The reasons for this are not easy to understand. Both countries have relied heavily on Basques and Italians for their immigrants. Both countries stretch from the tropical north to the frigid south. Both countries are largely agricultural. Both countries have relied on the same grape variety for the majority of the wines they consume, the País in Chile, the Criolla in Argentina. Despite all these similarities, the Chilean is not a wine consumer.

Notwithstanding the ready availability of wine at low prices, he drinks little more than the average Briton.

This lack of a domestic market may also account for the fact that there has been comparatively little investment in Chile in vineyards and wineries by the large multinational drinks companies.

The Chilean wine industry is at an interesting stage. It understands that it must develop in new directions, but it is not clear how or where. Yes, there is room for vineyard expansion, but this must be either to the north or to the south, where the climate may present problems. Certainly, in the past few years there seems to be a willingness to experiment with new grape varieties and there seems to be no reticence about the offering of icon wines at very high prices. Some critics consider that there is a certain smugness on the part of the leaders of the wine industry in Chile. Will over-confidence be rewarded with a fall? The renaissance of the Argentine wine industry must be giving cause for concern.

Despite all this Chile is a major force in the world of wine. Whilst it has the same acreage of vineyards as Greece, for example, its wines have conquered the world in a way that those of Greece have not. Despite a troubled recent history, Chilean wines can be considered a success. Let us hope that this continues.

HISTORY

The history of Chile and its wines can be split into two periods, that before the arrival of noble French grape varieties in the 1850s, and that after their arrival. Chile was the first country in the Americas to create a fine wine industry, based on the noblest varietals.

As in other Latin American countries, the vine arrived with the Spanish conquerors and history has it that the priest Francisco de Carabantes was the first to introduce it to the country that was to become Chile in 1548. However, existing already among the indigenous natives, there was a tradition of alcoholic drinks, based upon fermented grains. As Samuel Morewood says in his *History of Inebriating Liquors* (1838): 'The aboriginal Chilians, long before the landing of the Spaniards, employed leaven in making bread, and they were, besides, acquainted with the process of fermentation, by which they obtained from their grain and fruits, several kinds of inebriating liquors which they kept in jars after the manner of the

Greeks and Romans.' The vine was not, however, native to South America.

The first recorded vintage dates from just three years after the arrival of Francisco de Carabantes. Don Francisco de Aguirre produced wine on his estate of San Francisco de la Selva, which is right in the north of Chile, where the city of Copiapó now is. Shortly afterwards, the first vines were planted in what is now the heartland of the Chilean wine region. The soldier, Juan Jufré de Loaiza y Montesa, who had accompanied Pedro de Valdivia on his campaign, which culminated in the foundation of Santiago in February 1541, was rewarded with the grant of estates in Macul and Nuñoa, where he planted extensive vineyards.

Chile was considered to be the most fertile of Spain's American possessions and particularly suited to growing the fruits and grains of the home country. Morewood quotes Ovalle's *History of Chile*, when he says, 'Grapes were so plentiful in 1646, that they could not be disposed of; and the wine was a source of great injury to the Indians by their drinking it to excess. White wines were made from that species of grape called *Uba* (Uva?) *Torrontés* and *Albilla*, which were much valued; red wines were made from the ordinary grape and a species called *Mollar*.' According to one writer, wine production in the region of Santiago, at the beginning of the seventeenth century, amounted to 4.6 million litres of wine a year, with the vineyards being not just in the hands of the Spaniards, but also of the natives. In addition to wine, *chicha*, or part-fermented grape must was also a very popular drink.

Interestingly, at the end of the eighteenth century, one of the most important centres of wine production was La Serena, now at the northern limits of wine vineyards. Perhaps the main reason for its importance was it closeness to the silver, and other, mines. A parallel can be drawn with the vineyards of Amador County in California, where vines were planted to provide alcohol for the hearty thirst of the local miners, during the Gold Rush.

By the beginning of the nineteenth century, when the Chilean fight for independence reached its climax, wine was a major industry. The French writer Jullien, whose *Topographie de Tous les Vignobles Connus*, appeared as the Spanish hegemony in South America was in its last stages, said, 'The province of Arequipa, which stretches along the coast of the Pacific Ocean, to the foothills and slopes of the Andes mountains, is the most beautiful and most fertile of the four great provinces of the Vice-Royalty of Peru. The vine is grown everywhere and yields large crops.'

Chilean independence added further impulse to the country's wine industry. This was spurred on by a number of developments within the infrastructure of the country. The first of these began in the 1830s with the arrival of foreign engineers, who constructed the first major new irrigation channels since those built by the Incas. These opened up new areas to the possibility of vineyard plantation. Increased national pride, led to the creation of such bodies as the National Agricultural Society in 1838, the National Agricultural School, a few years later, and the Agricultural Credit Bank in 1855. Distribution on a national, rather than a local scale, was made easier with the arrival of the railways, largely financed by the British, in the 1860s.

At the same time as all this was happening, Chile gained wealth, and importance, as a crucial staging post on the shipping routes to California, where the Gold Rush was taking place. It was also beginning to exploit its nitrate reserves from the Atacama Desert. For the wealthy, the trip to Europe became a necessity and all things French became fashionable. Initially, it was a country house designed by a French architect that was the vogue, but this soon was extended to planting your vineyards with French varietals and constructing cellars on the Bordeaux model.

Whilst Silvestre Ochagavia is generally credited with being the first to have imported French vines into Chile in 1850, small parcels had, in fact been imported earlier. In 1845, the French-owned Viña La Luisa, which later became part of the National Agricultural School, was planted with French vines. Similarly, another Frenchman, Pierre Poutays, planted the short-lived Viña La Aguada with vines from his home country.

Within a very short space of time, many of the leading wine estates had their resident Frenchman, generally as winemaker or viticulturalist, but occasionally as master-cooper. Most of these specialists came from the Bordeaux region and Chile was to benefit, as did Rioja, from the mass exodus from that region as the result of the spread of *phylloxera* in the 1870s.

The spread of French varietals took place over several decades and, to some extent, it is still not complete with such traditional varieties as País and Moscatel still being widely grown. However, some idea of the role that they came to play can be gathered from the following quotation from the *Étude sur les Vins Exotiques*, which was written by Raymond Sempé to coincide with the Universal Wine Exhibition, which took place at Bordeaux in 1882. At that time, Chilean wine production was calculated at a million hectolitres a year and the author says, 'It is mainly plants from Bordeaux and Burgundy that have been imported into Chile. Little by little, the Chileans have abandoned their traditional methods of cultivating their vineyards and making wine, so that they can adopt the methods of the countries from where they have imported their vines. Thus, for some years, in a variety of regions, particularly in the centre of the country, they have produced excellent quality wines; to such an extent that they have become a source of riches to the country.'

'The part of Chile most suitable for growing the vine stretches from the northern frontier as far as Bio-Bio in the south; but in the south the dampness of the climate prevents the grapes from ripening naturally.' (It should be pointed out that the northern frontier was then much further south than it is now.)

'Vines in Chile can be classed either as French vines, or as Chilean vines. The French make up a considerable vineyard area in the central region. The main French varieties, which have been introduced into Chile, are the Pinot, the Gamay, the Sauvignon, the Cabernet, the Malbec, the Cot-Rouge, the Meunier, the Sémillon Blanc, the Folle-Blanche, amongst others. You can also find the Chasselas de Fontainebleau growing on trellises in gardens and orchards.'

'Chilean vines can generally be found in the south and the north; normally these vines, which grow in damp soil, receive little attention, whilst French vines are well looked after.'

The author concludes that the wines are unlikely to be competitive on a global scale, because their production was not sufficient to satisfy local demand. However, he foresees that they will play an ever-increasing part in the wealth of the local economy.

Whilst Viña La Rosa (1824) and Carta Vieja (1825) might dispute as to which is the Chilean wine company with the longest continual history, it was the second half of the nineteenth century which saw the foundation of many of the most important wine houses. Concha y Toro was created in 1883, Santa Rita in 1880, San Pedro in 1865, Undurraga in 1885 – and in many cases wine was no more than a hobby indulged in by someone who had made his fortune in mining or cattle-ranching, or who was an important political figure. There was also a great deal of intermarrying between the wine aristocracy families.

At the beginning of the twentieth century, there grew up a new class of wine merchants, as opposed to growers. Many of these immigrated to Chile from Catalonia and established themselves in Santiago and the leading ports. Often they handled a broad range of imported wines and spirits, as well as distributing the produce of Chilean bodegas. Some of them, such as the Mitjans family, went on to own vineyards and wineries themselves. Chilean wine production, at this time averaged about 2.5 million hectolitres a year, though for the three years of 1913–15, the figure totalled more than 4 million hectolitres each year. This placed it not far behind Argentina in overall production figures.

The 1930s were difficult years for the Chilean wine industry, with over-production and a powerful lobby for prohibition. This latter even had the support of a number of politicians including the presidents Jorge Montt and Arturo Alessandri, with Alessandri even grubbing up his vineyards and replacing them with fruit trees as a gesture of solidarity. These sentiments were reflected in a law, introduced by the Minister of Agriculture Máximo Valdés in 1938. Whilst its stated aims included support for the wine industry, its priority was 'to improve the living conditions of the working classes', who were stricken by alcoholism. The main effect of the law was to restrict the production of wine to 60 litres per head of population and to increase the taxes on both wine and beer. The result was that there was to be no extension of the area under vines – and this law remained in force until 1974.

The following period was one of stagnancy in the Chilean wine trade. Of consumption on the domestic market, probably no more than 5% was of fine wine and between 1939 and 1966 on only three occasions did exports account for more than 5% of the production. Of the exports that did exist, 90% were in cask. Great Britain, which was the most important customer for bottled wine in Europe, in 1964 shipped fewer than 150 cases. Little investment was made in either the vineyards or the wineries; hard currency was not available. As the winemaker Alejandro Hernandez said in 1969, 'For the past forty years or so, Chile has been resting on its wine-making laurels.'

It was also a time of growing agricultural unrest, with the

workers beginning to resent the almost feudal conditions under which they had been living. They tried to unionise themselves, often against fierce opposition from the winery owners. Whilst the Christian Democrat government of Eduardo Frei, elected in 1964, attempted limited agrarian reform, it moved too slowly for the socialists and too quickly for the right and it was succeeded in 1970 by a left-wing coalition, under Salvador Allende. This survived, whilst the economy crumbled about it, until September 1973, when there was a military putsch led by General Augusto Pinochet. Under his brutal regime, which lasted until 1989, the economy stabilised, but the price that was paid is considered by many to have been too high. Some leading members of the wine trade, such as Augustin Hunneus, went into voluntary exile and many overseas consumers boycotted Chilean wine.

The fall of Pinochet opened the doors. The Chilean economy was the most stable one in South America and proved to be immediately attractive to foreign investors. As the title of an article in the American magazine, *The Wine Spectator*, proclaimed, there was a 'Mad Rush to Chile by Californian and French Vintners'. Whilst there has been a boom in the price of suitable land for the planting of vineyards, this has not put off the speculators. From the 150 cases of bottled wine imported by Britain in 1964, the figure has now risen to more than 5 million cases, making it Chile's most important export market.

Is the future secure? There are certain dark clouds on the horizon. In common with many other countries, Chile over-valued the future market for white wine and it now has a surplus of Chardonnay. Whilst the United States is a very important market for the wines of Chile, it is a market that is largely based on price – and such markets can be very fragile. Finally, as I write this towards the end of the year 2000, sales to Britain during the past six months have fallen by 2%. Some of the Chilean companies I have spoken to dismiss this as no more than a blip in the figures, which can be laid at the door of just one company, whose sales of own-label wine to Britain fell dramatically. Others are beginning to question whether the roller coaster may have reached its summit?

On the other hand, there are many positive aspects that promise a bright future for Chilean wines. The Japanese seem to have overcome the indigestion that came about as a result of millennium optimism in the first half of the year 2000; Concha y Toro alone increased its sales in Asia by 147%. More promising, however, is the domestic market. At last, the Chileans themselves seem to be showing interest in the quality wines that their vineyards produce. A sign of this is the rash of new wine shops that has spread through the capital Santiago. Such outlets as El Mundo del Vino in Providencia and Vinopolis at the airport bear witness to a new demand for fine wines, not just from Chile, but from the world over. Perhaps the most telling sign of the growing confidence is the fact that the Agrosuper agroindustrial group (every roadside hoarding seems to encourage you to have a Superpollo chicken) is entering the world of wine with an initial planting of 1,000 hectares of vines!

THE WINE REGIONS

Chile is a long, narrow country; 4,000 km long and an average of no more than 175 km wide. It also has two mountain ranges, the Andes, which provide the country's eastern frontier and the coastal cordillera, which rises over 2,000 m. It is this second, much lower range, which gives me some reason to doubt the first quotation at the beginning of this chapter. From the deck of his cruise liner, or the playing fields of Viña del Mar, it would have been impossible for him to see 'the vineyards and fruit trees of all kinds stretching back to the Andes'.

To its west lies the Pacific Ocean. All these factors help to create a complex climate. Within this narrow band, the vineyards stretch for almost 1,300 km, from Copiapó, 800 km north of Santiago, to the Bio-Bio Valley, some 500 km south of the capital. Whilst this may appear a broad range, it pales into insignificance besides the vineyards of Argentina, which lie to the north of the most northerly in Chile and to the south of the most southerly.

These natural barriers of the Andes, the ocean and, to the north, the Atacama Desert, have been given as reasons why Chile has managed to avoid totally the scourge of *phylloxera vastatrix*. Other reasons have also been advanced; for instance, the traditional flood irrigation. Nevertheless until now, this has not been a problem. The implications of this extend beyond just the damage that the insect can wreak. It also means that vineyards can be planted with ungrafted vines, at much lower cost. However, the introduction of drip irrigation has led to potentially greater problems from nematodes, therefore many viticulturalists are choosing to plant grafted vines.

Structurally, there have been many attempts to give names to the various wine regions, including those where irrigation was the norm and those where it was not practised. With a lack of imagination, the government numbers its different regions from north to south, I to XIII, though they do also have more historical names such as Aisén del General Carlos Ibañez del Campo.

In order to sell into the European Union, the Chileans, have been forced to come up with more tightly controlled regions, whilst giving themselves sufficient flexibility to cross-blend. Initially they used, and abused, a small range of valley names such as Maipo Valley or Rapel Valley. This has since been developed, in order to give more individuality to the labels, into a hierarchy of Regions, Sub-Regions, Zones and Areas. Thus a wine produced solely from grapes from the neighbourhood of the town of Cauquenes, might give as it source Cauquenes, Valle de Tutuven, Valle del Maule or Valle Central, just as a red Burgundy from Savigny might call itself Savigny, Côte de Beaune Villages or Bourgogne. Each of the different sources named, however, does have different price implications.

Here then is the hierarchy from north to south:

Region:	Atacama		
Subregions:	Copiano Valley	Huasco Valley	
Region:	Coquimbo		
Subregions:	Elquí Valley	Limarí Valley	
Region:	Aconcagua		
Subregions:	Aconcagua Valley	Casablanca Valley	
Zones:	Panquehue		
Region:	Central Valley		
Subregions:	Maipo Valley	Rapel Valley	
Zones:		Cachapoal Valley	Colchagua Valley
Areas:	Santiago (Peñalolén, La Florida)	Rancagua (Graneros, Mostazal, Codegua, Olivar.)	San Fernando
	Pirque		Chimbaronga
	Puente Alto	Requinoa	Nancagua (Placilla)
	Buín (Paine, San Bernardo)	Rengo (Malloa, Quinta de Tilcoco)	Santa Cruz (Chépica)
	Isla de Maipo	Peumo, (Pichidegua,	Palmilla
			Peralillo

	Talagante (Peñaflor, El Monte) Melipilla	Las Cabras, San Vicente)	
Subregions:	Curicó Valley		
Zones:	Teno Valley	Lontué Valley	
Areas:	Rauco (Hualeñé) Romeral (Teno)	Molina (Río Claro, Curicó)	
Subregions:	Maule Valley		
Zones:	Claro Valley	Loncomilla Valley	Tutuven Valley
Areas:	Talca (Maule, Pelarco) Pencahue San Clemente	San Javier Villa Alegre Parral (Retiro) Linares (Yerbas Buenas)	Cauquenes
Region:	Southern Valley		
Subregion:	Itata Valley	Bío-Bío Valley	
Zones:			
Areas:	Chillán (Bulnes, San Carlos) Quillón (Ránquil, Florida) Portezuelo (Ninhue, Quirihue, San Nicolás) Coelemu (Treguaco)	Yumbel (Laja) Mulchén (Nacimiento, Negrete)	

If we look at the various regions, the most northerly, the **Atacama**, consists solely of vineyards for growing grapes for eventual distillation into pisco. Most of the vines will be various types of Moscatel. Table grapes are also grown.

Of the two valleys comprising the **Coquimbo** region, the **Elquí**, which comes to the sea at the beautiful city of La Serena, is the heartland of quality Chilean pisco production, with a solitary hectare of vines dedicated to table-wine production. Pisco is the big spirit of Chile, mostly drunk as pisco sour. Generally it is distilled just once and sold at a variety of strengths around 40°. Something rather special is El Fraile Reservado, which is distilled twice and aged in French oak barrels. It retails at about US$20, as opposed to the more normal pisco price of US$7.

Indeed, a village up the valley was renamed Pisco Elquí, in the 1920s, in order to give some justification to the Chileans' use of the name. Also of interest is the village of Vicuña, some 60 km up

ACONCAGUA REGION

Valparaiso

R. Aconcagua

ANDES

Santiago

R. Maipo

1 — Aconcagua
2 — Casablanca
3 — Maipo
4 — Rapel
5 — Curico
6 — Maule
7 — Itata
8 — Bio Bio

Major Valleys

CENTRAL VALLEY REGION

R. Rapel

Cachapoal Valley

Rancagua

R. Cachapoal

Colchagua Valley

R. Tinguiririca

ARGENTINA

Curico

Teno Valley

R. Metaquito

Lontue Valley

Constitucion

R. Claro

Talca

Claro Valley

R. Maule

Pacific Ocean

Tutuven Valley

Loncomilla Valley

R. Itata

R. Nuble

Chillan

Concepcion

R. Bio Bio

N

SOUTHERN REGION

0   Kilometres   300

Inset map

La Serena

Elqui

Ovalle

Limari

COQUIMBO

ANDES

ACONCAGUA REGION

Valparaiso

Mendoza

Santiago

CENTRAL VALLEY REGION

ARGENTINA

Constitucion

0   km.   150

Concepcion

SOUTHERN REGION

Area of Main Map

Chile

the valley from La Serena, which has gained a mystical reputation similar to that of Glastonbury. Not only does it appear to be on every available ley-line, but is a regular dropping-off point for UFOs! For the more down to earth, I can recommend the unsophisticated seafront restaurant *El Pequeño*, at the fishing-port of Guanaqueros, a few miles to the south of La Serena.

The second valley, the **Limarí**, centred on the busy town of Ovalle, is also important for pisco production with a number of distilleries. However, with the expansion into wine of the dominant pisco group, there are now over 400 hectares of vines for wine production, as well as some for table grapes. The one winery based in the valley, Francisco de Aguirre, is the major owner, but there are a number of independent growers. The Kendall-Jackson-owned winery, Las Viñas de la Calina based in Talca, comes to the Limarí Valley for some of its Chardonnay grapes.

Despite its being the most northerly region for the growing of wine grapes, the climate is mild, with summer temperatures rarely rising above 27°C. The important factors here are broad differences between day and night temperatures and sea mists every morning. The rainfall is very low: between 60 mm and 80 mm per year. The vineyards are drip-irrigated.

A third valley within the region, though it has no separate appellation, is that of Choapa, around the town of the same name. At present there are very few vines here, though in the ever-expanding search for vineyard lands, it is likely that there will be further development.

The **Aconcagua** region comprises two disparate zones; to the north is the Aconcagua valley, and, tagged on like a panhandle in the south, is the Casablanca valley.

The **Aconcagua Valley** lies across the Pan-American Highway some 100 km to the north of Santiago. Whilst there are vineyards lower down the valley, to the west of the main road, most of the major plantings are up the valley to the east, which leads to the main pass across the Andes. Here, in the zone of Panquehue, Don Maximiano Errázuriz established a winery in 1890. Whilst this company is still the dominant force in the valley, there have been new plantings by Viña Gracia and by such small companies as Viña Sanchez. Errázuriz has expanded its plantings, and those for its joint venture Seña along the valley and now has a number of vineyards, with plantings totalling more than 250 hectares. Within the valley, there is a broad range of microclimates; for example, the grapes at El Ceibo, on the valley floor, will ripen some three weeks later than those at the home vineyard of Maximiano. At its centre, the valley is not only the hottest, but also the driest vineyard area in Chile. Overall, the climate is arid, with winter rainfall varying between 100 mm and 300 mm a year. One of the important factors is the wind coming in from the ocean; this is reflected in the name of one of the local town Llay-Llay, which, in the native language means 'windy'.

With the effect of the ocean naturally being more important towards the lower end of the valley, it is here that mainly white varieties of grapes are grown, whilst the black grapes are grown further inland.

Throughout Chile, ripening periods are considerably longer than in Europe. In Burgundy, for example, one talks of a 100 days from flowering of the vine to harvest. Generally, in Chile, it is no fewer than 130 days and in the Aconcagua Valley it can be as much as 150 days.

The **Casablanca Valley** was first planted as recently as 1982, on an experimental basis, by Pablo Morandé, then winemaker at Concha y Toro. At the time he came in for a considerable amount of criticism as being foolhardy, for this was far away from the traditional vineyard areas. In fact, it lies on the main road to Santiago from Viña del Mar, at its closest little more than 20 km from the ocean. Here there is no coastal range to protect it from the winds coming off the sea and the maritime fogs. Spring frosts are a regular problem with both smudge pots and heated wind machines being used as protection. It is likely that these might be banned as they are helping to contribute to the invariable smog that seems to blanket Santiago. Sprinkler systems, as used in Chablis, for example, are not a viable alternative for, exceptionally in Chile, Casablanca cannot rely on melt-water from the Andes for irrigation; no river runs through the valley. All the water used comes from artesian wells and it is a finite resource.

Surprisingly, *phylloxera* is perceived as a potential problem by Ed Flaherty, the winemaker at Errázuriz. This is surprising for two reasons; first the vineyards of Casablanca are planted on sandy soil, which is anathema to the bug and secondly, until now, Chile has never suffered from *phylloxera*.

Rainfall averages between 400 mm and 500 mm a year, falling mainly in the winter, but occasionally also in May and September.

Despite the initial criticism, the Casablanca Valley is now considered to be the place for growing white grapes and currently there are approximately 3,000 hectares under vines. By the absorption of land that is currently used for dairy farming, this could be doubled. This must accentuate the already expensive price of suitable land.

To give some idea of the importance that Casablanca plays in the Chilean white wine scene, in the annual rating in 2000 carried out by the highly respected Guía de Vinos de Chile, five of the top 10 Chardonnays and four of the Sauvignon Blancs came from grapes grown in the region.

The **Central Valley** region is the heartland of Chilean viticulture, stretching from the city of Santiago more than 300 km south to the country town of Cauquenes. With the one exception of Errázuriz, every historically important Chilean wine producer comes from within this area. As sub-regions it has the four great wine valleys of Chile: the Maipo, the Rapel, the Curicó and the Maule. These account for more than three-quarters of the total vineyard area of the country and for more than 90% of the production of wine for export.

The **Maipo Valley** was where the first French varietals were planted, for the most part in the suburbs of the city of Santiago itself. Those who had made their fortunes in mining or cattle ranching built magnificent country houses surrounded by parks and vineyards. Some of these have now been overcome by the urban sprawl. The vineyards lie between the coastal range and the Andes, with many being on the lower slopes of the latter up to 1,000 m. This naturally accentuates the difference between day and night temperatures. Annual rainfall is 300–450 mm and the soils are varied, with sand, lime, clay and stones all featuring. This is primarily Cabernet Sauvignon country and a number of Chile's Cabernet-based 'icon' wines use fruit from this region.

Apart from those wineries based in and around Santiago (the few remaining lie between the city and the mountains), there are two main centres in the Maipo Valley. The first of these is near Buín, some 30 km to the south of Santiago on the Pan-American Highway. Here are Santa Rita and Carmen; to the west around the busy town of Isla de Maipo, are Santa Inés/De Martino and Tarapacá. Whilst to the north of them, near Talagante, are the Undurraga cellars.

For fine wine vineyards, the sub-region of the **Rapel Valley** is the most important, with over 13,000 hectares planted. Rather bizarrely, no river called the Rapel flows through the vineyard areas, for above the reservoir created by the Rapel dam, the river splits into two with the Cachapoal flowing from the east and the Tinguiririca from the south. To add to the confusion, the vineyards around the latter river come from the Colchagua Valley zone. Here the annual rainfall is greater than to the north with approximately 700 mm falling every year. Whilst temperatures are about the same with an annual average of 14°C, because the coastal range is lower, the ocean has a cooling influence. Soils are generally fertile.

Most of the major wineries in the Cachapoal Valley lie tucked in against the Andes, with their best vineyards on the well-drained soils of the foothills. Just off to the east of the Pan-American Highway, here, lies Los Lingues, perhaps Chile's most highly rated country hotel. Whilst I admire its location, its furnishings and its facilities, I personally have found it disappointing.

The growers of the Colchagua Valley are the most fiercely independent in Chile. They have grouped together to market their region, organising gastronomic tours. Other ideas include the restoration of a disused railway and the construction of a luxury hotel in Santa Cruz. One of their objectives is that their wines should appear separately on wine lists and on wine-merchants' shelves from other Chilean wines. They are not just Chilean wines; they are from the Colchagua Valley!

This again is primarily red wine country, with the Merlot being particularly important. Perhaps the wines find their best expression in the Apalta Valley, near Santa Cruz. From here come two of Chile's greatest red wines, the Alpha 'M' of Montes and the Clos Apalta of Casa Lapostolle.

Lontué, in the Curicó Valley, could be described as the capital of the Chilean wine trade. Within just a kilometre or two all the major companies seem to have cellars or vineyards: San Pedro, Santa Carolina, Concha y Toro, Valdivieso and La Fortuna. The largest single vineyard of all, that of San Pedro, lies just to the south of the town. Here the valley floor is broad and mainly flat, ideal for cultivation on the grandiose scale.

For staying in the region, I would recommend the Villa El Descanso at Curicó, which despite being on the main road is very comfortable. To avoid disturbance from the traffic, ask for a room at the back of the hotel, or, better still, one of the cabins in the garden.

Until comparatively recently the **Maule Valley** was considered to be the southern frontier of quality production in Chile. It is, however, the most important region as far as the area under vines is concerned, though many of the vineyards are planted in the traditional País, for ultimate sale in tetrabriks on the domestic market. For white wines, the Sémillon is the most widely planted variety. Such companies as Carta Vieja and Las Lomas de Cauquenes realise that to have a sound future, export markets have to be conquered and that the future is in bottle, rather than in bulk – or tetrabrik. The fact that the important Californian wine company, Kendall Jackson, has invested heavily in the area, building a winery and planting vineyards, suggests that this is an area of future expansion.

The climate here is wetter, and colder, than to the north. The annual rainfall can be as high as 800 mm and cold winds blow in from the sea. Frosts, too, can be a hazard and some wineries have installed fan heaters to minimise this danger. On the other hand, many of the vineyards are dry-farmed and this cuts out the cost of installing drip irrigation.

The capital of the region is Talca, which has a fire-fighting museum and a university with a wine school, though this does not rival the long-established schools of the Catholic University and the University of Chile in Santiago. For the tourist looking for somewhere to stay, I can recommend the Hotel Marcos Gamero. Whilst not quite completed when I visited, the Guest House at Viña Tabontinaja, seems most appealing.

The **Southern Valley Region** has two sub-regions, the Itata Valley and the Bío-Bío Valley. Together they account for about a fifth of the vineyard area of the country.

Despite the fact that it is so far south, the **Itata Valley** has a Mediterranean climate. Notwithstanding this, there has been very little attempt until recently to plant other than basic grape varieties, the País for red wines and the Italia, a clone of Ugni Blanc, for white. However, there was considerable investment in the area from 1989 onwards by Fundación Chile, an American-sponsored organisation. It has planted 170 hectares of noble varietals, such as Chardonnay, Cabernet Sauvignon and Syrah. However, there is no commercial winery of any importance within the region. Other grapes grown in the area include Gewürztraminer and Riesling.

Somehow I get the impression that the vineyards of the **Bío-Bío Valley** are something of an embarrassment to those who promote Chilean wines. Whenever I have tried to go there, I have been told that there is little to see, there are no wineries and, on the last occasion, everything is under floodwater.

The vineyards lie on both banks of the river, which flows south from the port of Concepción. Here the main problem is not the climate, for the mean annual temperature is 13°C, with good differences between day and night temperatures. However, the rainfall can be as much as 1250 mm a year, causing potential problems with rot. For fine wines, the most successful grapes are Pinot Noir and Chardonnay, Gewürztraminer and Riesling.

THE GRAPES

Chile has followed California down the varietal route; most of its wines are sold under the name of a single grape variety and just four of these dominate, Cabernet Sauvignon and Merlot for red wines and Chardonnay and Sauvignon Blanc for white wines. However, during the past few years there have been two disparate trends. First, the growth of blended wines; most of these being red and the best known of them in the 'icon' sector. Secondly, there has been an increasing willingness to experiment with a much broader range of grape varieties, though because of restrictions on the importation of vine-cuttings, the range is still somewhat limited.

However, at this stage two things must also be said. The second most widely planted red variety is the País and the second most widely planted white is the Moscatel de Alejandría. The first is never mentioned on a wine-label and the second rarely. Why? Because they are primarily used in basic blended table wine sold on the domestic market in either tetrabriks or demijohns.

The second important point to make is that there have been two recognition crises in the Chilean grape world. The first, and perhaps more important of these, is concerning Sauvignon Blanc. As Jancis Robinson says in *Vines, Grapes and Wines*, '. . . Only some of Chile's "Sauvignon" is Sauvignon Blanc. In the past, most was the more ordinary Sauvignonasse or Sauvignon Vert, thought by the Australian A. J. Antcliff to be Italy's Tocai Friulano. Both Chilean variations on the Sauvignon theme have a marked sweetness, almost floral character, not associated with French Sauvignon Blanc.'

Whilst this problem was recognised many years ago, there appears to have been little attempt to solve it. Much Sauvignonasse is still sold as Sauvignon Blanc and I know of no more than two wineries that have been bold enough to offer it as Sauvignon Vert. It is true that much is no more than a constituent in the basic varietal wine (Errázuriz 30%, Undurraga 40%), but nevertheless it seems surprising that since the problem was recognised 10 years or more ago, little effort has been made to remedy it.

In some ways, the second identification problem is more surprising. Following research by a French ampelographer as recently as 1994, it is now accepted that much of what was sold as Merlot was, in fact Carmenère, in its native Bordeaux, a moribund grape variety. As Carmenère has much harsher tannins than the Merlot and ripens up to three weeks later, it seems that the two have been long planted, and harvested, together indiscriminately. To resolve this problem, a number of steps have been taken. Some growers have marked individual vines in their vineyards, so that the two varieties are now harvested at different times. The disadvantage of this is that it precludes machine-harvesting. Alternatively, there has been a certain amount of head-grafting, though it appears that it is possible to graft the Carmenère on to Merlot rootstock, but not the other way round.

Before looking at the individual varieties, there is one very important factor that has to be taken into consideration with regard to the quality of the wine that they give; that is the question of yields. As there are no maximum yields laid down by legislation, and that, until recently, the price paid depended solely on the weight and not on the sugar content of the grapes, or their condition, there was a tendency to overcrop. Obviously, this had a serious effect upon the resultant quality of the wine. Now companies are much more quality conscious. At San Pedro, for example, each level of product category has a maximum yield imposed, whilst at Casa

Lapostolle, some of their growers are paid per hectare of crop, rather than per ton. Such moves are leading to quality improvements, but it is still apparent that at the 'commodity' end of the business, yields are excessive.

Red varieties

Cabernet Sauvignon: This is now the most widely planted red varietal with something over 16,000 hectares. The figure has doubled in the past 12 years. Whilst the grape is widely planted in the Central Valley, it is probably at its best in the Maipo Valley. The wines are much softer than their equivalents from Bordeaux, due to the grapes reaching optimum ripeness. The dominant flavours are ripe black fruit, such as cassis and blackberry. Eucalyptus hints are also often noted.

País: The classic grape variety of Chile, being of the same family as the Criolla of Argentina and the Mission of California. It was probably brought over by the earliest Spanish missionaries, possibly from the Canary Islands. Whilst this variety is widely denigrated, and is mainly used for everyday table wine, producers, such as Las Lomas de Cauquenes and J. Bouchon, have shown what can be done with low yields and careful vinification. During the past 15 years, the area under País has halved and now stands at about 15,000 hectares. It is mainly grown in the south, on dry-farmed land in the Maule and Itata Valleys.

Merlot: This grape variety has recently had much success, particularly on the American market, because it gives soft easy-to-drink wines, often with black cherry flavours. As a sign of its success, in 1993 there were just 12 Chilean Merlots on offer, by 1998 there were 75. There are approximately 5,500 hectares of vineyards with this variety. Probably its best wines come from the Colchagua Valley.

Carignan: After the 'big three' there is a rapid drop to the fourth most widely planted variety. The Carignan has approximately 550 hectares planted and the grapes are generally used for blends; it is often grown in the south as an alternative to País. One exception is the Gillmore straight varietal from Viña Tabontinaja.

Malbec: This is another historical varietal from the south-west of France, where it is sometimes called Cot. Following its success in Argentina, where it is widely planted, there are now just over 500 hectares planted in Chile, where it can achieve full ripeness and gives rich, meaty wines. It is grown in a variety of locations from Cauquenes in the south to Isla de Maipo in the north.

Pinot Noir: Despite the fact that this variety was the first one to be mentioned by Sempé in his list of French varietals planted in Chile, which he wrote in 1882, a century later there were no more than a 100 hectares planted. Now the figure has risen to just over 400. This may well be because it is a notoriously difficult variety from which to produce good wine. Nevertheless it is available from a broad range of producers, at a broad range of prices. Viña Gracia now claims to have the most important plantings, mainly in the Bío-Bío Valley in the south, though the best wines probably come from Valdivieso.

Carmenère: Whilst it is unlikely that the official statistics have been able to separate this variety successfully from the Merlot, under which guise it masqueraded for many years, they claim that there are 330 hectares planted. This is likely to be an underestimate. An historical Bordeaux variety, it has almost totally disappeared there because it is very susceptible to poor fruit-set. (It is rumoured that the only planting left there of this variety is a one hectare plot at the wine-school in Blanquefort.) In many ways it is well suited to Chilean conditions where it gives wine with a certain herbaceousness on the nose and rich fullness on the palate. There are many who hope that they can develop this as Chile's answer to the Zinfandel of California, the Malbec of Argentina and the Tannat of Uruguay.

Syrah: This is a comparatively recent introduction to Chile, probably as a result of its success in Australia. It is planted from the steep hillsides at Errázuriz in the north to the Itata Valley in the south. There are just over 200 hectares planted.

Cabernet Franc: For those used to Loire wines made from this variety, those from Chile will come as a complete surprise, for they lack the stalkiness that comes with incomplete ripeness. It is used as a blending agent as well as a single varietal. Among the better wines are those from Francisco de Aguirre in the Limarí Valley in the north to Gillmore in the Maule Valley in the south.

Other red varieties that are planted include the *Cinsaut* (200 hectares), *Alicante Bouschet* (22 hectares), *Zinfandel* (22 hectares, Canepa and Montgras), *Mourvèdre, Sangiovese, Portugais Bleu* (Morandé), *Garnacha* and *Petit Verdot*.

White varieties

Sauvignon Blanc: The one certain thing about Sauvignon Blanc in Chile is that much of it is not what it seems to be. Quite what it is remains open to dispute. Conveniently much of it is now called, but not labelled, Sauvignonasse. Is this the same as the Sauvignon Vert? Jancis Robinson and Hubrecht Duijker believe that it is, but others are not so sure. To complicate things further, there is also a grape called the Sauvignon Gris. Additionally there is the feeling that there might have been some intermingling with strains of Sémillon. All this is too much for the Chilean wine authorities, so they have taken the easy way out and grouped everything together. As a result it has been decided that Sauvignon Blanc is the most widely planted white varietal in the country, with more than 6,500 hectares.

Despite all this, or perhaps because of it, the Sauvignon Blanc in Chile generally lacks the concentrated flavours, and certainly the grassiness of its French sisters. The best examples often come from the Casablanca Valley.

Two wineries proud enough to sell wine labelled as Sauvignon Vert are the Co-operative Cellar at Curicó and Pueblo Antiguo.

Muscat d'Alexandrie (or Muscatel Alejandría): There are a number of members of the Moscatel family grown in Chile and they are generally used for distilling into pisco or for blended cheap table wines. However, Francisco de Aguirre sells a straight Moscatel de Austria. Despite its rare appearances on a wine-label, there are almost 6,000 hectares planted for winemaking, outside distillation.

Chardonnay: This variety has had perhaps the most spectacular increase in plantings of any in Chile. In 1983, the variety was not recorded at all and in 1988, Jan Read could write, 'The

Chardonnay crops sparsely in Chile and there are barely 100 hectares in cultivation.' Now the figure is approaching 6,000 hectares, of which more than 20% are in Casablanca. This is the most successful area with five of the six highest-rated wines in the 2000 *Guía de Vinos de Chile* coming from there.

As in other parts of the world a broad range of styles is produced, and this is the white wine most frequently barrel-aged.

Sémillon: Whilst this is generally considered to be a noble grape variety, in Chile it is a case of familiarity breeding contempt. Sempé records it as being widely grown in 1882 and Jan Read says that in 1988 it was responsible, often blended with Chardonnay, for 87% of Chilean white wine. Official statistics dating from 1983 also show it as having more than half the acreage of white wine vineyards; the current figure is less than 10%, mainly in the Maule Valley. It is still used widely for blending, but, because most of the vines are very old, can make outstanding single varietal wines.

Torontel: This is the same as the Torrontés of Argentina and gives elegant, highly flavoured, wines. There are just over a 1,000 hectares planted and the wine is generally blended into low-cost table wine.

Riesling: Whilst there are now only just over 300 hectares of Riesling remaining, German-style wines have a long tradition in Chile and the name Rhin is still used by Undurraga and Carmen, indeed the latter is just being relaunched on the domestic market with a poster campaign.

Other white varieties that are planted include the **Chenin Blanc**, the **Gewürztraminer**, the **Pedro Ximinez**, the **Viognier**, and the **Pinot Blanc**.

THE WINES

One of the problems about writing about the wines of Chile is that the foreign visitor is never exposed to a large proportion of them. Whilst the situation has altered considerably over the past 10 years or so, the fact still remains that the Chilean consumer, in the main, drinks totally different wines from those found on export markets. Eighty per cent of the wine sold officially in Chile is bought in litre tetrabriks or demijohns. In addition, particularly in the Maule Valley, you see roadside signs offering *chicha* for sale. This is sweet, part-fermented must and is a very popular drink. Also on offer, in season, is *vino pipeño*, the equivalent of the *vin bourru*, or new wine, as drunk in Alsace at harvest time. Of course, it is true that much of *vin de table* drunk in France is not of export quality, but, in Chile, even at higher levels, there are wines that do not find their way to the export market and which are never offered for tasting to foreign visitors. Some of these are for labelling reasons. For example, we are never likely to see in Britain the Margaux Cabernet Sauvignon of Carmen or the Corton Cabernet Sauvignon of Errázuriz. However, it seems strange to me that the Santa Rita Casa Real Cabernet Sauvignon sold on the Chilean market is different from that sold on export markets – though the latter is available on the domestic market as Casa Real (Etiqueta Export) at a considerably higher price. There appears to be a firm wall of separation between what a company does on the domestic market and what it does abroad.

At the same time, another point that is worth making is that the image of Chilean wines on the US market is different from that on the British. In the United States, Chilean wines are primarily a price item, with the market leader, by far, being Concha y Toro. In Britain, the market is much more fragmented and prepared to pay higher prices. This has made it particularly attractive for such newcomers as Caliterra and Cono Sur.

Until recently, on the British market, Chile was a four varietal supplier: Cabernet Sauvignon, Merlot, Sauvignon Blanc and Chardonnay, but, as can be seen by the broad range of varietals that is now being planted, the situation has opened up. Nevertheless, with few exceptions, on export markets, the wines are sold as straight varietals. Bordeaux-style blends are now beginning to appear.

As opposed to most wine regions, the ripening period in Chile may be as much as eight weeks longer. This has a number of results. First of all, many red varieties achieve a degree of ripeness in Chile that they never do in their home country. This is particularly true of the Bordeaux varietals, not just the classic Cabernet Sauvignon and Merlot, but more particularly with such lesser grapes as the Malbec, the Cabernet Franc, the Carmenère and the Petit Verdot. In

Bordeaux they have been all but abandoned, because of the difficulty they have in achieving full maturity. If they are used at all, it is often to add firm tannins. For the uninitiated, a bottle of Chilean Cabernet Franc, for example, may surprise with its rich, soft flavours.

There is a corollary to this. Some varieties, and I am particularly thinking of the Pinot Noir, often have such a degree of ripeness that they lose the finesse and elegance that can make them great wines. This also means that Chilean wines can be surprisingly alcoholic. It was only by chance, when I was looking at the tasting-sheet at a winery that I noticed that not one wine was less than 13.5°, and many were 14° or more. I must admit that I rarely pay attention to the strength of a wine, but it does provide a potential pitfall for the Chilean wine consumer.

A further extension of this is that very few wines are made for ageing. On my last trip to Chile, I am not sure how many hundred different wines I tasted, but I was only offered one that was five years old and four or five that were four years old. It is not that the wines do not age well, it is just that they are made for immediate consumption on release – and all wines are released young. Perhaps it is not strange that the Chilean producers have little interest in creating wines with complexity and tannins that will benefit from ageing in the bottle. Such a concept can have a bad effect on cash flow!

One expression on a Chilean wine-label that should be treated with care is the word *Reserve* or *Reserva*. Whilst this generally means that the wine has received some oak treatment, not necessarily in a cask, it has absolutely no official backing and, in effect, means absolutely nothing at all than that the price is higher than wines whose labels do not say this. Certain producers have been instructed by the authorities in Germany to remove the word from their labels.

This takes us on to another comparatively recent development, the launch by a number of wineries of 'icon' wines, nearly always red and 'Bordeaux blends'. That this has happened is not surprising. If you are selling your wine under a varietal name, it is very difficult to give an impression of added quality. This is a problem that has confronted the growers of Alsace for many years. They have come up with two main answers, medals and the *grand cru* vineyards. The first possibility is available to the Chilean growers and they make the most of it, though the multiplicity of wine fairs around the world has rather devalued many of their awards. As for giving certain sites exceptional status, this possibility has largely passed. The single vineyard, or even domaine-bottled, concept is rare in Chile. Indeed the pragmatism with which the valley appellations were used in the early days has considerably lessened their credibility. It is true that Casablanca has created a great reputation for its white wines, with a corresponding increase in land values, and the price of wine, but nowhere else has managed anything similar. The growers of the Cachapoal Valley are claiming a similar status for their red wines, but not surprisingly, this is strongly disputed by those who do not own land there.

The demand for the creation of prestige wines has been spurred on by foreign investors, often coming from Bordeaux or California. In both these regions, exceptionally high prices are paid for the top wines, be they *grands crus classés* or 'meritage' blends. An important proportion of these prices is not because of their integral quality, but either because of their rarity and the hype that surrounds them.

The concept of Chilean 'First Growths' is a comparatively recent one; the oldest member of the group is Don Melchor of Concha y Toro, which first appeared approximately 10 years ago. How do they reach this status? On their visit to Chile in March 2000, the Masters of Wine tasted 10 aspirants to this level and it is interesting to see that wines were selected largely on price, though it could be claimed that they were, for the most part, the produce of very old vines. These were the wines in the tasting, all of the 1997 vintage:

Domus Aurea, Viña Quebrada de Macul, Maipo Valley. Cabernet Sauvignon 95%, Cabernet Franc 5%. 10/14 months in one- and two-year-old French oak. Stated retail price in UK: £22.

Finis Terrae, Viña Cousiño Macul, Maipo Valley. Cabernet Sauvignon 50%, Merlot 50%. New French oak. Stated retail price in UK: £20.

Casa Real Cabernet Sauvignon (etiqueta export), Viña Santa Rita, Maipo Valley. Cabernet Sauvignon 100%. 14 months in new French oak. Stated retail price in UK: £20.

Gold Reserve, Viña Carmen, Maipo Valley. Cabernet Sauvignon 100%. 17 months in new French oak. Stated retail price in UK: £20.

Don Melchor, Viña Concha y Toro, Maipo Valley. Cabernet Sauvignon 100%. 12 months in new and one-year-old French oak. Stated retail price in UK: £20.

Almaviva, Viña Almaviva, Maipo Valley. Cabernet Sauvignon 72%, Carmenère 23%, Cabernet Franc 5%. 16 months in 85% new French oak. Stated retail price in UK: £45.

Don Maximiano Founder's Reserve, Viña Errázuriz, Aconcagua Valley. Cabernet Sauvignon 87%, Merlot 13%. 20 months in new French oak. Stated retail price in UK: £18.

Seña, Viña Errázuriz/Robert Mondavi, Aconcagua Valley, Cabernet Sauvignon 84%, Carmenère 16%, 16 months in new oak. Stated retail price in UK: £30.

Montes Alpha 'M', Viña Montes, Colchagua Valley. Cabernet Sauvignon 80%, Merlot 10%, Cabernet Franc 10%. 18 months in new French oak. Stated retail price in UK: £30.

Clos Apalta 1997, Casa Lapostolle, Colchagua Valley. Merlot 50%, Carmenère 30%, Cabernet Sauvignon 20%. 18 months in new French oak. Stated retail price in UK: £30.

It is perhaps interesting that the five cheapest wines are all produced by Chilean companies and that four of the five most expensive are from companies with either French or American investment. Whilst I have not tasted all of these wines, I gather that there was no direct correlation between price and quality.

If price were the only qualification in the creation of a Chilean *premier cru* status, then the following seven wines would also have to be considered:

Porqué Nó, Viña Gracia.
Gran Araucano, Viña Gran Araucano, Cachapoal Valley.
House of Morandé, Viña Morandé, Maipo Valley.
Catalina, Viña Santa Ema, Rapel Valley.
Caballo Loco, Viña Valdivieso, Lontué Valley.
Grand Cru, Viña Santa Amalia, Château Los Boldos, Requinoa Valley.
Milenium, Viña Tarapacá.

On re-reading what I have just written, I note that white wines go virtually unmentioned. There are reasons for this, of which the main one is that the production of red wine is almost twice that of white wine. More important, the Chileans appear to accord much less status to even their best white wines than they do to their reds. For example, I have just mentioned 17 red wines in Chile that regularly retail for over 12,000 pesos, and five of them sell for over 25,000 pesos. There is not a single Chilean white wine that sells for as much as 12,000 pesos. Despite the fact that the best white wines come from Casablanca, which has arguably the most expensive vineyard land, and that a French oak barrel costs the same for either red or white wine, the best white wines cannot command equal prices.

One aspect of white wines that does deserve a mention, is that of late-harvest wines. These are produced by a small number of companies and are generally made from *botrytis*-affected Sémillon or Sauvignon grapes.

THE WINERIES

Viña Francisco de Aguirre S.A. Limari Valley, Coquimbo Region. Whilst this is one of the newer wine companies in Chile, being founded only in 1993, it has great ambitions to be one of the Big Four Chilean producers within 10 years. These ambitions do not appear unreasonable, when you consider that the Capel group, which has 95% of the Chilean pisco market, owns 85% of its shares. With the two leading brands, Capel and Control, it has not only enormous resources but also is able to apply great pressure on buyers on the Chilean market, where it sells over five million cases of pisco a year. With a stable domestic market, and little demand overseas for its product, the company realised that to expand it needed to diversify and producing wine seemed a logical step. Indeed, its power has made it the number four brand on the Chilean market after Concha y Toro, San Pedro and Santa Rita, though this has been achieved mainly by selling lower quality wine in tetra-pak, produced in a separate winery.

The winery currently has 60 hectares of steeply sloping vineyards and is planting a further 250 hectares. As the minority shareholders are also local vineyard owners, in all, it controls the production of 420 hectares. Of these two-thirds are planted in Cabernet Sauvignon and almost a fifth in Chardonnay. The balance is made up of Merlot, Sauvignon Blanc and Cabernet Franc. Any further grape requirements are bought from local independent growers. All these vineyards are in the Limarí Valley, some 400 km north of Santiago, an area that has historically produced only grapes for distillation into pisco.

Despite it being the most northerly wine-producing area in Chile, the climate is quite cool, due to sea fogs rolling in from the ocean 35 km away. About 60–80 mm of rain falls each winter, with nothing for the rest of the year, so the vines are all drip-irrigated, from three reservoirs.

The winery is cut into the hillside, so is gravity-fed. A cellar has also been tunnelled out and whilst this is used currently for receptions, there are plans for the ageing of bottle-fermented sparkling wine. The winery is equipped with all the latest technology and has a storage capacity of five million litres. There are 1,500 barrels of French and American oak.

Apart from speciality wines, which include a late-harvest Muscat of Alexandria and a sparkling Muscat, the wines are split into five ranges. The basic range is the Tierra Arena Classic of young Sauvignon Blanc, Moscatel, Pedro Jiménez and Cabernet Sauvignon. These wines have no oak contact except for a small fraction of the last one. The Palo Alto wines include both partly oaked (Chardonnay, Cabernet Sauvignon and Cabernet Franc) and unoaked wines (Sauvignon Blanc and Merlot). There are also three oaked Reserve wines under the same label. The Tierras Altas Reserve wines have a proportion of new French oak and, at the peak is Tempus, where only French oak is used. These wines, which at my visit had not yet been released, are Cabernet Franc/Cabernet Sauvignon, Cabernet Sauvignon/Merlot and Chardonnay/Viognier blends.

Despite its recent arrival on the scene, it seems likely that this winery will have a big impact.

Wines I particularly enjoyed: Tierras Altas Chardonnay 1999, Palo Alto Cabernet Sauvignon 1999, Cabernet Franc Reserve 1999, Tempus Cabernet Sauvignon/Merlot 1998.
Other labels: Doña Gabriela, La Serena, Santa Andrea.

Viña Almaviva, Maipo Valley. Again a new star in the Chilean firmament, this winery is an equal joint venture between Concha y Toro and Baron Philippe de Rothschild from Bordeaux. The vineyard, which was first planted by the Chilean partner in 1978, lies just south of Santiago. The partnership was established in 1997, though the first vintage sold on the market was 1996.

There are 41 hectares of vineyards and current production is under 4,000 cases, though the ultimate objective is 25,000 cases per year. Yields are low, very low by Chilean standards, and the wine is aged in French oak for 16 months. The proportion of new oak seems to vary between 85% and 95%. Just one wine is made and this is the country's most expensive wine, retailing at about US$70. Like every other premium Chilean red wine, it is ready for drinking on release, though it has the structure to last.

At a tasting of Chilean 'First Growths' given to the Masters of Wine during their visit to Chile, in 2000, this was widely considered to be the best wine.

In a separate development, Baron Philippe de Rothschild has recently released a range of three Chilean varietal wines under the brand name MAPA.

Viña Anakena, Cachapoal Valley. Jorge Gutierrez created this wine estate at Requinoa in 1984 and also owned the Viña Porta brand, which he subsequently sold to Viña Gracia (q.v.). Anakena takes its name from a beach on Easter Island and the labels feature an exploding volcano. Current production is approximately 60,000 cases per year from a 70-hectare estate, but there are a further 100 hectares to be planted. Sales are aimed at export markets.

The vineyard has its own very cool microclimate, which makes for late ripening.

Wines I particularly enjoyed: Chardonnay Reserva 1997.

Viña Aquitania, Domaine Paul Bruno, Maipo Valley. The name of this winery gives some hint as to the origins of its ownership. It is a partnership between Bruno Prats, the former owner of Château Cos d'Estournel and Paul Pontallier, from Château Margaux, with, as minority shareholder Felipe de Solminihac, one of Chile's best winemakers.

The vineyard of 25 hectares is in the Quebrada de Macul, threatened by the urban sprawl of the city of Santiago. Only one wine is produced, with the label Domaine Paul Bruno, and this is a Cabernet Sauvignon. Despite the Bordeaux connection, only half of the blend spends any time in oak, and then no more than 10 months.

Araucano is the brand name for the Chilean wines produced by the ubiquitous Lurton brothers, Jacques and François. The grapes for these are mainly sourced in the Colchagua Valley and the wines are made at Viña Santa Laura (q.v.).

Aresti Family Vineyards, Curicó Valley. This is a family company, run by Vicente Aresti and his three sons. Whilst they have been making wine for almost 50 years, they only started bottling it at the end of 1999. To cater for this, an enormous bottling hall and underground cellars have been built at Bellavista to the south of the town of Molina. The capacity of this winery is 8 million litres and there is also a smaller one, with a capacity of one million litres at Micaela, near Lontue. In total, the estate has 355 hectares of vines in production; these are split between five different vineyards.

Whilst it has been exporting wine in bulk since 1973, the move to selling bottled wine means moving in a different direction. The target for the first year in bottle were 80,000 cases, but there is capacity for 400,000 cases a year.

Wines I particularly enjoyed: Montemar Cabernet Sauvignon 1999.

Viña El Aromo, Maule Valley. This bodega, situated in the centre of the town of Talca, firmly aims its wines at the domestic market. No barrels are used and any oak flavours come from chips. Its top-level wines are sold as Sello Gran Reserva and Sello Reserva Privada.

The company has an estate of 158 hectares and supplements this with bought-in grapes.

Viña Atenea, Curicó Valley. The Ojeda family have been vine-growers for more than a 100 years, though it is only recently that they have started selling bottled wine. The estate of 130 hectares is in the Teno Valley and at Sagrada Familia. It is planted in Cabernet Sauvignon, Cabernet Franc, Merlot and Carmenère for red wines, and Sauvignon Blanc and Chardonnay for white wines.

The winery is at San Juan de Peteroa and has recently been modernised, to include improved cooling systems and micro-oxygenation equipment.

Viña Balduzzi, Maule Valley. This is yet another family-owned company that has turned completely from selling nothing but wine in bulk, to nothing but wine in bottle – and this almost exclusively on export markets. The historic estate of 30 hectares was planted around the winery, but this was increased about five years ago by a further 70 hectares, solely planted in Cabernet Sauvignon. There are only three varieties planted: Sauvignon Blanc, Chardonnay and Cabernet Sauvignon. Current production is about 50,000 cases a year, but this is rising steadily.

There are more than 250 oak barrels in the cellar and also some classic *rauli*-wood vats. However, these are a deception, for they have all been lined with fibreglass.

Balduzzi is one of the comparatively few wineries in Chile positively to encourage visitors.

Bisquertt Family Vineyards, Colchagua Valley. This company would like to describe itself as 'the biggest boutique winery in Chile', but, with 800 hectares of vineyards, I have the feeling that it has somewhat outgrown its desired image. It also prides itself on the number of women who work there – but the company is firmly in the hands of the patriarchal Don Osvaldo Bisquertt and his sons.

The vineyards are split between five separate farms, all in the valley of the Tinguiririca River, the furthest being no more than 10 km from the winery. The company uses nothing but its own grapes for its wines and it came as a surprise to me how recently it was established.

Whilst the name is a historical one in Chilean wine history (the family began producing wine at the end of the nineteenth century), it was not until the beginning of the 1970s that this estate was created, when Don Osvaldo began planting vineyards and built the winery in a restored farmhouse. This is one of Chile's most attractive wineries and features a carriage museum.

As one of the many interests of the family is a stainless-steel fabrication plant, its vats can be seen here and in many other wineries. The barrels that it uses include a number of 500-litre French oak puncheons.

For many years the family sold only bulk wine to other companies, but launched its own bottled wines in the early 1990s. With an annual production capacity of more than 600,000 cases and current export sales of 200,000 cases, this is a company with plenty of room for expansion. It also means that it produces a big range of wines (and labels). In any given vintage, it might make six different Cabernet Sauvignons, six Merlots and six Chardonnays.

The company is also one of the leading proponents of the independence for the Colchagua Valley movement. This aims to create a separate image for these wines from others in Chile and to have them shown separately on wine-merchants' shelves. Don Osvaldo is not afraid of knocking the opposition. As he said to me at the end of the evening, 'No good wine comes out of Curicó'.

Wines I particularly enjoyed: Don Osvaldo Sauvignon Blanc 2000, Château la Joya Barrel-Fermented Chardonnay 1999, Château La Joya Cabernet Sauvignon 1998, Château La Joya Carmenère Grande Réserve 1999.
Other labels: Château La Joya (Casa La Joya in U.K.), Don Osvaldo, Los Pedrones.

Viñedos J. Bouchon y Cía. Ltda., Maule Valley. The Bouchon family is proud of its Bordeaux connections. It was from there that they emigrated to Chile at the end of the nineteenth century and the current head of the company, Julio Bouchon, returned there to take a degree in oenology.

However, its winery, at Santa María de Mingre, is of Australian design and was constructed in 1991/92, with such novelties for Chile as Potter rotary fermenters. The capacity is 2.3 million litres in stainless-steel and oak barrels and there is a further winery in Talca with a capacity in stainless steel only of 1.4 million litres.

Because of the distances between Santiago, where Sr Bouchon has property interests, and the winery, an airstrip has been built and a small fleet of planes is kept for commuting purposes.

In total it has 350 hectares of vineyards on three estates all in the Maule Valley. Here, comparatively far south as far as Chile's vineyards are concerned, the climate is somewhat different. With higher rainfall, most of the vineyards are not irrigated and this results in low yields. Whilst summer temperatures in the day time might average 32°C, at night they average no more than 16°, and throughout the year there are cooling breezes from the Pacific each afternoon. All this helps to concentrate fruit flavours. However, spring frosts can be a problem and there are heated wind fans in the vineyards to counteract this.

The company has a policy for its red wines of only using the term 'Reserva' for those that have spent some time in barrel.

Wines I particularly enjoyed: Cabernet Sauvignon Reserva 1998. *Other labels:* Chicureo, Las Mercedes, Convento Viejo.

Las Viñas de la Calina, Talca. That this winery sells 99% of its production in the United States is not surprising when you learn that it was created by the Californian company Kendall Jackson. When it started in 1993, it had the somewhat revolutionary concept of operating without either vineyards or a winery. Now things are changing.

In the beginning, the idea was to buy the best parcels of grapes from the best wine regions and vinify small lots. For example, Itata, the Limarí Valley and Casablanca were considered to be the best place for Chardonnay grapes, so they were bought there. As a winery, the second facility at Tabontinaja (q.v.) was used. Now, 700 hectares of vines have been planted at Cauquenes in the Maule Valley, and a winery, El Maiten, has been built at Talca.

Two levels of wines are produced, Calina, at the lower level, and Viñas de Calina, at the higher. Barrel ageing is a particular feature of this winery.

Viña Caliterra, Colchagua Valley. This winery describes itself as belonging 'to the new generation of Chilean wineries' and this is true, but at the same time misleading, as it could be said that it itself is now in its second generation. It was originally established, in 1989, by the Chadwick family, as a sister operation to Errázuriz. However, the idea was not to be an 'estate' winery, but, rather, one that would source the best grapes available from a variety of regions.

As a partner at that time, they had Augustin Huneeus, the Chilean-born owner of Franciscan vineyards in California. This partnership lasted two years. In the meantime, Robert Mondavi, also from the Napa Valley, had been seeking to invest in Chile and he and Eduardo Chadwick turned Caliterra into a joint venture in January 1995.

One of the partnership's first priorities was to create a vineyard and the responsibility for identifying somewhere suitable was given to Pedro Izquierdo, the viticulturist at Errázuriz. He found La

Arboleda, a remote offshoot of the Colchagua valley. Here was a property of 1,000 hectares, largely scrubland and hillsides, with some winter wheat growing on the valley floor. Its remoteness was a problem. A road had to be built and water and electricity had to be brought 4.5 km. The whole valley had to be drained, before planting could begin and drip-irrigation could be installed.

Planting began in February 1997 and there are 310 hectares planted to red varieties (Cabernet Sauvignon, Merlot, Carmenère, Syrah, Malbec and Sangiovese), with a further 40 hectares available. The vineyard is between 220 and 260 m above sea level and there is an average annual rainfall of about 600 mm. While the Pacific Ocean is 60 km away, cooling sea breezes have an important role to play in the climate. On the property there is a broad variety of soils, including loam, sandy, clay and rocks, with all combinations in between. There are 7,000 vines to the hectare and composted pumice is the only fertiliser used.

A gravity-fed winery with an initial capacity of 6.5 million litres in 128 stainless-steel vats of a broad range of sizes, was built in 1998 and wines of the 1999 vintage were made there. The first grapes from La Arboleda estate were picked in the 2000 vintage. At present only 30% of their grape needs come from their own vineyards; the rest is supplied by growers with long-term contracts. The next stage of development will be a barrel cellar on the property.

Caliterra was conceived primarily as an export operation and here it has achieved its objective. With annual sales approaching 700,000 cases and set to rise, all but 5% are exported. This makes the company the third largest exporter of Chilean wine. Here are quality modern wines at reasonable prices.

Wines I particularly enjoyed: Cabernet Sauvignon 1999, Central Valley, Cabernet Reserva 1998, Maipo Valley, La Arboleda Merlot 1999, La Arboleda Syrah 1999.

Camino Real S.A., Cachapoal Valley. This is a company that, whilst it produces a full range of wines, has concentrated its efforts on marketing just one. This is a Cabernet Sauvignon *Reserva Especial*, sold as Vino de Eyzaguirre, San Francisco de Mostazal. The bottles are each presented in a hessian sack, the story being that this was the packaging adopted by the first producers of the wine, the

Franciscan monks, in order to minimise breakages in transit. The main disadvantage of such a presentation is the difficulty that it presents to sommeliers to serve the wine – these have now been given a special set of opening instructions!

A Merlot Reserva Especial is shortly to be launched.

Wines I have particularly enjoyed: Vino de Eyzaguirre Reserva Especial 1998.

Viña Canepa. This is a family winery run by the redoubtable Luciana Garibaldi de Canepa, who almost takes it as a personal insult that visitors are not able to talk to her in her native Italian. She took charge of the company at a particularly difficult time, when her husband died and his three sisters inherited the bulk of the family vineyard estate, which had been built up over the years. They went on to establish the Hacienda El Condor and the TerraMater wineries (q.v.). She was left with the original Canepa winery in a Santiago suburb and the surrounding 18-hectare vineyard. Not deterred, she has recreated a powerful domain, with over 500 hectares at Trinidad in the Colchagua Valley, as well as two other properties in the Rapel Valley. A new vinification plant has also been built at Trinidad.

The location of the mother winery, now in the middle of an industrial estate, scarcely prepares the visitor for the quality of the wines. But Canepa has always been in the forefront of technology. Together with Miguel Torres, it introduced the Chilean wine-trade to stainless steel. It was also one of the first wineries to use oak casks, and it now has more than 3,000 French oak barrels.

The reliability and quality of Canepa wines mean that they are major suppliers of own-label wines to European supermarket chains. In all they export, in bulk and bottle, 5.5 million litres of wine a year, with almost two-thirds of this going to the British market. They sell a further 4 million litres on the Chilean market, where they distribute such brands as Beck's beer, San Pellegrino mineral water and Marqués de Riscal Rioja.

Amongst their specialities are a Zinfandel and premium oak-aged Cabernet Sauvignons called Finísimo and Magnificum.

Wines I have particularly enjoyed: Riesling, Maule 1999, Oak aged Sémillon, Rapel 1998, Syrah, Colchagua 2000, Sangiovese 2000, Carmenère Private Reserve 1998, Colchagua, Merlot Private

Reserve 1997, San Fernando, Finísimo Cabernet Sauvignon 1997.
Other brands: Peteroa, Rowan Brook, Las Taguas.

Viña Carmen. The life cycle of this winery has been a complicated
one. It was founded in 1850 and had a 50-hectare winery near Buín,
south of Santiago. Its wines soon gained an enviable reputation,
based largely on their long wood ageing. The winery passed into the
hands of the Ramila family and a 1911 advertisement has them
being sold under the brand name José G. Ramila, with the Pinot
selling at $16 a case and the Cabernet at $25. Interestingly enough,
the sales agent in Santiago at the time was Domingo Merry del Val,
for the company was bought by the brothers José and Felipe Merry
in 1930. For eight years it was in the hands of the Canepa family
and in 1985 it was bought by Ricardo Claro, the owner of Santa
Rita (q.v.). The existing vineyard estate was then absorbed into that
of Santa Rita and, for a few years the brand led a quiet, and largely
domestic, life.

In 1992, a state-of-the-art winery was built, within sight of that
of Santa Rita. The whole operation is highly computerised and
fewer than 10 people are needed to run it. This is facilitated by
the fact that the bottling is carried out at Santa Rita. Whilst
Carmen does not have a separate vineyard estate from Santa
Rita, it does have additionally contracts with 80 growers for the
supply of grapes. As well as this it has an experimental vineyard of
25 hectares given over to organic cultivation. This is the personal
interest of their winemaker Alvaro Espinoza, who originally
was their full-time employee, but now works for Carmen on a
consultancy basis. Organic wines have fascinated him since he spent
some time working with Fetzer in California. The organic wines are
sold under the name 'Nativa'.

The 'New Carmen' was conceived from the beginning as an
export-driven winery and the results have justified this. From an
initial production in the 1993 vintage of 70,000 cases production
has now risen to approximately half a million cases.

The range of wines on sale is based soundly round the four
classic Chilean varietals, Merlot and Cabernet for red wines and
Chardonnay and Sauvignon Blanc for the whites. However, there
are plantings of a number of other varieties including Syrah and
Petite Syrah, Gewürztraminer and Viognier. All Reserva wines have
some barrel ageing.

Interestingly, there is now a move to recreate the image of Carmen on the domestic market, with roadside advertising hoardings extolling the merits of their white 'Rhin'.

Wines I have particularly enjoyed: Sauvignon Blanc Reserva 1999, Cabernet Sauvignon Winemakers Reserve 1998, Cabernet Sauvignon Gold Reserve 1997.

Carpe Diem (Bodegas y Viñedos de Itata), Valle de Itata. Whilst there are certainly vineyards further south in the Bío Bío Valley, this is probably the southernmost estate with international ambitions in Chile. It was established at Bulnes, in 1989, as a joint venture between the Fundación Chile (established by the Chilean government and the ITT Corporation of the United States to invest in the country) and Francisco Gillmore the owner of Tabontinaja (q.v.).

The soils and climate here are different from elsewhere in Chile and the finest clonal material was imported from France. Whilst almost half the estate is planted in Cabernet Sauvignon, it produced Chile's first varietal Syrah in the 1996 vintage. The premium Cabernet is called Insigne and a further speciality is a Late Harvest Moscatel de Alejandría.

As well as selling something over 80,000 cases a year of bottled wine under the brands Carpe Diem and Condor, bulk wine is sold to other wineries and Viñas de la Calina (q.v.) is a regular customer for grapes. The wine is actually made by Viña Rucahue (q.v.) in the Maule Valley.

Viña Carta Vieja, Maule Valley. This can claim to be one of the oldest wineries in Chile and certainly the one to have remained in the hands of the same family the longest. Vines were first planted around Villa Alegre, in the middle of the sixteenth century, by Bartolomé Blumenthal. In 1825 the Del Pedegral family arrived there from Asturias in northern Spain and planted its own vineyards. Now, six generations later, Alberto Del Pedregal Aldunate runs the company and it is under him that dramatic changes have been made. Until 1985, the company either sold its wine in bulk or grapes to other companies. Now it bottles and sells wine under its own labels. In addition the original estate of 300 hectares of vines has increased to 500. In 1992, the company sold 145,000 cases; short-term projections now come up with annual sales of 1.5 million cases.

Three things have helped the company in its rapid growth. The first is the investment in modern equipment, particularly stainless-steel tanks. The second is the average age of the vines; this is now somewhere near 45 years and this is reflected in the quality of the wines. The third is that the policy has been to make fruit-driven wines that are easily approachable and agreeable to drink when young. Prices, also, have been very reasonable. These wines generally represent very good value for money.

Wines I have particularly enjoyed: Cabernet Sauvignon 1997.

Viña Casablanca, Casablanca Valley. In 1991, Santa Carolina (q.v.) decided to construct a separate winery in the Casablanca Valley and the Santa Isabel Estate came into being. As this is a white wine area, naturally the emphasis is on Chardonnay and Sauvignon Blanc, though there is also a little Gewürztraminer and more surprisingly some Cabernet Sauvignon and Merlot.

The former winemaker, Ignacio Recabarren, is one of Chile's finest and he has profited from his travels to Australia, New Zealand, California and Bordeaux. For example, his Sauvignon Blancs are made in a Marlborough style; using clonal material brought in from Sancerre in the Loire Valley. He has recently been replaced by Joseba Altuna, from Guelbenzu in Spain. Amongst the Chardonnays is Neblus, which is a barrel-fermented wine made from grapes affected by *pourriture noble*.

Whilst Casablanca grapes are used for some of the red wines, others are brought in from the Maipo Valley and elsewhere, particularly for the Cabernet Sauvignons. Of particular note is the El Bosque Estate wine, made from 80-year-old vines. A new arrival is the super-premium Viña Casablanca Fundo 'Special Cuvée', which made its first appearance in the 1999 vintage.

The basic Santa Isabel estate is of 60 hectares, with, in addition, more than three times as many under long-term contract. Current production is just under 100,000 cases per year.

Wines I have particularly enjoyed: Santa Isabel Sauvignon Blanc 1999, Sta. Isabel Chardonnay/Sauvignon 1999, Santa Isabel Gewürztraminer 1999.

Viña Casas del Bosque, Casablanca Valley. Whilst the estate was started by entrepreneur Juan Cuneo in 1992, it did not make a wine for its own label until 1998 (when the wine was made at the TerraMater winery) and when I visited in August 2000, the winery was still being finished.

Potentially, there will be 236 hectares of vines, of which 70 were in production for the 2000 vintage, another 56 had been planted and 40 were about to be planted. In addition there are substantial plantings of artichokes and beans. Frost is a problem here and there are both wind machines and heaters in the vines.

Whilst the current production is about 380,000 litres a year, only 20,000 cases of the best wine are bottled and sold under the winery label; the rest is sold in bulk. Most of the wines made are Chardonnay and Sauvignon Blanc, but red wines are made from grapes brought in from Isla de Maipo and the Rapel Valley.

Wines I particularly enjoyed: Sauvignon Blanc 1999, Chardonnay Credas Negras 1998.

Casa Lapostolle, Colchagua Valley. There are a number of reasons why this winery is memorable for me apart from the outstanding quality of the wines. When I first visited it with a group from Britain, despite arrangements made with the office in Santiago, we were not expected, so we had to have an impromptu tasting on the lawn. On the second occasion, I was being flown to the airstrip at neighbouring Santa Cruz, when in a scene reminiscent of the Hitchcock classic film, *North by Northwest*, we almost mowed down a man walking along the runway.

Casa Lapostolle is a joint venture between the Marnier-Lapostolle family, who own Grand Marnier liqueur and the Château de Sancerre (51%), and José Rabat, who is in telecommunications and owns the Viña Manquehue (49%). The very active technical consultant is Bordeaux vineyard owner Michel Rolland.

The company has approximately 300 hectares of its own vineyards in the prime red-wine site of the Colchagua Valley, and the prime white-wine site of the Casablanca Valley. In addition it controls about half as much again through long-term contracts with growers. Small yields are very much the order of the day and this is reflected in the concentration of the wines.

The winemakers believe in very ripe fruit and no wine that they sell is less than 13.5°. For the red wines only wild yeasts are used and the wine may spend up to 30 days on the skins in Séguin-Moreau oak fermenting vats, with hand *pigeage*. The cellar holds 3,500 barrels, mainly of French oak.

Perhaps because of Monsieur Rolland's vineyard interests in Saint Emilion and Pomerol, Merlot is the particular strength of this winery. This is at its peak in the wine from the Clos Apalta vineyard. This is dry-farmed and the yield is no more than 4 tonnes to the hectare, rather than the eight in their other drip-irrigated red wine vineyards. The average age of the vines is between 40 and 50 years. The wine is actually a blend of 60% Merlot, 30% Carmenère and 10% Cabernet Sauvignon. The wine spends 18 months in new French oak and is bottled unfiltered. Total production is about 2,000 cases a year.

The total production of the winery is about 18,000 cases a year, of which all but 5% is exported; most of this goes to the United States. It is expected that maximum production will not ever be more than 10% above current levels.

Wines I particularly enjoyed: Rapel Valley Sauvignon Blanc 2000, Classic Chardonnay 1999, Cuvée Alexandre Chardonnay 1997, Cuvée Alexandre Merlot 1998.

Casa Rivas, Maipo Valley. The Salas-Browne group has a broad range of agricultural interests, including forests, fruit orchards and vineyards. In 1993, it acquired a 2,000-hectare estate at Mario Pinto, in the Maipo Valley, some 50 km west of Santiago. Here was planted a 215-hectare vineyard and 52 hectares of, mainly, almond orchards. The owners claim that the vineyards are 'virtually organic' and they have been advised by Dr Eaben Archer, of Stellenbosch University in South Africa. Three-quarters of the plantings are in Cabernet Sauvignon and Merlot, with smaller areas of Chardonnay and Sauvignon Blanc.

A winery was built in 1997 with a storage capacity of 1.6 million litres. All wines are estate-bottled.

Wines I have particularly enjoyed: Cabernet Sauvignon Reserva 1998, Merlot Reserva 1998, Chardonnay Reserva 1998.

Las Casas del Toqui (Viña de Larose), Cachapoal Valley. Whilst this is a comparatively new winery, being created in 1994, it benefits from having more than three-quarters of its 112-hectare estate planted with vines more than 50 years old. The company is a partnership between one of France's largest insurance companies, AGF, and the Granella family who had long been landowners in the foothills of the Andes at Totihué, a small village near Rengo. Over the years their patrimony had been eroded and they had suffered cruelly at the time of Chilean land reform. They were looking for partners and they found this French company, which had already purchased Château Larose-Trintaudon, the largest vineyard in the Haut-Médoc, from the Forner family.

Because of its closeness to the mountains, there is a difference of more than 20° between daytime and night-time temperatures during the ripening season. This makes for concentrated fruit flavours. However, there is a price to pay; frosts are a potential problem in a quarter of their vines and, to combat this, they have three tractor-hauled turbo propane heaters. They give instant protection, without the investment that would be needed for either a sprinkler system or heated wind-vanes. Yields are considered to be an important factor in the quality of their wines, and parcels of vines are aimed at producing differing qualities of wine, with pruning being planned to achieve this. For example, the yields for their top Cabernet Sauvignons might be no more than 50 hl/ha, whilst for their unoaked Chardonnay, they may well be more than double this.

Following Bordeaux tradition, there is only one bottling of the top wines each year, therefore guaranteeing consistency of quality. Much of the investment has been in a new winery, to which a *chai*, holding 2,000 barrels, is being added. Current production is of about 75,000 cases a year, of which 90% is exported.

Wines I have particularly enjoyed: Sémillon 2000, Cabernet Sauvignon Reserva 1999, Cabernet Sauvignon Légende 1999.
Other brands: Viña Anita, Viña Alamosa.

Viña Casa Silva, Colchagua Valley. For many years this winery belonged to the Bouchon family (q.v.), but it was part of the dowry when Maria Teresa Bouchon married a dentist, Mario Silva, about 30 years ago. Indeed the new name was not adopted until the winery first launched its own range of bottled wines in 1997. The size of the estate has been increased considerably and it now totals over 800 hectares, not all of which are yet in full production.

Marketing here concentrates on reasonably priced, easily approachable wines. Of particular interest is the Sauvignon Gris, which was identified as a separate grape variety in Chile to the Sauvignon Blanc as recently as 1997.

Château Los Boldos, see **Viña Santa Amalia.**

Concha y Toro. With such a colossus in the wine world it is rather difficult to know where to start. It is the largest Chilean wine group, where it also owns another major winery Cono Sur (q.v.). In Argentina, it has the Mendoza winery Viña Patagonia (q.v.).

The name can be traced back to 1718 when the king of Spain gave the title of Marqués de Casa Concha to one of his Chilean subjects. In 1883, one of his descendants, Don Melchor de Concha y Toro, a politician, founded the company, partly on the basis of a vineyard that his wife Emiliana Subercaseaux, who was of French extraction, had brought with her on their marriage. These vineyards had been planted with vines brought from Bordeaux and had been looked after by French vineyard managers, Marin Percheux and Germain Bachelet.

The company became a Sociedad Anónima as early as 1923, with the main shareholders being Emiliana's daughters, with their husbands as the directors. More recently the company has been listed on the New York stock exchange. By 1947, the company owned 330 hectares of vineyards, which by 1969 it had increased to 765 hectares. This rise in holdings came about because in 1967 the board realised that its own vineyards accounted for no more than 30% of its needs and things were likely to get worse. As a result it bought, almost immediately 220 hectares of vines in Maipo and Puente Alto.

By 1969 the company claimed to be responsible for a third of the exports of all Chilean wine, though it must be pointed out that, at that time, they accounted for only a twentieth of the country's production. (Interestingly, during the 1940s Concha y Toro took on the distribution of Coca-Cola, but quickly gave it up because it was not sufficiently profitable!)

Now the company owns approximately, 3,300 hectares of vines

in more than 10 locations, stretching from Casablanca in the north to Lourdes, west of Talca, in the south. There are also eight vinification centres spread around the country, to minimise the distance that the grapes have to travel. In the last decade sales have risen by more than a quarter to over 10 million cases a year. Exports have doubled in the same period to over 4 million cases a year, with the United States being the biggest market. Sales in this market achieved a million cases as long ago as 1995, when it became the second largest brand of imported wine in the country. Capital investment is on a continuing basis and seems to be running at about US$25 million a year with the Far East and Europe being targeted as the customers of the future. In addition to all this Concha y Toro has two daughter companies, which are run autonomously, Santa Emiliana (q.v.) and Cono Sur (q.v.).

One of the company's greatest strengths lies in its marketing, with product ranges aimed at different sectors of the market. Both traditional brands and new concepts are run side by side. At the bottom lie competitively priced blends and basic varietal wines. Then comes the Casillero del Diablo range of varietal wines, introduced in 1965. This takes its name from a part of the cellar where the best wines were kept, and it was called 'The Devil's Lair' to frighten off (timid) would-be pilferers. Explorer is aimed at the inquisitive consumer, looking for new varieties and new regions. Trio, which started with the 1995 vintage, claims to be 'based on the concept of climate, soil and oenologist working together as needed for each varietal'. Terrunyo, introduced in 2000, lays stress on individual sites; Marqués de Casa Concha has more barrel ageing. At the top of the pyramid are the Chardonnay Amelia, based on Casablanca fruit, and the icon red, Don Melchor. This last wine has been selected by the leading Chilean wine guide as the most consistently great wine in Chile. Ignacio Recabarren is the senior winemaker responsible for many of these concepts.

Chile is fortunate to have as its market leader, both home and abroad, a winery that is not afraid to be innovative and which makes excellent wines at all price levels.

Wines I have particularly enjoyed: Trio Chardonnay 1997, Casillero del Diablo Chardonnay 1998, Trio Cabernet Sauvignon 1997, Sunrise Merlot 1998.
Other brands: Subercaseaux (sparkling wines).

Hacienda El Condor, Curicó. After the break-up of the Canepa family holdings in 1996, the three sisters, Gilda, Antonieta and Edda, established TerraMater (q.v.) and this winery. It is based around a 220-hectare estate in Sagrada Familia, though additional grapes are bought in from local growers.

Production runs around 200,000 cases a year, with the best wines being a Cabernet Sauvignon Malbec made from 40-year-old vines. The wines are sold under the brand name Millaman.

Other brands: Campero, Millaman.

Cono Sur, Rapel Valley. This winery was established as a separate entity by Concha y Toro in 1993. As part of its dowry it was given the historical low-price brand Tocornal, to add to the two newly created ones of Cono Sur and Isla Negra. It was felt that, for its image, Concha y Toro had concentrated on history and the family. Cono Sur has adopted the slogan, 'No family trees, no dusty bottles, just fruit'. As the winemaker/general manager, Adolfo Hurtado, said in an interview in the Chilean newspaper, *El Metropolitano*, 'Chile is a new world country and is seen as such outside. New world countries have no history, or at least not beyond fifty or a hundred years. In Europe that is seen as nothing.' The modern image even extends to the use of coloured synthetic corks.

This winery is aimed unashamedly at export markets, with Britain its number one priority; and it achieves half its sales there. At present it is the second supplier of Chilean wine on this market, just one place in the league tables ahead of its parent company. As the main source of its supplies, it has a 300-hectare estate in Chimbarongo, in the Rapel valley, which was bought in 1997. It also has long-term supply contracts with 21 different growers and, as a fallback position, the stocks of Santa Emiliana and Concha y Toro. A winery has been built on the estate with a capacity of 6.5 million litres in stainless steel and 2,000 barrels. Bottling is done on the Concha y Toro lines at Pirque.

Currently sales are running around half a million cases a year, of which 150,000 cases are for own-label customers in Britain. Cono Sur has not been sold on the Chilean domestic market until 2000, and it achieved sales of 15,000 cases in its first year.

Whilst this winery is particularly known for its Merlots, Pinot

Noir has become something of a speciality, with Burgundian Martin Prieur acting as a consultant. Forty hectares have also been sat aside as a project for organic wines.

Wines I have particularly enjoyed: Viognier 2000, Gewürztraminer, Bío Bío, 2000, 20 Barrel Pinot Noir 1999, Cono Sur Reserve Merlot, Colchagua 1999.
Other brands: Tocornal, Isla Negra, 20 Barrel.

Conde del Maule, Viñedos del Maule, Maule. A new brand to appear on the market, offering Chardonnay and Cabernet Sauvignon. The former appears under the title of 'Optimus'. This company is based at Talca and is the result of what was the local co-operative company turning itself into a limited company in 1995.

Córpora Vineyards and Winery. The Córpora group in Chile is a multi-faceted group with interests in everything from mining to salmon farming. In 1989 it turned its attention to wine, buying 5,000 hectares of land split between three vineyards in the Aconcagua Valley and one each in the Maipo Valley, the Cachapoal Valley, where it has its winery, and Bío-Bío, in the far south. Over 1,000 hectares of this is now producing.

The original brand of the company was Viña Gracia, with its strikingly colourful labels, but in 1997 Viña Porta was bought from Jorge Gutierrez of Viña Anakena (q.v.). The company has very strong ambitions to be amongst the top five Chilean wine producers and sales are currently approaching 400,000 cases per year.

The company claims to be the largest producer of Pinot Noir in Chile and as well as the standard range of varietals, will soon be offering such rarities as Mourvèdre, Grenache and Viognier.

Wines I have particularly enjoyed: Cabernet Sauvignon Celebrado 1998, Carmenère Reserva Especial Callejero 1999, Chardonnay Reserva Superior Temporal 1997.

Cousiño-Macul, Maipo Valley. However much a region, or a country, might seek to change its image, there is always demand for tradition and traditional wines. In many ways, Cousiño Macul is there to satisfy that demand in Chile.

The company was established by the Cousiño family, who made their fortune in coal mining in Lota, in 1856. It planted a 250-hectare vineyard and a magnificent park with a collection of plants brought back from around the world by the family shipping-fleet. In 1870, it employed French architects to design a winery with two floors of arched cellars. Vines were imported direct from France and, for almost a century and a half now, replantings have been from cuttings from this original French stock, propagated in the company's own nurseries. All this happened in Macul, to the south-east of the city of Santiago. The company still belongs totally to the Cousiño family.

Sadly the city has sprawled and the original estate is an asset that is about to be realised. Three hundred hectares of vines have been bought near Buín, 30 km south of the capital, and a new winery has been built. In Macul, a core vineyard of 25 hectares, the offices, the original cellars and the park will remain. The rest will be sold for housing.

Rauli vats still have a role to play in the ageing of the cheaper red wines, though Reserva wines are aged in American barrels and the top wines in French oak. As for the quality of the wines, I have in my files a letter from their then agents in Britain, the Nitrate Corporation of Chile Ltd, dated December 1977. Amongst other things, this says, 'In particular the red wines from pure Cabernet-Sauvignon stock have been admired by French experts and producers who rate them with the best French wines from Bordeaux for their quality and fineness.' Certainly the current style of its wines has some fans, but just as many who dislike it. At the top of the range of red wines is Finis Terrae, a Cabernet Sauvignon 50%/Merlot 50% blend.

Vitivinícola Cremaschi Barriga, Maule Valley. The Cremaschi family came to Chile in 1940, having spent 50 years in the wine trade in Argentina, where the family is still represented by the Furlotti winery. The current winemaker, Christian Cremaschi, was trained both in Bordeaux and California and this shows through in the quality of his wines.

The company has an estate of 100 hectares and uses only its own fruit. About 25,000 cases are sold each year under the label Cremaschi-Furlotti. The balance is sold off in bulk to other companies.

The winery was totally refurbished at the end of 1998 and now has capacity for 2.5 million litres in stainless steel. Perhaps surprisingly *rauli* vats are still used for some wines.

Wines I have particularly enjoyed: Cabernet Sauvignon 1997.
Other brands: Cremaschi-Furlotti.

Viña Cruz de Triana, Cachapoal Valley. This is yet another winery making the transfer from being a producer of bulk wine, to selling in bottle under its own label. Its first appearance in bottle was in the 2000 vintage.

The company has 100 hectares of vines planted in the classic Chilean varietals, with a preponderance of Cabernet Sauvignon. Heavy investment has been made in equipping the winery with the most modern technology. At present, the winery does not have its own bottling-line and has no facility for ageing wines in cask.

Cooperativa Agrícola Vitivinícola de Curicó, Curicó. The co-operative movement in the Chilean wine trade has little international image, but the cellar of Curicó, established in 1943, took the important decision in the late 1990s to invest in new equipment. It has around 60 members, who own between them 800 hectares of vines, a quarter less than in 1947.

Whilst most of the production is in tetrabrics and demi-johns for the domestic market, the increased quality enables them to supply European supermarket chains and to vinify the Terra Andina range of wines for the Pernod Ricard group. For this, grapes and wine are brought in from a broad variety of sources. They also have two brands: Los Robles, whose best wines are sold as Gran Roble, and the historical F. J. Correa Errázuriz.

Other brands: Viña Los Robles, F. J. Correa Errázuriz.

Viña De Martino, see **Viña Santa Inés.**

Viña Domaine Rabat, see **Viña Manquehue.**

Viña Echeverria, Molina, Lontué Valley. The Echeverria family has been growing grapes in Chile for more than 250 years, but the family estate had fallen on hard times until Roberto Echeverria returned to Chile from the United States in 1977. There he had been studying for a Doctorate in Economics and he reckons that his stay in the United States gave him an insight into how the Chilean wine industry would develop; away from being aimed at an unambitious domestic market, to one that would look outward to a world of wine consumers ever eager for quality wines.

Notwithstanding this he spent his early years working as an economist in Santiago during the week and coming home at weekends to work in the vines. It was 15 years before he felt sure enough of himself, and his wines, to buy a bottling machine and launch the Echeverria label on the world.

The estate is of approximately 80 hectares, with about half planted in Cabernet Sauvignon and the rest in Sauvignon Blanc and Chardonnay, and a very little in Merlot. Most of his needs for this last varietal have to be bought in. Sr Echeverria is a firm believer in wood ageing and he makes use of *rauli* vats as well as both American and French oak barrels. His use of oak is shown by the Chardonnay Family Reserva, which has a rich oakiness of almost historical Californian proportions.

Roberto Echeverria was also instrumental in the formation of Chilevid, an organisation created to promote Chile's smaller wineries on an international scale.

Wines I have particularly enjoyed: Cabernet Sauvignon Reserva 1997, Sauvignon Blanc 1998.
Other brands: Casa Nueva.

Viña Luis Felipe Edwards, Colchagua Valley. The Edwards family arrived in Chile from London in the middle of the nineteenth century and soon established themselves in the wine trade. Perhaps the most famous member was Guillermo Edwards, who was Senator for Nuble at the end of the First World War. At that time drink was a very serious problem amongst the working class and, being asked how this might be dealt with, suggested a threefold remedy: the number of bars should be restricted, taxes on imported drinks should be tripled and drunkards should be whipped.

The current Edwards estate consists of about 300 hectares of vineyards split between two farms: the Fundo San José at Puquillay in the Tinguiririca Valley and the Fundo Barnadita at Pupilla to the west. Both these sites include hillside vineyards. Current production is about quarter of a million cases a year, and rising.

Here the Cabernet Sauvignon is the dominant grape variety, with a range of four different styles being produced: Pupilla is at an entry-level price and Bodega Privada is the top of the line. This winery also has the reputation for regularly producing Carmenères to rank amongst the best in the country.

Wines I have particularly enjoyed: Carmenère 1998, Cabernet Sauvignon Reserva 1997.
Other brands: Edwards Ridge.

Viña Errázuriz, Aconcagua Valley. It is not quite clear when the Errázuriz family arrived in Chile from their native Navarra in Spain; it was probably towards the middle of the eighteenth century. What is clear, however, is that, by the middle of the nineteenth century, it had become one of the most influential families in the country. The winery was established by Don Maximiano Errázuriz in 1870. At the time he was a Member of Parliament and he went on to be Senator for Arauco and Ambassador at the Court of St James's in London. One brother, Crescente, was Archbishop of Santiago and his other, Federico, was in turn Minister of Justice and President of the Republic. His sister, Mercedes, married the owner of Viña San Pedro and Viña Lontué and his son, Rafael, also became a Senator and, later, Ambassador to the Holy See.

The estate, at Panquehue, in the Aconcagua Valley, north of Santiago, was, at 700 hectares, the largest single vineyard in the world under the ownership of one person. The philosophy of Don Maximiano was, 'From the best land, the best wines'. It had a well-earned reputation of being at the forefront of technology. It brought in its own master cooper, Eduardo Saez, from Spain, and his sons and grandsons continued in that role. One of the first motor tractors in Chile was imported to work in the vineyards. It became a showpiece.

The Errázuriz family decided to sell the property after the First World War and it passed through a series of owners, and declined in importance. By 1947, it was no more than 120 hectares and was now in the hands of the Bulnes family. In 1981, it was sold to Alfonso Chadwick, whose mother was a direct descendant of the Errázuriz. The company is now managed by his son Eduardo Chadwick, who studied industrial engineering at the Catholic University in Santiago, and oenology in Bordeaux.

Currently, the estate consists of almost 400 hectares of vines in production, but there is a regular programme of plantings in hand. The vineyards are split between five different sites in the Aconcagua Valley, one in Casablanca, one just south of Santiago and one far to the south, beyond Curicó. This last vineyard has its own winery at Sagrada Familia. This broad range of soils and climates helps with giving Errázuriz wines complexity and enables them to offer a broad range of wines.

The 'home' vineyard, the Don Maximiano Estate, totals 75 hectares and is largely planted on steep hillsides in an amphitheatre sun-trap site. On the steepest slope, Syrah has been planted amongst the cacti, with the vines planted 10,000 to the hectare and pruned to resist the wind, just as in the Rhône valley. It is from this 'home' vineyard that the premium wine, Don Maximiano Founder's Reserve, is produced. For this wine, in the 1998 vintage a blend of 87% Cabernet Sauvignon and 13% Merlot, the individual lots are aged apart and blended shortly before bottling. The other premium wine, the result of a joint venture with the Mondavi family, is Seña. The 1997 vintage of this wine is 84% Cabernet Sauvignon and 16% Carmenère and, in contrast to Don Maximiano, is blended young and then aged in oak.

A separate vineyard for Seña has been purchased. It, too, is in the Aconcagua Valley, but is some 20 km closer to the sea. So far 35 hectares have been planted in Cabernet Sauvignon, Merlot, Petit Verdot, Carmenère and Malbec. For the existing wines, the grapes have been sourced from a variety of regions, but it has been agreed that the wine can always have first call on up to 50% of prime fruit from the Don Maximiano vineyard. The head winemaker for this project is Tim Mondavi.

The chief winemaker for Errázuriz is Ed Flaherty, who trained at Davis and worked at Sonoma Cutrer before coming out to Chile. He works closely in conjunction with Pedro Izquierdo, the vineyard manager.

Production is running currently at about 450,000 cases a year, of which 10% is destined for the domestic market. Here, the top selling Cabernet Sauvignon is peculiarly called Corton, and there is a white wine to match under the same name.

Wines I have particularly enjoyed: Pinot Noir Casablanca Reserva 1999 ('Pinot Noir is a white wine in drag', Ed Flaherty), Sangiovese

Don Maximiano Estate 1999, Cabernet Sauvignon Reserva Don Maximiano estate 1998, Don Maximiano Founder's Reserve 1998, Chardonnay Wild Ferment Casablanca 1998.

Viña William Fèvre Chile, Maipo Valley. Ten years ago, William Fèvre took the decision that one vintage a year in Chablis was not enough and he decided to spread his wings in Chile. Together with a local partner, Victor Pino, who was able to contribute land in San Juan de Pirque and San Fernando, he established a winery, which is currently producing something under 50,000 cases a year. The aim is to increase this by about 60%. Recent developments include the construction of an air-conditioned cask-ageing cellar, which will hold 1,200 barrels.

Originally only white wines were produced, but vines have been head-grafted and the range now includes Cabernet Sauvignon, Merlot and Pinot Noir, as well as Sauvignon Blanc and Chardonnay. The wines are French in style, regularly striking only 12.5°, rather than the Chilean norm of 13.5°. Some of the wines have been shipped in bulk and bottled in France.

Other brands: Don Victor, La Misión del Clarillo.

Viña la Fortuna, Lontué Valley. Until now this winery, established by Daniel Guell in the early 1940s has been one of the most traditional in Chile, relying on *rauli* wood and concrete vats, rather than on stainless steel and selling most of its production in bulk. However, there are suggestions that the butterfly is emerging from its chrysalis, with Sergio Traverso, a Chilean winemaker, who honed his skills in California, being employed as a consultant.

At present exports are a lowly 35,000 cases a year but the plans are to increase these sixfold in the next five years. These are obviously wines to look out for in the future.

Other brands: Maison Blanche, Gran Fortuna, La Serrania, Traverso.

Viña Gracia, see **Córpora Vineyards and Winery.**

El Huique, Agrital Ltda, Colchagua Valley. The estate of San Miguel del Huique consists of three blocks of vines in the Colchagua Valley, of which approximately 90 hectares are in production. This is predominantly a red wine company, with Cabernet Sauvignon as its major feature. There is also a little Merlot produced.

Agrícola y Vitivinícola Itata, see **Carpe Diem.**

Viña Doña Javiera, Maipo Valley. This winery takes its name from Javiera Carrera, a member of one of the most famous families in the history of the fight for Chilean independence. The family of the current owner, Francisco Correa, has also had an important role in Chile's wine history. It left Castille in Spain and came to Chile via Peru in about 1700. It was originally made up of cattle-ranchers, and wine was a secondary interest until the brothers Bonifacio and José Gregorio founded what were to become two of the country's largest vineyards, Viña Lontué (founded 1875) and Viña San Pedro (1865).

Beside these two giants, Doña Javiera is a minute 80 hectares, but it has the potential for considerable expansion in its production, which is currently just over 20,000 cases a year. White wine is a strength here, with specialist equipment imported from New Zealand.

Wines I have particularly enjoyed: Chardonnay Reserva 1998.
Other brands: Rio Claro, Bodegas El Monte, Tamarugo, Arlequín, Status, Arrayán.

Viña Lomas de Cauquenes, Covica Ltda, Cauquenes, Maule Valley. This co-operative cellar was created as the result of a disaster. In 1939, an earthquake destroyed the town of Cauquenes shortly before the grape-harvest was due to be gathered in, so all the local growers got together and decided to create a communal cellar.

Currently there are 284 members of the co-operative (in 1973 there were 400) controlling 2,200 hectares of vines. More than three-quarters of the members have fewer than 10 hectares of vines. In addition, the cellar has its own experimental vineyard of 60 hectares. Exceptionally for Chile, the cellar insists that members must bring their total crop for vinification.

The members come from a radius of 20 km around the town, which itself lies just 20 km from the Pacific. Here the soil is very poor and water for irrigation is scarcely available. The annual rainfall is about 600 mm a year and this comes between June and

September. In summer, the day temperature can reach 36°, while at night it falls to 14°. Another climatic factor is the strong, cold wind, which blows from the south.

Most of the vineyards are in dry-farmed bush vines. There is a little drip irrigation. Yields are very low, down to one tonne per hectare on the hillsides, and a maximum of 15 tonnes per hectare in the plains. Sixty per cent of the plantings are in the País grape, though the winery also handles more than 20 other varieties. Because of the climate, and the isolation of the vineyards, the vines are exceptionally healthy; hail is a problem about once every 12 years, but apart from that the liking of young vine-shoots in the diet of rabbits appears to pose the largest problem.

In a normal year, the winery will produce approximately 18 million litres of wine and 85% of this is sold on the domestic market. Here 70% of sales are in tetrabriks, with 19% in 5-litre demi-johns and the balance in bottle. Whilst, there are some export sales in bulk, the majority is in bottle to a broad range of markets.

The company is fortunate to have what could be described as Chile's most enthusiastic winemaker, Claudio Barria. He is always experimenting with new wines and new methods of vinification. One of his great successes is an organic wine, Las Lomas, made from the humble País grape. Here he shows what can be done with low yields and careful vinification. Similarly, in the 2000 vintage he took the same parcel of Cabernet Sauvignon grapes to vinify three different wines, one with traditional vinification, the second with cold maceration of the fruit and the third with micro-oxygenation. Of the three cask-samples, it was the last that showed best in my tasting.

He also is a great proponent of the concept of *terroir* or *terruño*. He is determined to build up the reputation of the Cauquenes region not just for its wines but for its local foods and its hospitality. He is convinced that it is only by joining all aspects of local life in the promotion that the area's image can achieve the status it deserves.

Wines I have particularly enjoyed: Merlot 1999, Cabernet Sauvignon Reserva 1997.
Other brands: Las Lomas, Antu Mapu.

Viña Martínez de Salinas, Cauquenes, Maule Valley. This is a company established recently by Alfredo Bisello, who has Italian roots, in Cauquenes in the south of Chile. The first vintage to appear on the market was 1998, and this met with much acclaim across the range of varietals.

Wines I have particularly enjoyed: Cabernet Sauvignon Gran Reserva 1998.
Other brands: Primitivo.

Viña Manquehue, Viña Domaine Rabat, Colchagua Valley and Maipo Valley. When José Rabat joined forces with the French Marnier-Lapostolle family to create Casa Lapostolle (q.v.), he kept back some of his private estates and still sells, mainly on the domestic market, wine under the two labels of Viña Manquehue and Viña Domaine Rabat. These have an important share of the market.

The estate was, for long, based around the farm of Santa Adela de Manquehue, bought by the family in 1932, which lay to the east of Santiago. This has now been consumed by urban development, so new land was bought at Pirque and in the Colchagua Valley.

Wines I have particularly enjoyed: Viña Manquehue Gran Distinción Cabernet Sauvignon 1998.

Viñedos del Maule, see Conde del Maule.

Viña Montes, Curicó Valley. Few Chilean wineries can have been created with as much thought as this. It began life as Discover Wine in 1988 with four partners. Aurelio Montes was the master winemaker, having worked for Undurraga and San Pedro. Pedro Grand brought a wine estate just outside Curicó. Douglas Murray brought knowledge of wine markets around the world, having been export director for a number of leading Spanish wine companies and finally, Alfredo Vidaurre, as Dean of the economics faculty at the Catholic University brought contacts in the world of finance.

The original concept was to be no more than a boutique winery, but now Montes has grown to be a major international brand synonymous with quality Chilean wine. They are wines that I have enjoyed from Beijing to Birmingham and world-wide sales are now approaching 300,000 cases a year of which 95% is exported to 42 different countries. The estate of 250 hectares is based in the Curicó

Valley with some vines going back 100 years. Here they are planted with a density of 6,000 vines to the hectare and each vine is pruned to give a yield of 1 kg of grapes. For Aurelio Montes, it is the vine that makes for the quality of the wine. He is a great believer in clonal selection and would like to move more towards dry-farming his vineyards.

There is also a hillside vineyard, Finca Apalta, of 120 hectares in the Colchagua Valley, which many producers now consider to be the premium area for red wines. The vineyard has 10-year-old vines and has a slope of 25°. As it faces towards the south-west, exposure to sunlight is restricted and the result is the necessity for a longer ripening season.

The winery, at Curicó, seems to be under perpetual pressure to absorb the increase in sales. There is now stainless-steel capacity of 4.5 million litres and to this can be added more than 3,000 barrels, an equal split of French and American oak.

The range of wines produced is ever extending with Syrah and Petit Verdot being added to the range of varietal wines being made in the 2000 vintage. Until quite recently, the top quality wines, both red and white were Montes Alpha, but further heights have now been scaled, in red wines at least, with Montes Alpha 'M', a Cabernet Sauvignon (80%), Merlot (10%), Cabernet Franc (10%) blend aged for 18 months in new French wood. Only 2,000 cases of this wine are produced, when the vintage is good enough. Another wine of interest is their Late Harvest, a 50/50 blend of Gewürztraminer and Riesling, with 12.8° alcohol and 100 g of residual sugar.

Wines I have particularly enjoyed: La Finca de Apalta Cabernet/Carmenère 1999, Merlot Special Cuvée 1999, Montes Alpha Merlot 1998, Montes Alpha Cabernet Sauvignon 1999, Syrah 2000, Montes Alpha 'M' 1998.

Viña Montgras, Colchagua Valley. This is yet another Chilean winery that was created from nowhere less than 10 years ago and has managed to create a substantial market for its wines. Interestingly for a winery of this style, more than a third of its sales are achieved on the domestic market, which is, for the most part, conservative.

The company has an estate of 450 hectares, of which, at present about 250 hectares have been planted. The focal point of its vineyards is the Ninquén hill where the first of the plantings (currently about 50 hectares) are coming into production. Whilst currently most of the vines are Cabernet Sauvignon, Chardonnay and Merlot, there are also such interesting varieties as Zinfandel, Viognier and Malbec.

The winery was purpose built at a cost of US$15 million and is centred on a gravity flow system. The capacity is 5 million litres. The winemaker is Debbie Christiansen, who comes from New Zealand.

It is not surprising that the wines are aimed at the upper end of the market and is regularly introducing new wines. Amongst the most recent of these is Quatro, a blend of Cabernet Sauvignon, Merlot, Carmenère and Malbec.

Wines I have particularly enjoyed: Quatro 1998, Carmenère Reserva 1998.

Viña Morandé. There is an uncertain future for the site of this winery built by the side of Ruta 5, the Pan-American Highway, at Pelequén, south of Santiago. At present it is putting a brave face on things, with a new facility for tourists, but, as the main road is upgraded to motorway standard, there are plans for an enormous junction and flyover on the site for a new road to the container port of San Antonio. Whilst the current site may appear to have many advantages, it does seem rather peculiar for a company that bills itself as 'The Pioneers of the Casablanca Valley'.

That the winery should come under such a threat seems particularly sad as it crushed its first grapes as recently as March 1997. It is also the first winery in South America to have received ISO rating and has a capacity, in stainless steel, of 11 million litres. Either this threat of destruction is an idle one or someone has not looked into long-term planning.

The House of Morandé is, with its sister company Vistamar, a subsidiary of Impresas Lourdes. It was created in 1996 by Pablo Morandé, who for 20 years had been winemaker at Concha y Toro. It was at that company that he had 'discovered' Casablanca and recognised it as the ideal region for the production of white wines. In a personal capacity, he still owns 100 hectares of vines there, whilst the company owns just four! Indeed, it is supplied mainly by contract growers, not just there, but also in the Maipo, Rapel, Maule and Itata Valleys.

Notwithstanding its minimal vineyard holdings, the company has achieved remarkable sales in a very short period of time. In 1997, it exported 21,000 cases of wine; in 1998, 133,000 cases; in 1998, 240,000; and in 1999, 350,000 cases. In addition, in 1999 it sold 4 million litres of wine in bulk, 40,000 cases from a new winery in Maipú in Argentina, and became the largest producer of kosher wine in Chile!

The company must be one of the most ambitious in the Chilean wine-trade, and, to achieve its aims it has a very broad range of products with seven different label families. One of these, Aventura, includes such unexpected varietals as the Bouschet, the César, the Cinsault and the Portugais Bleu. All these different groups of wines do, however, have the common feature of the name Morandé being present on the label.

As far as sweet wines are concerned, they are produced in two different ways. There is a classic Sauvignon Blanc, made with very late harvested grapes from the Casablanca Valley and there is a Chardonnay where the sugar content of the grapes has been concentrated in a deep-freeze.

Wines I have particularly enjoyed: Malbec Reserva 1999, Late Harvest Sauvignon Blanc 1998, Terrarum Sémillon 1998, Vitisterra Chardonnay 1998, House of Morandé Cabernet Sauvignon 1997.
Other brands: House of Morandé, Vitisterra, Dueto, Aventura, Nova Terrarum, Pionero, Vista Sur and Niebla. (The last two are brand names of the associated company Vistamar.)

Viña Las Nieves, Rengo. This company was established by the Paredes brothers, who also own Torreón de Paredes (q.v.). It has an estate of 100 hectares and also buys in grapes.

Domaine Oriental, Agrícola Salvi S.A., Maule Valley. La Oriental Estate, which lies just to the east of Talca, was the first in the Maule Valley to be planted with French grape varieties. At that time, and until 1989, the property belonged to the Donoso family. It was then sold to a group of French expatriates, living in Tahiti, who also bought another neighbouring property, La Finca de Las Casas de Vaquería. This gives a combined total of 130 hectares of vines, with about half being planted in Cabernet Sauvignon. The vineyards are run to the ISO 14.001 environmentally friendly standards. The total production is about 100,000 cases a year.

There are three levels of wine made solely from estate grown grapes, Domaine Oriental, fermented in stainless steel, Clos Centenaire, which are aged in oak casks and the recently launched Casa Donoso 1810, premium Cabernet Sauvignon/Carmenère blends.

There is also a secondary brand, Piduco Creek, in which some purchased grapes are used.

Other brands: Casa Donoso.

Viña Portal del Alto. This company belongs to Chile's leading wine academic, Alejandro Hernandez, who is the Professor of Viticulture and Oenology at the Catholic University in Santiago. It was established, primarily to sell on export markets, in 1970, and some wines have been available for domestic consumption since 1994.

In all, the Professor owns 100 hectares of vines, split between four different farms. The 'home' vineyard of 8 hectares is near Buín, some 30 km south of Santiago. It is here that all his wines are bottled. Near San Juan de Pirque, at an altitude of 800 m is a second vineyard and a further 100 km to the south is an estate of 20 hectares near San Fernando. Here are some very old Merlot vines, and it is here that all the wines are made. The last property, and the largest, is in the Maule Valley. Here the traditional País has been grubbed up and replaced with a broad range of varieties including the Viognier and the Sangiovese.

Wines I have particularly enjoyed: Merlot Reserva 1998.
Other brands: Oriente Estates, Valle San Fernando, El Oriente, Millahue.

Viña La Posada Ltda., Colchagua Valley. This winery in Santa Cruz was originally an inn (*posada*) and this is how it gets its name. The Diaz family, originally from Asturias in northern Spain, settled in the region in 1905 and it was Eduardo Diaz, the current owner, who first planted vineyards 40 years ago and started to sell wine in bulk. In 1985 he started selling wine in bottle and in 1996 he first began to export.

The company has two vineyards; one, close to Santa Cruz is of

90 hectares and the second, in La Patagua, now has 50 hectares of Cabernet in production. Their premium wine Valdaz Cabernet Sauvignon comes from 60-year-old vines and has been aged in oak barrels for 12 months.

Wines I have particularly enjoyed: Valdaz 1997.
Other brands: Valdaz.

Viña Pueblo Antiguo, Colchagua Valley. The Toretti family, who own this winery only settled in Nancagua as recently as 1961, growing grapes and plums for sale on export markets. In 1978, it bought what had been the local co-operative cellar, established in 1940, and created its own winery. Initially sales were just of bulk wine, but, in 1999, it bought a bottling line and currently bottle 15% of production.

The family has 72 hectares of vineyards in production, but has as much again available for planting and a number of further growers under contract.

Wines I have particularly enjoyed: Cabernet-Syrah 1999.

Viña Quebrada de Macul, Maipo Valley. For many years Ricardo Peña, the owner of this estate, sold his grapes to such exalted names as Viña Aquitania, Concha y Toro and Santa Rita, but, in 1996, he took winemaker Ignacio Recabarren as a minority partner and it was decided to make and bottle their own wine.

Two wines are made: a red Domus Aurea and a white Domus Proa. The first wine is based on Cabernet Sauvignon, with traces of Cabernet Franc and Merlot and is aged in French oak for up to a year. The first vintage to arrive on the market, the 1996, was voted the fourth-best Chilean Cabernet of the year, by the highly respected *Guía de Vinos de Chile*. The white wine is an unoaked Chardonnay.

Viña Requingua, Curicó. Whilst this vineyard was first planted in the 1920s, it was taken over by Santiago Achurra and his family in 1961. The total area of the estate is over 1,000 hectares, surrounding a beautiful old manor house. There are 432 hectares planted in vines with more than three-quarters being Cabernet Sauvignon. There is also some Merlot, Sauvignon Blanc and Chardonnay. This is another of those wineries just beginning to create an image for itself by offering bottled wine. Its top Cabernet Sauvignon is sold as Torre de Piedra.

Wines I have particularly enjoyed: Chardonnay 2000.

Viña la Roncière, Cachapoal Valley. The wines from this winery made their first appearance, to some acclaim in 1999. The best appears to be a Cabernet Sauvignon Reserva 1998.

Viña la Rosa, Rapel Valley. This winery is part of the giant Sofruco company, which has almost 2,000 hectares of fruit trees, and which belongs to the Ossa family. This is yet another of those companies that has expanded rapidly on the back of own-label business with supermarket chains. It only started bottling its own wines in 1994 and is forecast to pass the million case mark within the next few years.

The original estate was founded in 1824 and has been in the hands of the same family ever since. The family arrived in Chile from northern Spain in the eighteenth century and amassed a fortune from silver and saltpetre mines. One branch of the family bought Viña Santa Teresa, an estate which disappeared in the 1970s, whilst another bought La Rosa. At present the company has 600 hectares of vineyards in production, but this is set to increase by a third.

It has a broad range of wines. For example at the beginning of the year 2000, it was offering four different Cabernet Sauvignons: La Rosa 1998, La Palma 1998, Don Reca Reserva 1998 and La Palma Reserve 1997, all in different brackets, but all offering excellent value for money. For the consumer with a limited budget, these are certainly wines to seek out.

Other brands: La Palmería, La Palma, Don Reca, Cornellana, Quinta las Cabras, Casa Leona.

Viña Rucahue, San Javier, Maule Valley. Francisco Gillmore has extensive wine interests in southern Chile. These include Carpe Diem (q.v), Tabontinaja (q.v.) and this winery – not to mention a winery on Long Island in New York State. Rucahue is mainly a supplier of bulk wines from its 300 hectares of vines that are currently in production. The potential is there for much larger sales and, at present these seem to be confined to export markets.

Viña San Carlos, Colchagua Valley. Until 1966 the Viu family had been wine wholesalers, but wholesalers of some standing, for, in the previous year, Miguel Viu Manent formed part of a commission reporting on the state of the wine industry to the new President, Eduardo Frei. In 1966, the family bought the long-established wine estate of San Carlos de Cunacó in the heart of the Colchagua Valley. Initially sales were in bulk to the major producers, but, since 1990, the company's brand has been developed with bottled wine. All the wines are estate-bottled.

The estate has two vineyards; the first, San Carlos, was amongst the first in Chile to be planted with French vines, and is irrigated by a network of channels, constructed by the Incas. This vineyard is of the about 150 hectares, though not all is yet in production. The second, La Capilla, of about 50 hectares, is at Peralillo, some 30 km closer to the Pacific Ocean.

Wines I have particularly enjoyed: Sémillon 1999.
Other brands: Viu Manent.

Viña San José de Apalta, Colchagua Valley. This is a new face on the Chilean wine scene, backed by a 100-hectare estate in Apalta, belonging to the Donoso family. The company has Alvaro Espinoza and Angela Muir MW as advisers. Its first wines to be released are of the 2000 vintage under the brand names Envero and Apaltagua.

Viña San Miguel del Huique see **El Huique.**

Viña San Pedro, Lontué. I first visited this winery in 1991. Then it was run-down and seeking to sell off surplus vineyards; now it is one of the most impressive wineries in Chile and is number three in both domestic and export sales. Its history is an interesting one. Established by the Correa family at the beginning of the eighteenth century, it was planted with noble French varieties in 1865. Having stayed in the hands of the Correas for almost 250 years it was sold in 1941 to the Stein and Wagner families. Matters were not helped by the workers coming out on strike in 1953, for better working conditions. In this they were backed by the church and the right-wing Falange party. For a time it fell into the hands of the infamous Spanish wine and banking conglomerate Rumasa and its importance was in steady decline.

Its renaissance is due to two important factors. In 1994 a

majority holding in the winery was bought by Compañías Cervecerías Unidas, the largest brewery group in Chile, a major pillar in the commercial empire of the Luksic family. It brought in the capital that was needed. The second factor was that it employed Jacques Lurton, from Bordeaux, as a consultant. Has the investment been a good one for the brewery? At the beginning San Pedro accounted for only 3% of the group's profits, now it accounts for 15%.

In all the winery has more than 2,100 hectares of vines in production; the 'home' vineyard, near Molina in the Rapel Valley, is the largest single planting in Chile, with 1,200 hectares in one block. It has further holdings in four different locations, including the prestigious Colchagua Valley. The winery's capacity in stainless-steel tanks is 15 million litres and there are 6,000 small oak barrels. To obtain better colour and fruit extraction, there is a battery of rotary fermenters. In the abundant 2000 harvest, even these facilities proved insufficient and space had to be rented in 11 other wineries. A team of 16 winemakers, under the control of New Zealander, Brett Jackson is employed.

Whilst certain individual wines are produced, most wines come within four different quality ranges. At the entry-price level is the Gato line: Gato Negro for red wines and Gato Blanco for white wines. These are easy-drinking varietals and account for about a quarter of the total production. Any oak influence comes from either chips or stave treatment.

Next comes 35 Sur, followed by Castillo de Molina Reserva wines. At the top comes a Cabernet Sauvignon, Cabo de Hornos, produced from 60-year-old vines and given 18 months ageing in new French oak casks. One of the major factors that affects the different quality levels is the yields. For the Gato range these are between 18 and 20 tons to the hectare, for the 35 Sur, 13 to 15 tons, for the Castillo de Molina 8 tons and for the Cabo de Hornos, no more than 4 tons.

Amongst the other wines produced are a vintage 'Champagne', made from Chardonnay (90%) and Pinot Noir (10%) and a Late Harvest Riesling, from partially botrytised grapes.

Two other labels are found on the domestic market, Las Encinas, which, as the label says, 'has an oxidation which reminds us of sherry', and Urmeneta, with a Sauvignon Blanc and a Cabernet Sauvignon.

The Santa Helena range of wines is also produced at the winery. This brand is marketed separately and was purchased by San Pedro in 1976. The wines come in three levels, in ascending order: Gran Vino, Siglo de Oro and Selección del Directorio.

Wines I have particularly enjoyed: Castillo de Molina Reserva Sauvignon 1999, Late Harvest Riesling 1998, Gato Negro Cabernet Sauvignon 2000, Gato Negro Merlot 2000, Castillo de Molina Reserva Merlot 1998, Cabo de Hornos Cabernet Sauvignon 1996. *Other brands:* Gato, 35 Sur, Castillo de Molina, Las Encinas, Urmeneta, Cabo de Hornos, and Santa Helena.

Viña Santa Alicia, Maipo Valley. Whilst this winery was built almost 50 years ago the brand of Santa Alicia did not appear until 1994. Its wines are labelled as 'Estate Bottled' but it is not clear whether it uses only grapes its own estate of 150 hectares. Total production is approaching 250,000 cases per year.

Its top Chardonnay comes from El Ciprés vineyard and its top Cabernet Sauvignon from Los Maitenes.

Viña Santa Amalia, Requinoa, Rapel Valley. In Europe, the Massenez family is known for its fruit *alcools blancs*, distilled in the Vosges mountains, but in 1990 it decided to diversify and bought what had been the co-operative wine cellar at Requinoa. Part of the property is used for the distillation of pears and the majority for making wine, which is generally sold under the brand Château Los Boldos.

There is an estate of 250 hectares of vines on stony, low-yielding soils and many of the vines are over 40 years old. Peculiarly, those wines, which are labelled as Vieilles Vignes, do not necessarily come from the oldest vines. The top wine, Château Los Boldos Grand Cru, is a Cabernet Sauvignon (80%)/Merlot (20%) blend, produced from genuinely old vines.

The annual production is 180,000 cases, but this is set to increase as recently planted vineyards mature. None of the wine is sold on the Chilean domestic market.

Other brands: Château Los Boldos.

Viña Santa Carolina. The Pereira family arrived in Chile, from northern Spain, via Buenos Aires at the beginning of the nineteenth century. It immediately made a fortune from mining and, in 1875, Luis Pereira did the fashionable thing of the time and commissioned a Frenchman to find him a vineyard and replant it with French vines. The site he found was no more than 6 km from the centre of Santiago and it was named in honour of Sr Pereira's wife, Carolina. The vineyards have long been consumed by the industrial development of the city, but the magnificent vaulted cellars, which were built at the same time, still remain and are used by the company for storing casks. They have been declared a national monument.

The Pereira family remained the company's owners and oversaw its expansion until it went public in 1963. It also had interests in insurance and in the 1960s Julio Pereira was a Conservative Senator for Santiago and became Minister of Defence. A branch of the family is still the major shareholder.

Santa Carolina is currently ranked number four in sales of Chilean wine, with 11% of the market, just behind San Pedro, but some way behind Santa Rita and Concha y Toro. Its total sales are something over 3 million cases a year. The company has 580 hectares of vines in production, split between Santa Rosa in the Maipo Valley and San Fernando in the Colchagua Valley. In addition, its subsidiary company, Viña Casablanca (q.v.) has 60 hectares. As might be gathered by a comparison of the vineyard area and the sales figures, by far the majority of this company's needs are satisfied by bought-in grapes. There are four separate wineries. For many years, Ignacio Recabarren was the chief oenologist, but this position is now held by Maria del Pilar Gonzalez.

Perhaps it is not surprising that such a large winery should offer many different wines: for example, in any given vintage, there may be a seven different Cabernet Sauvignons and six different Chardonnays on the market. Some names are common to different varietals. For example, Tres Estrellas appears as an entry-point wine for both Cabernet Sauvignon and Sauvignon Blanc; at a higher level, Antares for Cabernet Sauvignon, Merlot, Chardonnay and Sauvignon Blanc. Then come Dallas Conte, Estrella de Oro, Reserva and, at the peak as far as Cabernet is concerned, Reserva de Familia. This last wine is partly made from low-yielding centenarian vines in the Maipo Valley.

A secondary label used by the company is Ochagavia. This is the name of a family, which reputedly emigrated from Portugal and arrived in Chile after some time in Argentina. It established its own winery in 1851 and this was subsequently bought by the Pereira family.

Wines I have particularly enjoyed: Chardonnay Dallas Conte 1998, Barrica Selection Syrah 1998.
Other brands: Ochagavia, Miraflores, Planella.

Viña Santa Ema. The owner of this winery, the Pavone family, came to Chile from Piedmont during the First World War. In due course, it bought vines at Isla de Maipo and began to sell wine in bulk to the major wineries. Now most of its 300 hectares of vines are in the Rapel district and its sales of bottled wine, largely to the United States, have reached 350,000 cases a year.

Most of the wines reflect its success on the American market, having overt fruit and, often, surprisingly high levels of residual sugar. The top red wine Catalina, which is a Merlot (50%)/Cabernet Franc (25%)/Cabernet Sauvignon (25%) blend, is a more serious wine, spending at least a year in new French barrels. This is normally a minimum of five years old before it is released.

Wines I have particularly enjoyed: Cabernet Sauvignon Reserve 1996.
Other brands: La Playa, Marqués de Los Andes, Maison du Lac.

Viña Santa Emiliana. This company is part of the Concha y Toro (q.v.) family, though it is run totally separately. It was created in 1986 to answer the new demand for young, fruity varietal wines; wines that, at that time, were outside the style that Concha y Toro was supplying. One of its first export managers was Thierry Villard, recently arrived from his success selling the Australian Jacob's Creek wines around the world. He went on to set up his own winery, Villard Fine Wines (q.v.) with the support, and minority participation of, Santa Emiliana.

The winery has vineyards in nine different farms spread about the country and has over 1,400 hectares of vines planted with a further 300 hectares available for planting. In addition it sources grapes from as far south as the Bío-Bío Valley. Winemaking techniques are designed to extract maximum flavours of fresh fruit, with grapes being pressed as close to their source as is possible. Cask ageing is considered to be an unnecessary luxury, wood flavours being provided mainly by stave treatment. Generally speaking, the name Palmeras Estate on the label means that the wine has been treated in this way.

The wines are always sound and represent good value for money. On this basis, Santa Emiliana has built up sales around the world of a million and a half cases a year.

Wines I have particularly enjoyed: Merlot 1998.
Other brands: Palmeras Estate, Andes Peaks, Walnut Crest, Santa Isabel (shared with Viña Casablanca).

Viña Santa Helena, see **Viña San Pedro.**

Viña Santa Inés, De Martino, Sociedad Agrícola Santa Teresa Ltda., Maipo Valley. Basically this family-run winery produces two parallel ranges of wine, one aimed at the restaurant trade, called De Martino and one aimed at the off-trade called Santa Inés. In addition, the family is an important grower of table grapes and has a plant for the production of concentrated grape must, a product that is in increasing demand around the world.

The estate, of about 300 hectares, is at Isla de Maipo, to the south-west of Santiago and the family, of whom five members run the company, has not hesitated to hire the best advisers. These include, for advice on canopy management, Dr Richard Smart, an Australian, who has come to be called 'New Zealand's viticultural guru', and, on winemaking matters, Aurelio Montes. (One thing of interest that can be seen here in the table-grape vineyards is propagation by layering.) Certainly this gives the impression of being one of the 'tidiest' vineyards in Chile.

One particular matter of pride for the De Martino family is that it was amongst the first to recognise that much of what had, for generations, been called Merlot in Chile, was in fact Carmenère and it was the first to label it as such in the 1996 vintage. The wines are estate-bottled, with the exception of its highest level Chardonnay, the *Reserva de Familia*, which is made from grapes bought in from Casablanca.

This is one of my favourite producers in Chile and it takes a great deal of care with its wines, using both American and French oak barrels. The names Enigma and Legado de Armida are used on the Santa Inés label for some of the superior, reserve, wines; the equivalent De Martino wines are called Prima Reserve.

Wines I have particularly enjoyed: De Martino Malbec 1998, De Martino Reserva de Familia Chardonnay 1998, Santa Inés Legado de Armida Carmenère 1998.

Viña Santa Laura, Colchagua Valley. This is a recently established boutique winery at Santa Cruz, in the Colchagua Valley. Whilst there are 80 hectares of vineyards, the owners, the Hartwig family, have decided to limit production to a maximum of 14,000 cases. There are three basic varietal wines: a Cabernet Sauvignon, a Merlot and a Chardonnay, and a premium wine called Gran Reserva, which is barrel-aged for a year and is a predominantly Cabernet Sauvignon blend, with an eighth each of Merlot and Carmenère. The wines are all sold under the Laura Hartwig label.

Viña Santa Monica, Rancagua. This winery is one of those trying to maintain the best of traditional Chilean wines, whilst, at the same time, offering wines that are acceptable for export markets. To achieve this there are both *rauli*-wood vats and stainless-steel tanks, but the winery is being steadily modernised. Still, however, two-thirds of the production is sold in bulk rather than in bottle. Most of the bottled-wine sales, currently running at something over 80,000 cases a year, are exported.

At the top of its product range comes Tierra del Sol barrel-aged Cabernet Sauvignon and Chardonnay. Then there is a Cabernet Sauvignon and a Sémillon, sold without a vintage as Reserva de Bodega, and finally a range of varietal wines including a Riesling and a Cabernet Sauvignon Rosé.

The company, which belongs to Emilio de Solminihac and his wife Monica, has more than 80 hectares of vineyards in production, for the most part around the winery.

Wines I have particularly enjoyed: Riesling 1999.

Viña Santa Rita. The Santa Rita winery is at Alto Jahuel, in the shadow of the Andes, some 30 km south of Santiago. In a country with many beautiful wine estates, this is one of the prettiest with a park of mature trees and an imposing Victorian château, complete with its own chapel. This now serves as an exclusive luxury hotel and restaurant.

The estate was created by Domingo Fernandez Concha in 1880, on a site which was already important in Chilean history, for during the fight for Chilean independence in 1814, Bernardo O'Higgins took refuge here with 120 of his men after being defeated by the Spanish at the *Desastre de Rancagua*. On its creation the property was perceived as a very model of modernity, with its own horse-drawn railway constructed to connect with the main line at the nearby town of Buín.

Until 1978 the company belonged to the Garcia Huidobro family, but it had suffered serious financial losses during the government of the Unidad Popular, under Salvador Allende. In 1977, a deputation went to General Pinochet to ask the then government for a loan of 2 million dollars to help carry them over the difficult period. This was refused and they had to seek else-where. Salvation, of a kind, came in the form of the entrepreneur Jorge Fontaine. As the price for his support he took control of the company, buying the shares of the family, and those workers who had invested in the company, at a price imposed by him. At the same time he told the workers that he was freeing them from the conditions of 'serfdom' that they had suffered under the previous owners.

The ownership of Sr Fontaine did not last long. He, in turn, sold it in 1980, to a consortium led by Ricardo Claro Valdés, a businessman amongst whose business interests are a company producing 90% of the country's bottle needs, and the shipping line Sur Americana de Vapores. One of his partners in the buy-out was Owens-Illinois Glass Company of the United States, but its shares were subsequently bought by Sr Claro.

Santa Rita is the second largest wine company in Chile, with sales of over 6 million cases. It has 22% of the domestic market, as opposed to the 24% of Concha y Toro, with sales of over 5 million cases, four-fifths of which are accounted for by tetrabriks. It sells 1.1 million cases on export markets, but is particularly proud of being the leading exporter of premium wines. It claims the highest average export price of all the major companies: US$30, in contrast to the overall average of US$24 – and US$19 for Concha y Toro and US$18 for San Pedro. In addition, its subsidiary company, Viña Carmen (q.v.) sells a further 340,000 cases a year.

Currently, the company has almost 1,600 hectares of vineyards, with a further 400 yet to be planted or to come into production. Half of these are in the 'home' vineyard in the Maipo Valley, the rest are spread between Casablanca (284 hectares), the Rapel Valley (339 hectares) and the Maule Valley (101 hectares). As far as the varieties planted are concerned, the most important, by far, is Cabernet Sauvignon with 673 hectares, followed by Chardonnay (319 hectares) and Merlot (271 hectares). The company also owns the Viña Doña Paula in Mendoza, in Argentina, with 150 hectares of vines.

In order to produce the wine, the company has two major vinification centres at Buín and at Los Lirios in the Rapel Valley, and two lesser facilities at Palmilla, again in the Rapel Valley, and Lontué in the Maule Valley. Between them they have a total storage capacity of 65 million litres. In all they have 12,000 barrels (60% American oak and 40% French), of which a third are replaced each year. All bottling, including the wines of Carmen, takes place at Buín. The winemaking is under the control of Cecilia Torres and Andrés Ilabaca.

For the international consumer, there is likely to be some confusion as to the wines that are offered. For example, on the domestic market, anything up to eight different Cabernet Sauvignons might be available. One of them is called Casa Real, but this is not the same as the Casa Real sold on export markets, which is more than twice the price. If you want to drink this in Chile, you must ask for Casa Real Export Label. To show its strength in depth with this varietal the 2000 edition of the well-respected *Guía de Vinos de Chile*, lists the outstanding Cabernets in seven different price-brackets. Santa Rita is represented in four of these and is the best in two of them, with its Casa Real Export Label 1996, being the outstanding wine of the year.

On export markets, the varietal label hierarchy appears to be, from the top downwards: Casa Real (for Cabernet Sauvignon only), Medalla Real, Reserva and 120 (in memory of the refugees from the battle of Rancagua). In addition there is an elusively rare wine called Triple C, a blend of Cabernet Sauvignon, Cabernet Franc and Carmenère.

Wines I have particularly enjoyed: Medalla Real Sauvignon Blanc Rapel Valley 1999, Reserva Chardonnay, Casablanca 1999,

Reserva Merlot, Maipo Valley 1999, Medalla Real Cabernet Sauvignon, Maipo Valley 1998, Casa Real Cabernet Sauvignon, Maipo Valley 1997.

Seagram de Chile, Casablanca. This is a modern winery where Mumm sparkling wines are made both by the tank and traditional methods. Whilst Seagram has sold the mother company in Champagne, it has retained the production name in Latin America.

Viña Segú Ollé, Viña Segú, Maule Valley. The Fundo Mirador Estate of the Segú family is in the heart of the valley of the River Loncomillo, an area that traditionally gave ordinary table wines from the País and Moscatel grapes, for sale on the Chilean domestic market. It was here that this Catalan family came to settle in 1924. Before that it had had interests in brewing, but felt that the future lay in the production and distribution of wines. For over half a century, it cultivated the traditional varieties and it was not until 1981 that it began to plant classic European varieties. Now almost half its production of 80,000 cases a year is Cabernet Sauvignon and this appears under a variety of titles under the two different suppliers' names: Segú and Segú Ollé. On the domestic market, the latter name is used for Reserva wines under the Caliboro title, whilst the best wine from the former is Super Premium, which does not appear in all vintages. Amongst its white wines, Sauvignon Blanc comes highly recommended.

Other brands: Caliboro, Los Caminos, Doña Consuelo.

Seña, see **Viña Errázuriz.**

Viña Siegel, Colchagua Valley. This estate, with eight hundred hectares of vines in the Colchagua Valley, was established in 1975, by Walter Siegel Dauelsberg. Like many others, it is making the transformation from being a seller of wine in bulk for the major brands, to trying to create an image for itself with its own bottled wines. These it is selling under the brand name El Crucero.

Viña Tabontinaja, Agrícola Tabontinaja Ltda., Maule Valley. This winery is thought to take its name from the *tinaja*, or terra cotta, ali-baba basket-shaped, vats in which wine used to be aged in Chile

– and still is in certain parts of southern Spain. The estate was first created in the middle of the nineteenth century but was bought in 1990 by Francisco Gillmore, who has wide-ranging interests in the wine industry, both in Chile and in the United States, where he owns a winery on Long Island. Tabontinaja is managed by his daughter Daniella, who has worked on vintages in Australia and California. The family is of Scottish origin and has arrived in the world of wine by way of Brazil and raising goats.

This is a winery that aims very much at the ultimate consumer. On the property is a guesthouse (definitely not a hotel, I was told) where faithful customers have rights to free accommodation and where they can enjoy a very broad range of local attractions. In Santiago, there is a tasting-cellar and bistro for the promotion of the wines.

The estate has 60 hectares of vines, which are divided into 31 blocks. Many of these have their individual microclimates and the vintage can last from the end of February until the beginning of May. The grapes from each plot are vinified separately and great attention is paid to the individuality of each wine. Current sales are only about 10,000 cases a year, under the Gillmore name, and there is no intention of increasing this. 'We only want to increase our quality, not our production,' says Daniella. This quality comes at a price to the consumer!

One of the major interests of Tabontinaja is that, despite its small size, it has two winemaking facilities on the site. Until recently, one of these was used by the Calina company of Kendall-Jackson (q.v.), but it has now built its own facility.

Wines I have particularly enjoyed: Cabernet Franc 1999, Carignan 2000, Merlot 1999.

Cooperativa Vitivinícola de Talca, see **Conde del Maule.**

Viña Tarapacá Ex Zalava, Maipo Valley. This company has amongst the longest histories of any in the Chilean wine trade. It was first established by Francisco de Rojas y Salamanca in 1874, and was known during its early years as Viña de Rojas. In the 1920s, it was bought by the Zalava family and, as a result of a marital dispute, the husband came to own the name, whilst the ex-wife owned the vineyards. What was she to call the wines that she now had to sell? After a number of legal disputes, the well-known lawyer, later to become President of the country, Don Arturo Alessandri, came up with an ingenious solution. She could use on her labels the term *Ex Zalava;* she, as a gesture of thanks decided to add *Tarapacá*, the constituency that Don Arturo then represented in the senate. The estate then passed through a number of hands, including the Barros Hurtado family, which had extensive pastoral interests. They, in turn, sold it to Rafael Mery. When I first visited it in 1990, it had fallen on hard times and it was up for sale. It had just 70 hectares of vines planted, at Tobablaba very close to Santiago. Its winery was very run-down.

Now everything has changed. In 1992 it was bought by the important holding company, Compañía Chilena de Fósforos, which had a broad range of interests, comprising, inter alia, arms-dealing to asparagus plantations. Since then it has invested over US$50 million in the winery and the vineyards.

The re-created estate, some 45 km south-west of Santiago, is more than 2,500 hectares of which 600 are now producing vineyards. This has now raised the company from being a small, well-reputed producer, to a major player with annual sales of over a million cases. The company is strong on the domestic market, where it still sells a *Chablis* and a *Borgoña* as its basic wines. For the varietals, the hierarchy, moving upwards, begins with León de Tarapacá and moves to Gran Tarapacá and Gran Reserva (additionally for Cabernet Sauvignon, a black label Gran Reserva). These last wines tend to be heavily wooded in a traditional style. Their icon wine, which was launched at the end of 1998 is the 1996 vintage Milenium, a Cabernet/Merlot/Syrah blend. Whilst this initial vintage has received some criticism, the 1997 vintage of the same wine has been broadly acclaimed. On a lower level is a Cabernet/Merlot blend, entitled Triunfo.

Wines I particularly enjoyed: Leon de Tarapacá Sauvignon Blanc 1998, Gran Tarapacá Chardonnay 1998.
Other brands: Rosario Estate, Santa Cecilia, Terra Nova.

Viña Terra Andina, see **Cooperativa Agrícola Viti-Vinícola de Curicó.**

Viña TerraMater. This estate comes as a result of the splitting of the Canepa family holdings in 1996 after the death of José Canepa.

Whilst his widow inherited the Canepa company, the three sisters, Antonieta, Edda and Gilda, inherited almost all the vineyards. From these emerged two wineries, TerraMater and Hacienda El Condor (q.v.).

Whilst the winery is near Isla de Maipo, in the Maipo Valley, the vineyard holdings include Hacienda San Clemente, in the Maule Valley and Hacienda San Jorge, near Curicó. The former vineyard is a particularly good source for Cabernet Sauvignon, while much of the Merlot and Carmenère grapes come from the latter. Basic varietal wines are sold as Paso Del Sol, whilst superior wines, aged in French oak, are sold as Altum TerraMater.

Current production is about 300,000 cases of bottled wine a year, but there is the potential to triple this.

Wines I have particularly enjoyed: TerraMater Reserva Merlot 1999.
Other brands: Alma TerraMater, Casa Las Loicas, Paso del Sol.

Viñedos Terranoble, San Clemente, Maule. This winery is based on an estate in the San Clemente Valley, but as all its vines are not yet in full production, it has had to rely, to a certain extent on bought-in grapes. Its policy is also to use irrigation only for young vines; once they come into production, dry-farming is the rule. Currently production is around 80,000 cases a year, but the potential is for more than this. This is yet another winery, which in the past has made wine for Viñas de la Calina (q.v.).

Most wine consumers' exposure to carbonic maceration wines is with the ephemeral Beaujolais Nouveau, but here French wine-maker Henri Marionnet uses it for making his Merlots and they have been shown to maintain their fruit and flavour for five years and more.

Wines I have particularly enjoyed: Merlot 1994.
Other brands: Valle Andino, Sierra Vista.

Viñedos Torreón de Paredes, Rengo. This is an old-established wine property that was bought by the Paredes family in 1979. The current estate of 150 hectares of vines in production includes some on barren, stony soil, reminiscent of the *garrigues* of the south of France. Most of the production is of red wines and these are noteworthy for the vibrancy of their fruit.

One distinctive fact about this winery is that it is one of the very few to offer wines with bottle-age. At the end of 1999, for example, its Private Collection Cabernet Sauvignon 1993 and its more expensive Don Amado Cabernet Sauvignon 1993, were both still available on the domestic market. This latter wine is only produced in outstanding years and the composition of the blend, usually involving Cabernet Sauvignon, Merlot and Carmenère, can vary considerably.

Viña Torrealba, Curicó. The Torrealba bought its property, just south of Curicó in 1978 and began to plant vines. Initially its wine was sold in bulk to other wineries, but now it has a range of bottled wines under its own label.

It has 80 hectares of vineyards and 70% of its production is in red wine. The cellars have storage capacity of 800,000 litres and include stainless steel and 250 American oak barrels.

Wines I have particularly enjoyed: Cabernet Sauvignon Reserva de Familia 1998.

Sociedad Vinícola Miguel Torres, Curicó. If Miguel Torres can be said to be responsible for the renaissance of the Spanish wine industry, he can equally be said to be responsible for the birth of Chile as a wine-exporting country. When I first visited the country, the wines that were available on the domestic market were of a common, undrinkable, style. The sole exceptions were those of Torres. As a member of the Masters of Wine team to visit Chile in 1989 subsequently wrote, 'The Miguel Torres winery is small and simple, compared with others visited, but their influence, particularly in encouraging a trend to make fresher, fruitier whites acceptable locally, has been important.' What the company introduced to Chile, as it had introduced to Spain, were stainless steel and small oak casks. It is impossible to underestimate the influence that these have played in dragging Chile into the modern wine world. Whilst it is possible to exist by selling traditional red wines (as has been shown by some Rioja houses), it is now almost impossible to sell oxidised white wines. The contribution that Miguel Torres has made to the Chilean wine industry was recognised by his being awarded the Order of Bernardo O'Higgins in 1995. A further result of the success of Torres has been pointed

out by the Chilean wine historian, José del Pozo, namely the investment by a number of French wine companies. This led to a broader
recognition around the world of the merits of Chilean wine.

Miguel Torres went to Chile first at the invitation of a Chilean
winemaker who had been his colleague at Dijon University.
Immediately, he was attracted by the possibilities and invested, at
the beginning of 1979, in an estate, just to the south of Curicó, on
the banks of the Guaiquillo River. This investment, of US$200,000
must represent just a small percentage of what he has since spent. In
2000 a new low-roofed, red-tiled winery was his latest gesture.

As well as the original Fundo Manquehua at Curicó, the estate
also includes the Fundo Cordillera in the Claro Valley, the Fundo
San Francisco Norte in the Lontué Valley and land in the Claro and
Maule valleys. In all there will soon be available grapes from more
than 350 hectares of the company's own estate. The winery is also
run as a tourist attraction, being well situated just by the side of the
Pan-American Highway South of Curicó.

Production is now about 170,000 cases a year, and when all
the recently acquired land comes into production, it should be
substantially more. Torres were amongst the first to experiment
with such grape varieties as Gewürztraminer and it produces a
traditional method sparkling wine from the classic ingredients of
Chardonnay and Pinot Noir. There is a broad range of brand names
used, of which Santa Digna, Bellaterra and Don Miguel are perhaps
the best known on export markets. At the top end of the red wine
range come the Cabernet Sauvignon, Manso de Velasco, aged in
French oak, and Cordillera, a blend of Carignan, Syrah and Merlot.

It is interesting that the Masters of Wine, when they returned
to Chile in March 2000, did not include Miguel Torres in their
programme. Does this mean that it is now considered as a winery
that has little new to show? Certainly it seems to have lost some
of the impetus that made it for long one of the most important
wineries in the country. Have the pupils now overtaken their
master?

Wines I have particularly enjoyed: Santa Digna Sauvignon Blanc
1997, Santa Digna Cabernet Sauvignon 1998.

Viña Undurraga. This is one of the great historical names of the
Chilean wine industry. The Undurraga family is thought to have

arrived from the Basque country in north-west Spain, at the end of the eighteenth century. The founder of the company, Francisco Undurraga, was born in 1855, and spent part of his youth in Europe. His fortune was due largely to his father-in-law who gave him two cattle ranches as a dowry. Selling the cattle during the War of the Pacific against Peru and Bolivia (1879–1883) proved to be immensely profitable and this enabled him to buy the estate of San Vicente de Talagante for $157,000, at auction, in 1882. There is a story that Doña Isadora Goyenechea de Cousiño, one of the founders of Cousiño-Macul, also wanted to buy the property, but arrived too late at the sale. Her offer to Francisco Undurraga of a substantial premium above what he had paid was rejected out of hand. At this time there were no vines on the estate and the plantation and the construction of a winery took place under the supervision of two Frenchmen, Pressac and Dalbaie. The winery was modelled on the one recently built at Viña Errázuriz Panquehue. These cellars and the surrounding park are still in existence, though the former are now more of an attraction for foreign dignitaries than anything else.

The company still belongs to the Undurraga family, though they have the British-owned investment group, Hampton's, as minority shareholders.

Undurraga is a company that has always been present on export markets. When Jan Read wrote his book on Chilean wines in 1988, he claimed that, proportionally to total sales, it was, with 40% of sales abroad, the most important exporter. Fifteen years later, its total sales have tripled and exports now account for 60% of sales, but proportionally, there are a number of more important exporters. What it has managed to maintain, however, is high average prices for its sales.

What is more important is the rapid expansion of the vineyard holdings. In 1947, the company owned 120 hectares of vines, in 1969, 147 hectares and in 1985, 195 hectares; now it owns 995 hectares, split between four farms, two each in the Maipo and the Colchagua valleys. These account for approximately half of the company's needs. Total production is now well over a million cases a year. On the domestic market, the wines are distinctive for their bottle, which has been likened to the traditional *bocksbeutel* of Franconia; this is known as their *caramayola* bottle.

Whilst the company is perhaps best known for its range of

Cabernet Sauvignons, it also has a high reputation for its Gewürz-traminer and for its Cabernet Sauvignon/Pinot Noir blend.

Wines I have particularly enjoyed: Gewürztraminer 1999, Cabernet Sauvignon 1999, Cabernet Sauvignon Reserva 1996.

Viña Valdivieso. The town of Lontué might be described as the heart of the Chilean wine industry and right in the middle of the town, cramped up against the railway line, lies what was described to me as 'the ugliest winery in Chile', that of Valdivieso.

The company was founded in 1879 by Alberto Valdivieso, who had bought the Santa Elena estate, specifically to produce sparkling wines. In the 1920s, it was looked upon as one of the most advanced wineries in the country, having in its cellars 32 enormous vats of *rauli* wood, which had been built on site by Chilean craftsmen. At the time, they were considered to be 'unique in their size in Chile'.

Alberto lived until 1935 and after his death the company was taken over by the Mitjans family, which had first arrived in Chile from Catalonia in 1887. In 1914, they created, with another Spanish family, the company Mitjans, Ribas y Cía., which, in due course, changed its name to Fca. Licores Mitjans. This company manufactured alcoholic products and distributed others that it imported from Europe.

Valdivieso is still known for its sparkling wines; it is the most important producer of *méthode traditionelle* wines in Chile, with 80% of the domestic market, but it now makes slightly more still wine than sparkling. It also is a leader in supplying own-label wines to European markets. In this last field, its sales were suffering seriously at the time of my visit (mid-2000).

The company's vineyards are centred on the Primavera estate of 200 hectares near to Sagrada Familia, which provides it with 5% of its grape needs. This vineyard takes the form of an amphitheatre at the end of a valley.

Of its sparkling wines, the Brut and Extra Brut are bottle-fermented, whilst the Demi-Sec is made by the Charmat method.

Because of the important needs for Pinot Noir for its sparkling wines, this also is a speciality in its still wines, and it makes some of the best in the country. Perhaps the outstanding wine, however, is one called Caballo Loco (Mad Horse). This is produced from remnants of Reserva quality red wines blended together. Each blend is numbered (the current release is No. 4) and is sold without a vintage. (Though the No. 4 has a solid base of 1997 vintage wines.) The ingredients of each blend are unspecified, but, to give some continuity, approximately 20% of the previous blend will be included. Fewer than 1,000 cases of each blend are produced. Other Reserve quality wines are labelled 'Premium V'.

Wines I have particularly enjoyed: Pinot Noir 'Premium V' 1998, Malbec Barrel Selection Reserve 1999, Caballo Loco No. 4.
Other brands: Morillon, Mitjans, Stonelake.

Viña Los Vascos, Colchagua Valley. Whilst the arrival of Miguel Torres did much to lead to the renaissance of the Chilean wine industry, there is no doubt that the investment of the Domaines Baron de Rothschild in the Los Vascos Estate in 1988 set the seal on the validity of its rebirth.

The property had first been planted with vines as long ago as the middle of the eighteenth century by Miguel Echeñique, who had come over from Vizcaya, in Spain, as an army officer. The property still belonged to the same family at the time of the Rothschild investment; indeed, they remained for some time as minority shareholders, until they subsequently sold their holding to Viña Santa Rita.

Currently there are just over 300 hectares of yielding vines and these give an annual production of over 300,000 cases of wine. After failing to produce satisfactory Sauvignon Blanc, production is now concentrated on Cabernet Sauvignon and Chardonnay, though a little Merlot is grown for blending purposes.

Whilst production is firmly based on Bordeaux principles, it is surprising how little use is made of casks. Neither the ordinary Cabernet Sauvignon, nor the Chardonnay see barrels. These are reserved for the Grande Réserve Cabernet Sauvignon.

I have long used Los Vascos as a sound fall-back on a boring wine list. One is never disappointed, but I have always been surprised that the wines, given their parentage, have never been brilliant. Is there, something, therefore in what Jürgen Matthass says in his book, *Wines From Chile*? 'Whilst the team of oenologists, under the leadership of the experienced Lafite helmsman Gilbert Rokvam, would like to present a *Chilean red super wine*, the French owners are still resisting. It would appear that the full potential is not being developed, in order to keep competition at arm's length from French products.' Or, as others have expressed it to me, Château Lafite itself might not be able to withstand value-for-money comparisons.

Viña Veramonte, Casablanca. Generally speaking, Chilean wineries do not have the promotional pizzazz of, say, the wineries of the Napa Valley. Few of them go out of their way to attract tourists; one of the exceptions is Viña Veramonte. It is ideally situated for this. If you are driving from Santiago down to the main resort town of Viña del Mar, you arrive in the Casablanca Valley through the Zapata tunnel. Before your eyes can accustom themselves again to the daylight, there is a hoarding cajoling you to visit the Veramonte winery, just a kilometre further on the right. Here there is a tasting cellar and souvenir shop in the Californian mould; it is a hard-hearted tourist who does not leave without a bottle or two of wine and a sweatshirt!

If you consider the parentage of this winery, it is scarcely surprising that it has a Californian image. The brains, and much of the finance, behind the operation, is Augustín Huneeus, a Chilean who left the country when Allende came to power and who rescued the Franciscan Winery in California from bankruptcy.

He was one of the first to realise the potential of the Casablanca Valley as vineyard land and bought 3,000 hectares of land there. The estate comprises 450 of these at the eastern, and warmest, end of the valley. Because of their location, early-ripening red grapes, such as Pinot Noir and Merlot can also be grown with success, in addition to the more traditional Sauvignon Blanc and Chardonnay. This geographical advantage is stressed on the labels, with the source being given as Alto de Casablanca. Its premium Merlot is called Primus. Cabernet Sauvignon, and occasionally Merlot, grapes are brought in from the Central Valley.

Production is currently running at 150,000 cases a year and set to rise considerably.

Villard Fine Wines, Casablanca. By its nature, Chile is a country of immigrants, but one of the most successful of these is one of the most recent, Frenchman, Thierry Villard. After many years as export manager for the South Australian wine company, Orlando, and the responsibility for introducing the rest of the world to

'Australia's top drop', Jacob's Creek, Thierry gave up everything and moved to Santiago, his wife's home city in 1989. Initially, he was export manager for the Santa Emiliana winery, but he soon persuaded them, and some local growers in the Casablanca Valley, to support him in a new venture.

However, Thierry realised that there were other fields within the local wine industry that were ripe for exploitation. He took on an agency for a firm producing stainless-steel vats and also, throughout South America, for Nadalié casks from Bordeaux. These he now imports broken down and they are re-assembled in a Santiago cooperage, run by his son Sébastien.

Whilst the scale of the winery is still quite small, 18 hectares of vines and annual production of 25,000 cases, it is set to expand. Most of the production is exported, mainly to Britain. As well as relying on grapes from its own vineyards, there are also contracts with local growers and, particularly for the production of red wines, with the Maipo Valley. His Merlots and Sauvignon Blancs, particularly, are establishing reputations for themselves.

Wines I have particularly enjoyed: Sauvignon Blanc 1998, Merlot Reserve 1998.

Viña Viu Manent, see **Viña San Carlos.**

Cuba

The ubiquitous Chardonnay is now grown on
this Caribbean island in the tobacco-growing
region of Pinar del Río.
Jancis Robinson, *The Oxford Companion
to Wine*, 1999

That Jancis Robinson should have no more than this to say about
Cuba and its wines is not surprising; this Caribbean island is semi-
tropical and is probably best known for its cigars, its communism
and its rum. None of these are likely bedfellows for fine wine
production. Indeed, when the Spanish government decided, as part
of the celebrations for the 500th anniversary of the discovery of the
Americas, to commission a book on American viticulture and its
roots, 16 countries participated, including such unlikely grape-
producers as the Dominican Republic and Guatemala; Cuba does
not get a mention. Now it can claim to have a thriving, if limited,
wine industry.

Cuba was visited by Columbus in 1492, was conquered by the
Spanish at the beginning of the following century and was under
their rule for almost 400 years. There can be little doubt that
the early missionaries tried to plant vines, for the making of
communion wine, as they did elsewhere in the Caribbean.

In Britain, the first rumours that we heard of a modern wine
industry were at the end of 1998, when it was announced that wines
were now being made from a selection of grape varieties. Shortly
there would be more than a 100,000 cases of wine a year available
for the British market, and that they would be launched at a tasting
at the Cuban Embassy in London. Since then the wines seem to have
maintained a singularly low profile and initial requests for further

information were sidelined. However, there are vineyards and a winery in Cuba!

Vinos Fantinel is the result of a friendship between Dr Ardizones, the Cuban consul in Rome, and the Fantinel family, who have a 250-hectare estate producing Collio and Grave del Friuli wines in the north-east of Italy. This family started in the wine trade as recently as 1969, previously having been hoteliers and restaurateurs.

The Cuban project was launched in 1994 as a result of liberalisation of Cuban laws, which permitted the establishment of joint-venture companies. This company is a joint venture between the Fantinels and Coralsa, the Cuban Ministry of Food. After extensive research into the most suitable sites for the planting of vineyards, the first vines were planted in 1996 and there are, at present 30 hectares planted, though not all yet in full production. There are plans to plant a further six hectares in the near future. These vineyards are in the southern foothills of the Guaniguanico Mountains in the western province of Pinar del Río. These are around the sugar-cane producing towns of San Cristobal and Soroa, some 75 km south-west of Havana. The red soils are rich in minerals and iron, though drainage has proved to be a problem. The Fantinels claim that they are ideal for making full-bodied, Australian-style wines!

The sub-tropical climate has both advantages and disadvantages. On the plus side, there are two vintages a year in December and July; on the minus, fungal diseases are rife and cyclones occur regularly, with the capacity to destroy a crop totally.

Current plantings are of Tempranillo (selected because of Cuba's Spanish history), Cabernet Sauvignon, Merlot and Chardonnay (because of their current international appeal), and Pinot Grigio (because of the company's roots in Friuli). In addition, Sauvignon Blanc is imported from Italy in the form of grape must. At the moment production is running at about a million bottles a year, most of which is sold on the Cuban domestic market, where they are fortunate enough to have as a distributor the main rum brand. About 60% of the wine sold is red. A very recent development is the production of a sparkling wine, from Chardonnay grapes, by the tank fermentation method.

The winery, at Pinar del Río, is under the control of winemaker Gianpaolo Gabassi. At present, one gets the impression that he and the Cuban authorities are feeling their way with regard to production controls, and this is only natural in a nascent industry. However, they have big export plans and it seems probable that EU standards will have to be introduced. The office, in Havana, is under the control of Maria Elena Fantinel, from the third generation.

At the moment, there are three levels of wine being produced. At the basic level are red, white and rosé blended wines sold under the Soroa label, except in Cuba, where they are called Orchid Valley. In the local supermarkets, they sell for under US$5 a bottle. Above this comes the San Cristobal 'Reserva' range of varietal wines, with Pinot Grigio and Chardonnay as whites and Tempranillo and Cabernet Sauvignon as reds. They should sell at under US$7.50. Their top range goes under the name Castillo del Morro 'Gran Reserva', retailing at US$11, the red is 70% Cabernet Sauvignon and 30% Merlot; the white is Chardonnay and Sauvignon Blanc in the same proportions. They take their name from a castle that was built in the middle of the sixteenth century to protect the sea approaches to Havana harbour. The company is restoring the vaults in this castle as ageing cellars for the wine. (It should be pointed out that, at present, none of the wine is barrel-aged.)

What is the future for Cuban wines? With ever-increasing popularity of the island as a tourist destination, Fantinel has been wise to begin by concentrating on the domestic market, where it has established a sound position. However, its plant has a capacity of producing four million bottles of wine a year and is, at present, only making a quarter of that. Their vineyards are nowhere near in full production. Exports will soon become a necessity. Certainly there are parts of production and labelling that will have to be tidied up if the wines are to comply with EU regulations. Some wines are already being sold in Europe; beginnings are being made in selling to other Caribbean countries. The wines have been described as being 'not really exciting' though 'better than expected from a tropical country'. It will need more than such faint praise, if the company is ever going to achieve the once-mentioned target of 120,000 cases a year on the British market!

Mexico

Vines are cultivated in these settlements to great extent, and the wine in some places is not inferior to the best Spanish wine. In the environs of *Passo del Norte,* the vineyards produce such excellent wines, that they are preferred to those of Paras, in new Biscay, so much celebrated as being the produce of the *Vitis Vinifera* of Asia, planted by the first settlers. Under the old government, the vine could hardly be included among the territorial riches of Mexico, the quantity being so inconsiderable. But the political changes which have taken place in that country, have given encouragement to the plantation of the vine and the consumption of native produce, unshackled by the prohibitory and tyrannical laws of the mother country. The inhabitants of Mexico and New Spain will soon be enabled to supply not only their home consumption, but that perhaps of the whole of North America; and Mexico may yet serve to that portion of the globe, what France, Spain, Portugal, and Italy have long proved to the rest of Europe.

Samuel Morewood, *Philosophical and Statistical History of the Inventions and Customs of Ancient and Modern Nations in the Manufacture and Use of Inebriating Liquors,* 1838

Whilst Mexico is the northern boundary of the vineyards of Latin America, it has rights to be considered as the heart, for, whilst

Wine growing areas
1 Valles de Calafia
  y Guadalupe
2 Tecate
3 Valle de Mexacali
4 Valle de Santo Tomás
5 San Vincente

Mexico

Columbus attempted to plant vines on the island of Hispaniola on his second voyage, the first successful plantings were in Mexico. Also it is in Mexico that we find the oldest winery in the Americas, established around 1580, though, because of delays in communications, the official land grant was not signed by King Philip II of Spain until 15 August 1597. This winery is still in production. It is also to Mexico that the current Californian wine industry owes its conception – for Europeans it is often hard to accept that California formed part of Mexico until the Treaty of Guadalupe in 1848.

Spanish colonists did not introduce the vine to Mexico, for they found native American vines growing there in profusion. However, a number of measures meant that the vine played an important role in early agriculture. First, the Merchant Venturers of Seville decreed in 1519 that every ship leaving for the Indies should include a certain number of vine shoots in its cargo.

Secondly, wine was an essential part of the diet of the conquistadors and extended supply lines meant that it was in short supply. The capture of Tenochtitlan by Cortés in 1521 led to a drunken orgy of celebration, which finished the last of the wine that had been brought from Spain. As Hugh Thomas says in *The Conquest of Mexico* (1993), 'Whether demanded as tribute, under proper legal forms, or in any other way, the shortage of food was severe. The fields in the Valley of Mexico had not been sown during 1521. Thus during the last part of that year, and much of 1522, the lack of maize was so great that even the Castilians encountered hardship. There had hitherto been only a minuscule amount of trade from Spain and Hispaniola, and none from Cuba. So there was no wine, nor clothes nor flour.' In a later move to answer part of the problem, Cortés ordered in March 1524 that 'Every person who obtains a grant of land under the partition of the Indian estates shall be obliged to plant proportionally each year a minimum of one thousand vine shoots, until there shall be on each land grant a minimum of five thousand vines.' It seems from accompanying documents that it was expected that these figures should be achieved more by grafting on to native vines rather than by planting ungrafted Spanish shoots.

Finally, as in other parts of Latin America the influence of the church was of paramount importance and in Mexico Catholicism was embraced by the natives perhaps with more fervour than anywhere else. Of this Hugh Thomas says, 'The conquerors had by then covered the country with a network of monasteries, churches, shrines and parishes – first Franciscans, then Augustinians and Dominicans, finally secular clergy. Processions at Corpus Christi and in Holy Week, as well as masques, such as an annual battle of Christians and Moors had become popular. The turning point of the history of the Mexican church was, however, when the Virgin Mary herself was supposed to have appeared, with dark skin, on 9, 10 and 12 December 1531, to a newly baptised Indian, "Juan Diego", on the hill of Tepeyac just to the north of Tenochtitlan. Thus began the cult of the "brown Virgin", "*la virgen morena*", of Guadalupe, recalling the monastery of Guadalupe in Spain, and establishing that the Indians too could have their divine heroes.'

Whilst the major need of the church was for wine for the mass, it was important in other ways. As the eighteenth-century Jesuit Francisco Javier Clavijero wrote, 'The missions did not sell the wine, but they used it in the mass, at table and for the sick, with what was left over being given to benefactors or exchanged for provisions.'

As far as the history of Mexican, and Californian, wine is concerned, it is the religious orders that are particularly important. For it was their missionary zeal that took first the Jesuits and subsequently the Franciscans and the Dominicans to Baja California and later as far north as Sonoma in what is now the American state of California. Whilst there had been a short-lived Mission established at La Paz, just north of the tip of the California peninsula, as early as 1683, the first permanent Spanish settlement was established in October 1697 with the Misión Nuestra Señora de Loreto on the eastern coast. In the next 70 years, before they were expelled from the Spanish Empire, the Jesuits created 23 missions in Baja California and became the *de facto* rulers of the province. The hole left by their departure was filled by the Franciscans, who were particularly active in spreading to Alta (mainland) California. With them, the priests brought the Mission grape, which makes up for its lack of ability to produce quality wine, by being able to thrive in unlikely climates and with minimal tending. This variety went on to be the most widely planted grape in California until Agoston Haraszthy introduced a selection of European varietals at the end of the 1850s.

A further reason for the importance of the churches in the early history of wine in Mexico was the edict made by the King of Spain in 1699. In a bid to protect the interests of his domestic wine producers, he banned the planting of vineyards and the making of wine and brandy in his dominions in South and Central America. The sole exception to this rule was the making of wine for the church. With the seat of Spanish power in the Americas being based in Mexico City, this law was applied with some severity, whilst in more distant colonies, such as Argentina and Chile, it was all but neglected. This law was not repealed until Mexico gained its independence following the civil war, which started in 1810.

It was not until 1821 that the Viceroy finally agreed to withdraw and give up Spanish sovereignty. Power was seized by the commander of the army, General Agustín de Iturbide, who quickly promoted himself to Emperor Agustín. Whilst his rule lasted less than two years, he sought to promote the interests of Mexican wines by introducing punitive taxes on imported products. Despite such efforts there was little demand for local wines. And with more than a century of internal unrest, including one period of 22 years, which saw 36 changes of the President, as well as the same man coming into office on 11 occasions, there was no incentive for the industry to re-establish itself.

It can be said that wine production in the country was at a standstill until after the Mexican Revolution in 1916 when, the 'Constitutionalist' Conservative Venustiano Carranza overthrew the Liberals led by Francisco Madero, whose family, coincidentally, owned vineyards near Monterrey in the north-east of the country.

Whilst Mexico has just under 50,000 hectares of vineyards, the fourth largest area in Latin America, after Argentina, Chile and Brazil, it is neither an important consumer nor producer of wine. Annual consumption per person is just over a quarter of a litre, a figure more than matched by that for brandy. Beer, rum and tequila, too, are much more popular and, in addition, there is the highest consumption of Coca-Cola, per capita, in the world. Wine is drunk by the wealthy in the restaurants of Mexico City; but even here there is little tradition and little demand. Indeed there is no national pride in the product; those who can afford to drink wine, generally prefer to drink imported wine.

It is true that there has been a rapid increase in the production of table wine in the country, but this is starting from a very low base and is largely fuelled by burgeoning export demand.

Nevertheless, as little as 8.3% of the grapes grown are used for making wine. Almost eight times as many are destined for brandy production; close to twice as many are sold as table-grapes and just as more as raisins. In no way can Mexico claim to be a wine-loving country! Whilst there is some optimism as to an awakening of interest in wine amongst the Mexican middle classes, the realists are concentrating more of their efforts on export markets.

This lack of interest in wine is reflected by the nature of the Mexican laws controlling wine production. Basically, there are none, or as one winemaker put it to me, 'Here the only wine laws are in the conscience of the winemaker.' For example, each producer is free to decide what percentage of Cabernet Sauvignon he puts in a bottle that he labels as Cabernet Sauvignon. Of course, as far as wines destined for the European Union are concerned, they must contain a minimum of 85% of the grape variety shown on the label. However, it is not clear that there is anyone in Mexico deputed to police this! Another side effect of this indifference is that there is no government-led research into viticulture and vinification.

Where, then, are the Mexican vineyards? Over half of the area under vines is in the state of Sonora, which runs south from the American border, which it shares with the state of Arizona, along the eastern shore of the Gulf of California (or the Mar de Cortés, as the Mexicans call it). Most of the state is a continuation of the Arizona desert, with the triple advantages for grape growers of unlimited sunshine, little rain and artesian water available for irrigation.

Within the state, there are two major vineyard areas. The first, around the town of Hermosillo saw its first plantings in the early 1960s. Here yields are high, with most of the wine made going for distillation into brandy, though much base for wine coolers is also made. Not surprisingly, amongst the most widely planted varieties are the Palomino and the Thompson Seedless. The vintage here takes place between the beginning of July and the middle of August.

The town of Caborca lies north-west of Hermosillo, close to the American border. Here there is true desert, with sandy soil, and night temperatures which fall below freezing. The first vineyard, one hectare of Mission vines, was planted in 1964. There are now more than 13,000 hectares of vines planted, with much of the production, which is Thompson Seedless, being dried and sold as raisins. For brandy grapes, the harvest can begin as early as the third week of June.

Mexican quality wine production is concentrated in the northern part of the state of Baja California, where more than 90% of the country's quality wine is produced. In many ways the vineyards are a continuation of those of California to the north, for they mostly lie in a series of valleys running west/east where the high temperature is moderated by morning mists rolling up from the sea. These mists are caused by the cold Alaska current, which flows along the coast in a southerly direction. This also brings welcome humidity to the vines. (In California, there is a similar effect at Carneros, where the Sonoma and Napa Valleys join, in the Santa Ynez Valley and at Temecula, just north of San Diego.) In each case, the relieving effect of the ocean makes good winemaking possible.

These three valleys are, from north to south, the Guadalupe, the Santo Tomás and the San Vicente. The Guadalupe Valley begins at El Sauzal, which is on the coast road about 110 km south of the American border at Tijuana and some 3 km north of Ensenada, the self-styled wine capital of Mexico. Whilst this town has much to recommend it, it suffers from its closeness to the United States. At holiday time, its streets are thronged with students making the most of the more relaxed drinking laws, including a lower permitted drinking age, and with the elderly seeking to prolong their activity with the host of remedies permitted south of the border, that are forbidden north of it. It is truly abroad – yet it is only a 90-minutes quick dash down the motorway from San Diego. Every day, cruise ships put in, to disgorge their passengers seeking souvenirs in the myriad of shops ready to welcome them. The marriage between Mexican commercial port and centre of the fishing industry and a centre for American escapism is not a totally happy one.

El Sauzal has not only a number of fish-canning factories, but is also home to a number of assembly plants. Baja California is able to offer foreign companies a number of tax incentives and many American industries have established factories to take advantage of these and the lower labour costs in Mexico. Such plants are dubbed *maquilladores*, or make-up artists. The appeal of regular wages in these factories is impacting on the traditional local agricultural industries, including that of wine. It is becoming increasingly difficult to recruit staff to work in the vineyards and wineries. A further by-product is that increasing demands on the water supply, here mainly in the form of a subterranean aquifer, are placing pressure on the available water for irrigating the vineyards. What water is left is becoming increasingly impregnated with salt and has to be treated before it can even be used for irrigation.

At the ocean end of the valley where the climate is cooler, the best white grapes are grown, mainly Chardonnay, Sauvignon Blanc and Chenin Blanc. A subsidiary valley, here, is that of San Antonio de las Minas. Off the far end of the main valley leads the Valle de Calafia, home to the most powerful red wines. In early Spanish legend, Calafia was an island off the coast of California ruled by a warlike Amazon queen. In total the Calafia Valley has about 950 hectares of vines, whilst the Guadalupe Valley has approximately 3,000. The climate can be described as Mediterranean with an average rainfall of about 250 mm per year. This falls mainly during the months of winter. In the summer, the temperature may rise as high as 36°C; in the spring and autumn a mixture of clear and misty days is the rule. These sea mists permit a limited amount of dry-farming, though irrigation is generally practised. The soils are mainly alluvial, though on the valley sides, where the better vineyards are, they consist of decomposed granite. The sandy nature of the soil means that *phylloxera* is not a problem and one could plant ungrafted vines. However, nematodes are present and because of this all vines are grafted. The other main causes for concern are powdery mildew and *botrytis*. As already mentioned, increasing industrial calls on the water that is available, and salination, may well mean that drought will become an increasing problem. The vintage normally lasts from the first week in August until the end of October.

As in many other parts of the world, the past 10 years has seen a dramatic change in the varieties of grapes that are planted. In 1990 the Grenache, or Garnacha, was the most widely planted red grape variety, and the Chenin Blanc, the most widely planted white, with the Chardonnay not appearing at all. Now the concentration is on the world-wide favourites, Cabernet Sauvignon and Merlot for red wines and Chardonnay and Sauvignon Blanc (and still a good deal of Chenin Blanc) for whites. The Zinfandel has been planted in the valley for more than 60 years and some of the best wines come from the Nebbiolo.

Visiting the valley is easy, because the main road Mexico 3 passes through it. This runs from its junction with Mexico 1 at El Sauzal to the sleepy border town of Tecate, a distance of about 110 km. The last of the Missions to be built in the Californias was Misión Nuestra Señora de Guadelupe (1834) but it held out against Indian attacks for just six years, and now little of it remains. Its vineyards reverted to scrubland. Just after the turn of the century, a colony of White Russians was established in the valley. They were pacifist refugees, who had arrived in Mexico via, to them, a deeply inhospitable Los Angeles. It was they who planted the first non-ecclesiastical vineyards in about 1911. Initially they just made wine for their own consumption, but they expanded on a more commercial scale in the early 1930s. Whilst there are few families who have survived, and some still grow grapes for sale to the wineries though they do not make wine, their early life is shown in the Museo Comunitario de Guadalupe, just off the main road in the village of Guadalupe.

Whilst most of the valley is covered by vineyards, there are also extensive orange orchards.

Most of the vineyards are the property of independent growers, who then sell their produce to the major wineries. The two most important are situated facing one another, at the far end of the valley, in the Valle de Calafia.

Vides de Guadalupe – Domecq S.A./Casa Domecq. This winery is at the end of an extended tendril of the multi-national Allied Domecq. In Mexico, the name Domecq is synonymous with brandy; indeed it stands as one of the largest spirit brands in the world even though it is little seen outside the country itself. Whilst Domecq might also be the largest brand of Mexican wine, selling about 700,000 cases a year (of which, less than 10% is exported) it is scarcely considered to be a matter of much priority by its British owners. Policy is decided by a group of distillers who come down from Canada once a year. It is scarcely surprising that the wine-maker Ronald McClendon, who previously worked with the Phelps winery in California, gives the appearance of a somewhat lonely man.

Domecq do not have their own vineyards but have about 400 hectares under contract and source further supplies from about 70 independent growers. In all, the winery has a capacity to stock 16 million litres of wine of which 15 million can be in stainless steel.

New oak barrels, both American and French are widely used, with Seguin Moreau being the preferred cooper.

A broad range of wines is made; at the bottom comes Los Reyes including a red, a Barbera-based blend, and a rosé from Grenache. Next comes Calafia, the red a blend of Ruby Cabernet, Valdepeñas (Tempranillo) and Cabernet Sauvignon. Thirdly there is a range of straight varietal wines, including a Cabernet Sauvignon, a Merlot and a Chardonnay. Finally, the premium wines are called Château Domecq, the red being a Nebbiolo/Merlot blend and the white being based on Sauvignon Blanc, a third of which is barrel-fermented. Other brands they produce include Padre Kino, named after an early Jesuit missionary, and a range of kosher wines. The Padre Kino white is a blend based on Ugni Blanc, Palomino and Chenin Blanc. These brands between them account for approximately 45% of Mexican wine production. Despite the laxity, or non-existence, of Mexican wine laws, Domecq wines are 100% what they claim to be, both as far as the grape variety and the vintage are concerned.

Generally, I found the wines that I tasted to be sound rather than exciting, with white wines marred by an excess of oak. The wine that appealed to me most was the Château Domecq red 1993, which had deep fruit concentration with soft tannins.

On the back of its undoubted success in the market place, the Domecq winery projects itself as a tourist attraction and receives approximately 15,000 visitors a year.

Productos de Uva S.A./L. A. Cetto. In the 1920s Don Angelo Cetto emigrated from Piedmont to settle in Mexico, planted vineyards and began to make wine, but it was not until 50 years later that the decision was taken to sell any products under the family name. Now the 100% family-owned group is the largest producer of wine-products in Mexico, with 1,200 hectares of vineyards in the Guadalupe Valley and a further 1,600 hectares in the state of Sonora. Much of the wine from Sonora is used as a base for wine coolers or for distillation, and some of the grapes are dried. In all it produces between 400,000 and 500,000 cases of wine a year with 40% of its output being exported.

The group is based round three plants. The head-office, ageing warehouses and wine bottling lines are in downtown Tijuana, and are a major attraction for tourists from across the border. The winery (and a small bullring for particularly honoured guests) is in the Calafia Valley, and in Mexico City wine coolers and sangria are produced. In addition, the group owns the tequila brand Viuda de Romero.

Whilst they are close neighbours, facing each other across the valley, there are many contrasts between Domecq and Cetto. At the former, management may seem very remote, at Cetto it is very hands-on, with the president of the company, Luigi Cetto, appearing to be omnipresent. Whilst Domecq does not own vineyards, Cetto does. Whilst Domecq appears to be a passive participator in exporting, Cetto is very active with customers in 25 countries. At Domecq, little experimentation is apparent whilst at Cetto, there are trial plantings and trial vinifications of a host of different grape varieties, with red wines being made currently from 17 different varieties.

Since Cetto entered the market with wines under its own name, just over 20 years ago, it has made rapid gains. Overseas, its broad presence has led to it being almost synonymous with Mexican wine and on the home market its share has risen in the last 10 years from about 7% to approximately 40%.

Overall, two-thirds of the Cetto production is of red wine and they make wines at three different levels. First of all come the commercial blends, then a range of 100% varietal wines (though there are also a number of dual varietal blends) and at the top come the 'Limited Reserve' wines, these again being split into *Reserva Limitada* and *Reserva Privada*.

In Britain, Cetto is perhaps best known for its Petite Syrah, but amongst its outstanding red wines is also a Zinfandel, made from grapes from dry-farmed 60-year-old vines in Tecate. I also particularly enjoyed a Tempranillo and a Malbec, made from three different clones. All these wines had the very clearly defined characteristics of the varietal on the label. However, the red wines of which the Cetto family is most proud are their range of old vine Nebbiolo Reservas Limitadas, and still available is a broad range of vintages going back to 1986, when they first made the wine.

Its white wines range from a clean, fresh, commercial Chenin Blanc up to a superb selection of oaked and unoaked Chardonnays, of which my favourite was Chardonnay Reserva Privada 1996, which had spent seven months in new French oak. As a tribute to their Italian roots, the Cetto family makes a Passito wine, which spends 10 years in sealed casks before bottling.

The Italian-born winemaker, Camillo Magoni, a native of Friuli, can be proud of what he is making.

As well as the two giants of the valley, there are also a number of smaller producers. These include:

Monte Xaníc. This winery was established some 10 years ago by five Mexican partners, of whom one, Hans Backhoff, acts as director and winemaker. It has approximately 45 hectares of vineyards, planted in five white varieties (Chenin Blanc, Colombard, Sémillon, Sauvignon Blanc and Chardonnay) and five red (the Bordelais quintet of Cabernet Sauvignon, Merlot, Petit Verdot, Cabernet Franc and Malbec). It uses only its own grapes and makes between 20,000 and 30,000 cases of wine a year. In Mexico, its wines are sold only to restaurants and they are distributed in France by Château Lafite Rothschild and in the United States by Chalone.

Here no expense has been spared in a bid to make top quality wines. The winery also has a policy of holding back some wine from each vintage so that it can offer from stock, for example, Chardonnays going back to 1991 and Cabernets back to 1988.

The range of white wines includes barrel-fermented Chardonnays, a Late-Harvest Chenin Blanc and Viña Kristel, which is a Sauvignon Blanc (90%)–Sémillon blend, with three months in oak. Whilst they were very good, I found the red wines more interesting. There is a very concentrated Cabernet Franc, an intensely rich, but firm, Merlot, a full-flavoured Cabernet Sauvignon and my favourite, a 1995 vintage wine described as Cabernet-Merlot, but which is, in fact, made from the full range of the five Bordeaux varietals. This showed little sign of age and will become a truly great bottle.

Château Camou. This is a winery that wishes to model itself on Château Margaux and three million dollars have already been invested in its creation. It is a comparative newcomer on the scene having sold its first wines in 1995. At present it has 30 hectares of vines in production and these will rise to 50. Some grapes, particularly Chenin Blanc and Zinfandel, are bought in. The current 15,000 cases of wine made each year will rise to a maximum of 30,000. The intention is to become a winery aimed at export sales, as the feeling is that the Mexican market is not sophisticated enough to absorb much high-priced Mexican wine. At the moment exports are confined to the United States and a small beginning has been made in Quebec.

The winemaker, Dr Victor Torres (apparently no relative of the Torres of Penedés), trained in Barcelona and he is determined to make Mexico's finest wines. White grapes are picked at night by lamp-light; the team of 50 pickers going out at 10 p.m. and coming in at 6 a.m., in an effort to bring the grapes in at as a low a temperature as possible. The red grapes are picked between 5 a.m. and 11 a.m. All the grapes are sorted on arrival back at the winery, with any of doubtful quality being rejected. Up to 20% of stalks are left with the red grapes and both red and white grapes are given some pre-fermentation maceration, in order to extract the maximum fruit.

Of the white wines, my preference was for Fumé Blanc 1996, which came from 60-year-old vines, and the Chardonnay of the same year. The Gran Vino Tinto 1996 (a blend of 63% Cabernet Sauvignon, 24% Cabernet Franc and 13% Merlot) started softly in the mouth, but showed a firm finish.

Three other small wineries based in the valley are **Casa de Piedra**, **Viña de Liceaga** and **Bodegas Valle de Guadalupe**.

Casa de Piedra. This winery is the brainchild of Hugo D'Acosta, who is the general manager of the Santo Tomás winery. It was established to produce no more than 2,500 cases of a premium red wine. The first vintage was 1997, when only 500 cases were made from old Cabernet Sauvignon and Tempranillo vines, which had been dry-farmed. The winery is situated at the bottom end of the valley at San Antonio de las Minas and the wines are made to last, with mouth puckering tannins and very concentrated fruit. Of the production, 80% is sold *en primeur* to private individuals with a guaranteed buy-back price.

Viña Liceaga. This winery is less demanding in its pricing policy. It has 15 hectares of vineyards, again at San Antonio de las Minas, on granitic soil, planted mainly with Merlot, but with some Cabernet Franc. The first vintage was in 1996 and is labelled as a varietal Merlot. The intention is to produce just three wines, a standard

Merlot, a Merlot *Gran Reserva* and a Cabernet Franc/Merlot blend.

Bodegas Valle de Guadalupe. This is a small winery, producing currently no more than 800 cases of wine a year, which owes its origins to the White Russians who settled in the valley at the beginning of the twentieth century. It was founded by Alexi Dalgoff in 1930 and is still in the hands of the same family. It makes wines from Chenin Blanc, French Colombard, Cabernet Sauvignon and Zinfandel, which sell under the name of Bibayoff.

Bodegas de Santo Tomás. This is the main winery in Baja California to source its grapes outside the Guadalupe Valley. It has recently built a state-of-the-art winery in the valley of the same name. Its historical winery buildings in the centre of Ensenada, still contain its offices and a tasting cellar, but also include in what used to be the concrete vats, a bookshop, a restaurant, a wine-store, with wines from every winery in the region, and a Cuban ballet school!

Santo Tomás is the historical winery of Baja California, having been founded in 1888, though the vineyards it then bought had originally belonged in part to the Mission of Saint Thomas Aquinas, established in 1791. During its career, it was bought by Abelardo Rodríguez, later to become President of Mexico (it is interesting that despite the comparative insignificance of the Mexican wine industry, at least three Presidents have had interests in it). It was finally purchased in the 1960s by a wealthy industrialist, Senor Pando, who died in 1997 at the age of 102. Santo Tomás is still part of the Pando Industries Group, whose other interests include tuna and food.

Thirty years ago, the company sold 300,000 cases of wine a year; now it sells less than half that, with almost a third of its production being exported to the United States and Europe.

The company owns about 250 hectares of vines, but they are not all in full production, and it buys grapes as needed. Its vineyards are split between the Guadalupe, Santo Tomas and San Vicente valleys. In this last there is no irrigation and vines tend to be susceptible to Pierce's Disease, a bacterial disease common in southern California and Texas, which is capable of totally destroying a vineyard, and to which there is at present no known antidote.

The manager, Hugo D'Acosta, trained at Montpellier and their winemaker for the past six years, Christopher Gartner, is Swiss. Their aim is that the wines should have more flavour as a result of lower yields and that 'they should express the terroir of Mexico'. Certainly the wines that I tasted had exceptional varietal flavours, with my favourite being a Merlot 1997. In conjunction with the Livermore Valley winery Wente, they make what they like to describe as a NAFTA (North American Free Trade Area) wine, called Duetto. This is a classic Bordeaux blend.

Finally in Ensenada, there are two wineries, which share the same winemaking facilities, **Cavas Valmar** and **Mogor Badan**.

Cavas Valmar. This is a truly family-run winery, with the husband and wife team of Fernando Martain and Yolanda née Valentín. Not too much imagination was needed for the company name! They met when they were both working at Bodegas Santo Tomás and started in a modest way by making 300 cases of their first wine in 1990. The operation is still moderate; in 1998 they made 500 cases each of Chenin Blanc and Cabernet Sauvignon; the grapes for the former being sourced in the Guadalupe Valley and for the latter in the San Vicente Valley. They have recently bought eight hectares of land, which they hope to plant with Cabernet Sauvignon, Merlot and Chardonnay. Originally, they aged their red wines in second-hand Bourbon barrels; now they buy used casks from Monte Xanic and Santo Tomás.

Mogor Badan. This winery is on an even more artisanal scale. Senor Badan is a Swiss oceanographer, with two hectares of vines in production and two more that have just been planted. Perhaps with a touch of national pride he produces 150 cases a year of Chasselas, which despite the heat has typical delicate fruit and fresh acidity. More serious is the eponymous Mogor Badan, a blend of almost two-thirds Cabernet Sauvignon, one-third Cabernet Franc and a touch of Merlot. New oak from a Burgundian cooper makes for a firm tannic wine.

The viticultural region of La Laguna comprises the two states in north-east Mexico of Coahuila and Durango, which largely consist of desert crossed by the Sierra Madre chain of mountains. Viticulturally, with one exception, the states are of little importance, with three-quarters of the wine produced going for distillation. The one exception is around the small town of Parras de la Fuente, which lies more than 1,500 m above sea-level to the west of the major city of Monterrey. The translation of its name, vines of the spring, says it all. Here underground streams coming down from the mountains break forth and the first Spaniards to arrive here in 1521, a small group of soldiers and priests, discovered fields of wild vines. Wine was made from these grapes and the Mission of Santa Maria de las Parras was built.

About 60 years later, Don Lorenzo García created a wine estate some 6 km to the north of the town and built himself an imposing manor house. The land grant that he received in due course from the King of Spain is still in existence and the estate came to be known as the San Lorenzo winery. This continued to flourish, even through the centuries when the production of wine in the Spanish Empire was forbidden, by making altar wine.

Under Napoleon III the French occupied Mexico and the San Lorenzo winery was bought by a French company. In due course, it sold the winery and estate to Don Evaristo Madero, a man with broad international contacts. Parras was one of the first towns in the world to have both electricity and the telephone through his friendship with such notables as Thomas Edison and Alexander Graham Bell. In due course San Lorenzo changed its name to **Casa Madero**. The winery is still in the hands of the Madero family and, over the past 30 years the vineyards have been entirely replanted – twice. In this they have been advised by experts from the University of California in Davis – and this has probably been an expensive decision, for, as happened widely in the Napa Valley, the A×R1 rootstock was recommended and the vineyards were subsequently destroyed by *phylloxera*.

When the replanted vineyards are fully in production, there will be 485 hectares, split between three red varieties (Merlot, Cabernet Sauvignon and Ruby Cabernet) and four whites (Chenin Blanc, Chardonnay, Riesling and Colombard). The reason for the inclusion of large plantings of Colombard, particularly, is that much of the wine still goes for distillation into brandy – some of this is distilled in copper Charentais stills, bought by Don Evaristo 130 years ago.

The setting of the vineyards, winery and manor house in an oasis in the middle of arid mountains, must be one of the most beautiful in the world of wine – and it has its own airstrip so that you can fly straight to the cellar door.

Whilst brandies are the major item in the portfolio, the range of wines is as good as any from Mexico, though it is small compared to the Big Three of Baja California. The top of the range Cabernet Sauvignon, Casa Grande, is outstanding. Interestingly, the appellation Parras Valley is the first controlled wine region name in Mexico.

The final wine region of Mexico is Zona Central, the states of Aguascalientes, Zacatecas and Querétaro. Here the vineyards are amongst the highest in Mexico, lying as up to 1,950 metres above sea-level. The vineyards here had some historical importance, for the town of La Villa de Nuestra Señora de la Asunción de las Aguascalientes, (now rather less breathtakingly known as Aguascalientes) had extensive vineyards in the eighteenth century, which continued right throughout the prohibition of the Spanish Empire. Watered by the warm springs, for which the town is known, they provided enough wine to keep 25 stills busy.

Nowadays four-fifths of the grapes are distilled and the majority of what is left is table grapes for eating; grapes for winemaking are of very limited importance. Nevertheless, the Spanish multinational wine company, **Freixenet**, has established the Finca Doña Dolores in Querétaro Province in the highlands to the north of Mexico City. They have just under 40 hectares of vines, planted with Ugni Blanc, Sauvignon Blanc, Pinot Noir and Maccabeo. Not surprisingly, the plantings of Pinot and Sauvignon are being increased at the expense of the other two varieties. Their needs are filled out with grape purchases from local growers. Production is, at present, approximately quarter of a million bottles of bottle-fermented sparkling wine sold under the label **Sala Vivé** in the United States and Mexico itself. Small quantities of a still, red wine are made from purchased Cabernet Sauvignon grapes.

What is the future for the wines of Mexico? When one asks this question, it is also well to think of Brazil. Both countries have large populations that drink very little wine. In Brazil, great expectations for the wine industry lie in a hoped-for increase in domestic consumption. The Mexicans, on the other hand, appear to me to be more realistic and are building their hopes on increased penetration of foreign markets, reasoning that with the fashionable image they have already built up with foreign consumers for their beers and their tequilas, there is little reason why their wines should not follow. Land and labour are cheap, subterranean water for irrigation is available, the peso is plummeting, the climate is reliable, the future looks rosy!

Paraguay

═══

Paraguay has very little in the way of vineyards,
either because the land is not suitable, or because
the missionaries have seen that they do not
become too common, so as to prevent the
disorder that wine can lead to.

Jullien, *Topographie de Tous les Vignobles Connus*,
1816

Paraguay is a frustrating country; those government departments that bother to reply to your queries as to wine production in the country, tell you that they have no information on the subject, but give you five, much less likely, names of those who might. In addition, the one book to mention their wines in more than a passing fashion, *La Viticultura Americana y sus Raíces* (1992), says rather confusingly, 'Currently there are about 2,000 hectares of vines. Of the total of vineyards in production, 524 have an area of less than five hectares and the remaining 1,080 are up to fifty hectares'. Things just do not add up!

Vines were first brought to the country by missionaries from Buenos Aires and wine continued to be made by the Jesuits in their highly developed communities in the upper valley of the Río Paraná. With the expulsion of the Jesuits by the Spaniards in 1767 and the further persecution of the church by the first of Paraguay's many dictators, 'El Supremo' José Gaspar Rodríguez de Francia, who ruled from 1814 to 1840, the vineyards were reclaimed by nature. It was not until the coming of the Mennonites, in the 1920s that any were replanted.

The Mennonites are an Anabaptist Christian sect named after the sixteenth-century Dutchman Menno Simons. Mainly because of their pacifist beliefs, they have been continually persecuted and have moved from country to country. In 1921, the Paraguayan government passed a special law, the *Privilegium*, granting the Mennonite refugees certain rights including exemption from military service and autonomous government within their colonies in the country. There are now approximately 25,000 Mennonites living in Paraguay, refugees originally from Germany and Russia, though many came to the country from Canada. Most of them live in three colonies in the inhospitable *chaco*, in the north-east of the country, called Menno, Neuland and Fernheim, where they speak their own particular dialect of German. These are primarily agricultural colonies, where their small vineyards give them the wine to which they are accustomed.

When I arrived in the capital Asunción, to research the wines of Paraguay, I openly confess that I was feeling low after two full weeks in Brazil and Uruguay, so I thought I would take a soft option. I would go to the nearest supermarket, buy a number of bottles of the local wine and taste them in my hotel room. My laziness was well rewarded; there was not a single bottle of Paraguayan wine in the store. The shelves were laden with wines from Chile and Argentina, not to mention a broad selection of European countries! I had to work harder on my research.

The climate of Paraguay is not conducive to the production of wine; for much of the year the temperature is 30–40°C and rainfall is often up to 2,000 mm per year, much of it falling during December, when the grape harvest takes place. Because of this European grape varieties are unsuitable and largely American varieties and hybrids are planted. Half of the production comes from the Oberling grape, a cross between the Gamay and an American grape. This is also grown for grape juice and as a table-grape.

Whilst there are small vineyards throughout southern Paraguay, including the Horticultural Research Station at Caacupé, 50 km east of Asunción, the main plantings are at Colonia Independencia, some 200 km south-east of the capital. This lies at the foot of the Ybytyruzu Hills and it is here that 80% of the country's wine is produced. It is a very German agricultural community, largely established by refugees after the Second World War. There are also some Mennonite and three South African families. The vineyard holdings are for the most part very small and most of the growers are members of the local co-operative cellar, the **Cooperativa Agrícola de Producción Independencia**.

There is no village, or town, as such, where the tarred road finishes is the centre of the community with a supermarket, restaurant, bar and filling-station belonging to one of the independent growers, **Martin Fichter**. Whilst Herr Fichter was very pleased to entertain me to a typically German meal in his restaurant, he was unwilling to discuss Paraguayan wines and their production, muttering darkly in German about chemicals. Certainly, of those Paraguayan wines that I tasted his red, Fichter's Wein Princesse, was the best, with memories of a Cabernet Franc from the Loire, though the packaging left much to be desired.

A much more sophisticated label, though not wine, was the white Viñas del Ybytyruzu from the **Escher Group**, whose main business appears to be producing Paraguayan whisky from local cane spirit. A more serious-looking wine was the Riesling 1998 from **Bodega Gerhard Buhler**. The label talked of the family's origins in the Kaiserstuhl region of Germany, offered a *Deutsche Weinbau – und Kellertechnik*, with temperature control being applied on the fermenting wine when it reached 23°C!

Seemingly, most of the local production is consumed within the colony itself and in the local state capital of Villarica. Much of the sales are in bulk from the co-operative van and the locals appear to drink their wines mixed with soda water. It is rumoured that some is clandestinely shipped in bulk across the River Paraguay into Argentina, to be sent back in bottle baptised as Argentine wine.

Is there a broader future for the wines of Paraguay? The answer must be 'No', for the climate is against quality and, being in Mercosur, the growers will not be able to produce anything to compete with the quality of wines from Argentina and Chile. Indeed, whilst the Paraguayan Ministries of Agriculture and Stock-rearing and of Industry and Commerce were signatories to the agreement on the wine regulations that would be applied within Mercosur, that was promulgated in Buenos Aires in June 1996, no effort appears to have been made to put them into effect. With regard to such matters, it could be said that the government has a *laisser-faire* policy! Notwithstanding all this, I am sure that the Germans will continue to produce wines for their own consumption. It is a part of their heritage that they are unlikely to abandon.

Peru

Letter from a traveller in Peru – Peruvian Sherry –
Doubtful if made in Peru.
T. G. Shaw, *Wine, the Vine and the Cellar*, 1864

With some justification, Peru could be described as the saddest
wine-producing country in Latin America. It has the greatest history
of any of them, having at its peak, as the most powerful colony in
the Spanish Empire, more than 36,000 hectares of vines. Now, it
has no more than 11,000.

Whilst this is a book about the wines of Latin America, as far as
Peru is concerned it must also be about the local spirit, pisco. The
story of the two is bound tightly together, for every wine producer
seems to have his stills and also make pisco.

The early days of the history of wine in Peru are particularly well
documented, for they merited a chapter in the *Comentarios Reales
de Perú*, by Garcilaso de la Vega *El Inca*. Son of one of the fellow
conquistadors of Cortés, he was particularly noted for the humane
way in which he treated the conquered Incas – and married one. The
Comentarios tell how vines were first brought to the country by
Francisco de Caravantes, 'one of the earliest conquerors of Peru, a
native of Toledo, a noble man'. These vines came from the Canary
Islands. Elsewhere it is mentioned how the first wines were made in
1560 on the Finca Marcahuasi, eight leagues from Cuzco, by Pedro
López de Cazalla. 'Who was motivated more by honour and fame
as being the first in Cuzco to have produced wine from his own
vineyards' than by the prize (of two bars of silver and 50 ducats),
offered by the Emperor Charles V to those introducing Spanish
crops to the new colony.

Another writer, Pedro de Cieza, whose *Crónica de Perú* was

Wine growing areas

TUMBES
ECUADOR
PIURA
Piura
AMAZONAS
Iquitos
LAMBAYEQUE
CAJAMARCA
Chiclayo
SAN
MARTIN
BRAZIL
Trujillo
LA LIBERTAD
ANCASH
HUANUCA
Huanuca
Paramonga
PASCO
Cerro de Pasco
Huancho
JUNIN
LIMA
Lima
MUANCA
VELICA
MADRE DE
DIOS
CUZCO
Cuzco
Ica
ICA
Puquio
AYACUCHO
PUNO
AREQUIPA
Pacific Ocean
Arequipa
Puno
Mollendo
MOQUEGUA
BOLIVIA
TACNA
Tacna
CHILE

Kilometres
0   300

N

Peru

published in 1551, talks of how the vine established itself wherever the Spaniards went. When the colonists arrived in the Ica Valley in 1563, they planted vines. They were helped by the fact that there was already in place an efficient system of irrigation, which had been established by the Incas many years before. Part of this system is a channel 52 km long and 15 m wide, called La Achirana. Legend has it that this was built on the orders of the Inca king, Pachacutec, as a result of his being rejected by a girl from Ica. In honour of her virtue he offered her whatsoever she wanted; she asked that water be brought to her people's settlement. On the instructions of the king, his army of 40,000 men spent two weeks digging the channel. It is this superior irrigation system that has enabled Ica to be the centre of the Peruvian wine industry ever since.

It was from Peru that viticulture spread through South America through Bolivia to northern Argentina, and from Chile to Mendoza.

The importance of the Peruvian wine industry is confirmed by a number of sources. By the middle of the seventeenth century, according to Bernabé Cobo, in his *Historia del Nuevo Mundo*, there were a broad range of different varieties planted, including the Mollar, the Albilla and both black and white Moscatels. 'From just the one region of Ica, which is in the diocese of the city of Lima, each year set sail more than a hundred ships laden with wine bound for other colonies, not just of this kingdom but of others.'

So great was the competition created by this wine for the domestically produced Spanish product, that the Jesuit Diego Torres Bollo persuaded King Philip II, in 1614, to ban the export of wine from Peru to other Spanish colonies, notably Panama and Guatemala. There is little evidence, however, that this edict had any effect. Indeed, by the year 1630, 150,000 jars of wine a year were being exported through Ica alone. Soon, added to this were the sister products of brandy and vinegar.

By the middle of the eighteenth century, wine production was dominated by the Jesuits, who owned no fewer than 203 estates in the country. In addition, the churches received tithes from other landowners and it is not surprising that their wealth led to jealousies and the eventual expulsion of the Jesuits in 1767.

The Californian gold rush gave great impetus to both the Peruvian wine industry and to demand for pisco. When boats had sailed round Cape Horn, they would put into Peruvian ports such as Pisco to re-victual and they would take on casks of the local spirit to satisfy one of the needs of the miners. In addition its merits were recognised by the Royal Navy, then very active in the Pacific, as a preventative of scurvy. The Pacific Fleet relied on pisco rather than rum for the daily spirits ration. Just as the port of Oporto gave its name to the local wine, Port, so did Pisco give its name to the local spirit. For the sailors this became a more than acceptable local substitute for rum. Indeed, it is an English captain, Hugh Salvin, who is first credited with calling the spirit 'pisco' as early as 1829.

Agriculture, as a whole, and viticulture in particular, suffered from the independence movement of the nineteenth century. *Phylloxera* too caused a major setback to the industry. Despite the sandy nature of the soil, which limits its effects, it was spotted in the Moquegua Valley in 1888 and in the more important grape-producing regions of Chincha and Ica in 1896.

The end of the nineteenth century saw the introduction of better grape varieties, particularly the Malbec, to Peru, but the twentieth century has not been kind to the country. The political situation has been unstable and the country has been at the mercy of leftist guerrilla movements such as the *Sendero Luminoso* and the MRTA. Agrarian reform in 1970/1, following the revolution in 1968, broke up many of the big wine estates and, unlike in Bolivia, the *campesinos* have shown little interest in wine production. Cotton and then asparagus were to be the saviours of the Peruvian economy. Both of these have priced themselves out of the market.

A further problem for the industry is the prevalence of fraud. The wide availability of cheap spirit made from sugar cane has led to wide adulteration, particularly of pisco. The government recently carried out research into the situation and this showed that 45% of all wine on the market and 75% of all pisco is fraudulent. This has led to the rather sad and despairing slogan, '*Solo es pisco, si es 100% uva*'. 'It is only pisco if it is 100% grapes'. One has only to look at the stalls lining the Pan-American highway in somewhere like Chincha to gain an idea of the fertility of imagination of many of the 'wine-producers'. Sadly the government appears to be unwilling to take any steps to control the industry, whilst the genuine producers hold up the example of Uruguay as a country which has supported and strengthened its domestic product. As a result, all wine and pisco production in Peru is carried out on what might be described as an artisanal scale. Most of the equipment is out of date and, compared to other wine-producing countries, the wineries have the air of museums about them. Modern technology is, for the most part, a dreamed hope for the future. The situation is further exacerbated by the fact that, while there are laws controlling the production and naming of pisco, there appear to be few for wine, though, if a vintage is mentioned on the label, 95% of the grapes used in the production of the wine must come from that year. With regard to varietal wines, these are described, by a Peruvian authority, as being 'wines which owe their composition 100% to a single grape variety, or if not this, to at least 75% of this variety'. It appears, however, that there is little, or no, control of the legislation.

Officially, there are five different vineyard regions in Peru: the North Coast, the Central Coast, the South Coast, the Andean Sierra and the Selva. However, of the 11,000 hectares of vineyards in the country, 90% lie in the Central Coast region and it is only here that wines of anything more than local importance are produced. Elsewhere, table grapes are grown, as well as some grapes for pisco. The second most important region is the South Coast and this is given over, almost entirely, to pisco production.

It should be realised that the coastal region of Peru is desert, intersected by a series of valleys flowing from the Andes down to the sea. It is only in these valleys that irrigation can be carried out successfully and it is in these valleys that vines, and other crops, can be grown. In addition, the vineyards benefit, as do those of California and Baja California, in Mexico, from cool currents of air coming up the valleys from the offshore cold currents. The resultant humidity and daily contrasts in temperature give quality to the wines.

Rainfall in this coastal region is minimal and water needs have to be met by seasonal river flow, normally during the months of November to March, augmented by artesian wells drawing on subterranean aquifers. Traditionally, many of the vineyards have been planted in 'sunken gardens', which are filled when river irrigation is available. Whilst this form of flood irrigation may have helped against the spread of *phylloxera*, it did little for the quality of the wine.

The three most important valleys for grape production on the Central Coast are, from north to south, Chincha, Pisco and Ica. The towns of Chincha and Pisco lie on the coast some 200 km south of

Lima; Ica lies 70 km south-east of Pisco, 50 km from the sea and about 400 m above sea level. As a generalisation the average temperature in Ica is about 3°C above that of Chincha, reaching a maximum of 33°C in February and March and a minimum of 10°C in June to August. The average difference in day and night temperatures is approximately 15°C. This contrast in temperatures enhances fruit flavours. The relative humidity is much lower in Ica than in Chincha. The vintage generally takes place in February.

Of the grape varieties that are grown, distinction has to be made between the 'local' varieties used mainly for distillation into pisco and the 'new' varieties used for table wine. These are grown in approximately equal proportions. A similar area of vineyards is used for the growing of table-grapes. The traditional varieties are the Negra Corriente or Créole and Quebranta used for making the highest quality pisco, pisco puro, and the Albilla, Moscatel, Torontel and Italia, used for Pisco Aromático.

The most important grapes for red wines are the Malbec, Barbera, Cariñena, Garnacha, Ruby Cabernet and Alicante Bouschet; for white wines, the Sauvignon Blanc, Ugni Blanc, Chenin Blanc, Pinot Blanc, Riesling and Sémillon.

The Ica valley is said to have more than 400 producers of wine. Whilst many of these will primarily be pisco producers, a number make both wine and pisco. Of these, there is one, which has an international reputation, this is **Viña Tacama**, whose estate lies 7 km north-east of the town of Ica. This is one of the great historical estates of Peru. It was originally presented to the Augustinian Order of monks in 1589 by the King of Spain and it held a strategic position on the *Camino Real*, the road to the silver and mercury mines at Santiago Chocorro. It was purchased by the Olaechea family in 1889 and, at its peak, before the agrarian reforms in 1971, when much of their land was expropriated, there was a community of 800 people, with their own school, football team and swimming pool. Times must have been difficult, for it came under bazooka attack from guerrillas in the *Sendero Luminoso* movement. Even during my visit there appeared to be a large number of armed guards, though I was told that this was because the payroll was being delivered that morning! Despite all these problems, Tacama can probably lay claim to being the oldest continually producing vineyard in the Southern Hemisphere.

Since 1924, the estate has relied on French technical advice, with recent consultants having included Professors Jean Ribéreau-Gayon, Émile Peynaud and Max Rives. The winemaker, since 1961, is Robert Niederman, previously with Skalli in Algeria. Despite the similarities in the climate between Oran and Ica, he found that different techniques were needed for winemaking. 'To my surprise', he says 'when I arrived in Peru, having been used to winemaking in a hot country, I was faced with musts high in acidity and I have had to carry out malolactic fermentations, right from the beginning in 1961'.

The magnificent manor house is surrounded by an estate of 150 hectares, which is renowned not only for its wines, but also for its stud of traditional Peruvian 'pacing' horses, which are trained in a specialised form of dressage. Still and sparkling wines, as well as pisco are produced, and there are 30 hectares of table-grapes, planted on the insistence of the revolutionaries for the feeding of the proletariat. As well as having the historical local flood irrigation, there are a number of artesian wells and a dam to provide water to the vineyards.

Just as elsewhere in Peru, the availability of hard currency has made it difficult to import the latest winemaking techniques and stainless steel is only just beginning to make an appearance. Some Limousin oak barrels have been bought, but these are being currently used on an experimental rather than a commercial basis.

The varieties planted include the traditional Quebranta and Albilla, mainly for the production of wines for distillation into pisco; Sauvignon Blanc, Chenin Blanc, Ugni Blanc and Sémillon for white and sparkling wines and Malbec, Tannat, Petit Verdot and Cabernet Sauvignon for red wines. The sandy soil and flood irrigation had provided sufficient defence against *phylloxera* until 1968, when unfortunately, some imported infected vines were planted. Nematodes had not been a problem until the arrival of *El Niño* and a resultant increase in temperature. Now almost all the vines are grafted.

Its top white wine is probably Blanco de Blancos, which has, in the past won a major award in international competition in Paris. This is a blend of 70% Sauvignon Blanc and 30% Sémillon. It also makes an agreeable sweet wine in a Loire style from grapes from 115-year-old Albilla vines.

The current owner of Viña Tacama is lawyer Pedro Olaechea, but he says that any credit for the quality of the wines is due to his father and the winemaker. However, he feels that life is hard for the wine-producer in Peru. The government does nothing to restrict the sale of fraudulent wines and piscos, and with an annual production of the estate of 100,000 cases and only 150,000 wine consumers in Peru, he has to look for export markets. One potential recent success, with a British supermarket chain, came to little, when the map on the back label showed boundaries to Peru that were in dispute! This proved to be a most sensitive matter!

One of the saddest wineries I have ever visited, was that of **Viña Ocucaje**, founded in 1898, which now belongs to the Rubini family. At its peak, the estate had more than 1,350 hectares of vines and its own port from where its sailing boats would ship the wine to the city of Pisco for onward exportation. The vineyards were all confiscated during the agrarian reforms and the winery now seems like a museum to the past. There are more than 60 wooden open-top fermenting vats which are no longer used; there is a storage capacity of three and a half million litres in Italian oak vats, built in 1847; these are 70% empty. The winery floor is made of beaten earth, dampened to keep cool.

What wines that are still produced, are made from concentrated musts, and the wines, too, have an historical aspect to them. They include a range of solera-produced 'sherries' and a quinine-infused 'port'. Their table wines are sold under the brand name *Fond de Cave*.

However, the Rubini family has learnt how to adapt. The estate is now entitled 'Viña Ocucaje Sun, Wine and Resort'. The house has been turned into a hotel with full sporting facilities; dune buggies can be rented to drive over the desert that has now engulfed what was once the country's biggest vineyard. In the courtyard lies the fossilised skeleton of a whale, stranded 40 miles inland, in the unknown past. Is this a symbol of the once great wine industry of Peru?

Typical of many of the smaller wineries of the Ica region is that of **Bodega Alvarez** at Yanquiza. Whilst the company claims to have been founded in 1930, it still uses an oak wine-press that could have existed when wine was first made in Peru 450 years ago; the grapes are still trodden by foot. Here three brothers produce 30,000 litres of pisco a year, which they sell in bulk to merchants. They also make a little sweet wine. They have three copper pot stills which are fired with *huarango,* a local hard wood. Each brother has his own concrete vat in which to store his individually distilled spirit, which comes off, after one distillation at 44% alcohol. This is the traditional face of the Peruvian wine industry.

The 180 hectares of vineyards of **Bodegas y Viñedos Tabernero** are at Grocio Prado and at Chincha Baja in the Chincha Valley. Their cellars are in the centre of the town of Chincha itself. As is usual they produce a range of piscos from gas-fired stills, sparkling wines by both the tank and gas injection methods, and table and fortified wines. Here there has been considerable investment with a new Italian bottling line and a 100 new barrels on order for ageing their Cabernet Sauvignon.

In all, they produce about 125,000 cases of wine a year; for me the most exciting was their Gran Blanco, which is a classic Chenin Blanc varietal wine. There is little doubt that the owners, the Rotondo family, are ambitious for international recognition, and they already export to a number of markets, including Japan.

Another historical winery is that of **Santiago Queirolo**, situated in a colonial style building in the old Pueblo Libre quarter of Lima. If you are just passing through the city, this is well worth a visit, not just for the wines, but also for the collection of lovingly restored historic vehicles that they own and also for their restaurant, just around the corner, *El Boliviarano*, which specialises in local dishes. It is also very close to the Archaeological Museum and that dedicated to the memory of the liberator, Simón Bolívar.

Because of the cramped nature of its city site, the company has its vinification plant at Pachacama to the south of the city. Its vineyard, Viña La Lágrima, lies even further south at Cañete. Here there are approximately 100 hectares of vines, including Cot, Merlot, Barbera, Criolla, Rubired, Moscato and Isabella. As might be gathered from this esoteric selection, much of its sales are to locals in tetrabriks and demijohns. The wines that I tasted had a certain rustic appeal. Interestingly, whilst most of the vines are pruned along wires, some are allowed to sprawl along the ground in historic Italian fashion. A speciality of this company is *masco*, which is fruit-flavoured pisco.

I suggested at the beginning of this chapter that Peru is the saddest of the wine-producing countries in Latin America. It has had a long and glorious history, but lack of investment, a small domestic market and a lack of interest by a series of governments have all led to an industry that is in a sad way. The political instability is unlikely to encourage any outside company to invest and the competition from fraudulent domestic products makes it difficult for the honest local producer to generate enough profit to pay for new equipment. However, there are moves in the right direction and it may be that the quality wines of Peru will find their niche. The government needs to be persuaded that wine can be a regular earner of hard currency, but that encouragement is needed for this ever to happen.

Uruguay

―――――

I read recently that Uruguay was destined to be
the next 'In' wine-producing country. I ask myself
what has Uruguay got that Argentina and Chile
do not have?

Clive Coates, *The Vine,* January 2000

One regular problem in the wine trade is that of satisfying the consumer's constant demand for novelty, be it for sourcing, packaging or grape variety. This, too, is a problem for the wine-writer; constantly looking for innovations, particularly if they are matched with quality. During my more than 40 years in the trade, I have introduced the British consumer to wines from two different countries. The second was Uruguay; the first was . . . Well, that can wait until I come to write my autobiography!

I first became acquainted with the wines of Uruguay in the autumn of 1989, at Anuga, the enormous food fair that takes place in Cologne every other year. I was looking in the catalogue at the list of countries offering wines and amongst the classical suppliers and some more recent newcomers from the New World were Ethiopia and Uruguay. Now, I had been exposed to the wines of Ethiopia *in situ* in Addis Ababa and I could vouch for their lack of commercial interest. In addition I suspected that they were made in Eritrea, then part of Ethiopia, from imported Italian grape concentrate. So, I went over to the Uruguayan pavilion. There amongst a herd of meat producers and a bunch of citrus growers, was a small booth, no more than two metres wide, containing half a dozen wine producers. Behind the counter, looking like fledglings eager to receive a worm from their mother's beak, they stood clamouring for the buyers' attention.

What were they doing in Cologne? Their presence at the fair was one of the first initiatives of the Uruguayan National Institute for Vitiviniculture (INAVI), which had been established the previous year, partly in response to Uruguay's potential membership of South America's common market, Mercosur. This would open their domestic market to the cheaply produced wines of Argentina and, in due course, Chile. They had been given three tasks: first, to promote the wines more aggressively in Uruguay itself; secondly, to improve the quality of Uruguay's wines; and, finally, to seek out export markets for these wines.

In many ways, Uruguay is the odd man out amongst the countries of Latin America. It never really attracted the attention of the early Spanish and Portuguese explorers, as it has little in the way of natural resources and the first visitors, in the form of Juan de Solís and his party, were massacred by the local Charrua Indians in 1516. In the 1620s Jesuit missionaries established a series of colonies in the valley of the River Paraguay. Some 60 years later, the Portuguese sought to limit Spanish influence by constructing a fort at Nova Colonia do Sacramento, across the estuary of the River Plate from Buenos Aires.

Whilst it is probable that the Jesuit missionaries produced wine for their own use, the first mention of wine in Uruguay does not occur until 1776 – more than 220 years after it had been produced in Mendoza in Argentina and a 170 years after it was made in Buenos Aires. This first mention comes in the *Agricultural Observations* of José Manuel Pérez Castellano. The writer's family came from the Canary Islands and he speaks of grape varieties from there, including a selection of Moscatels.

Independence came to the country after a series of wars, first against Spain and latterly against Brazil. Peace was finally brokered by the British, who were beginning to have extensive commercial interests in the area, in 1828. Freedom gave impetus to the planting of vineyards and one was established at Bella Vista by someone called Gibernau. His wines were served at the inaugural banquet of Manuel Oribe, the second president, on 1 May 1835. A second vineyard was established in the same area in 1839 by Francisco Aguilar.

Traditionally, the two great men in the history of Uruguayan wine are Pascal Harriague and Francísco Vidiella. The former planted a 200-hectare vineyard at Salto, a town on the River Uruguay some

400 km to the north-west of Montevideo. The variety that he used was the Lorda, which he brought with him from Concordia in Argentina. This variety is none other than the Tannat from the French foothills of the Pyrenees, where it is best known as the base grape for the red wines of Madiran. This grape has now become the most wisely planted *vinifera* variety in Uruguay and, in his honour, is now domestically called the Harriague. During the 1880s, the vineyard, and a small winery, were bought by two British brothers G. and C. Dickinson. Their main contribution to South American oenology was in the field of microbiology, as they were among the first to establish a wine laboratory in the continent.

Francisco Vidiella is a rather more unlikely man to be considered as a father of the wine industry. Originally from Catalonia, he had been in general business for more than 40 years when, in 1874, he established a winery at Colón, in the outskirts of Montevideo. With absolutely no agricultural experience, he planted a 36-hectare vineyard with Folle Noire and Gamay Blanc, imported directly from France. His first vintage was completed in 1883, with the First National Vintage Festival being celebrated on 25 February of that year. In his honour, the Folle Noire is now known locally as the Vidiella.

During the 1870s and the 1880s a broad range of quality *vinifera* grape varieties was brought in by immigrants from France, Spain and Italy. At about the same time the American variety, the Isabella, was introduced from Brazil. This was to become the most widely planted variety in the country, under the local name of Frutílla.

Rural enclosures, also during the 1880s, led to real dangers of unemployment and this resulted in the creation of what now claims to be Uruguay's oldest winery **Sociedad Vitícola Uruguaya** or **Vinos de la Cruz**, in May 1887. In the same year, an Italian immigrant Pablo Varzi established his own vineyard and winery at Colón. Later, in 1914, he established the first co-operative cellar in Uruguay. Partly this was to give support to those growers who had suffered from the arrival of *phylloxera* in 1893, but also it was an effort to improve the quality of local wines. Interestingly, the co-operative system has had little success in Uruguay, and their cellars account for less than 3% of the total production.

The new century was a busy time for the wine industry. In 1903 the first wine laws were promulgated and these stressed the import-ance of 'honest' wines. As A. N. Galanti says in his monumental work, *La Industria Vitivinícola Uruguaya* (1919), 'The production and sale of wine in Uruguay is controlled by laws, which, when taken as a whole, seem totally suitable. They are, without any doubt, more practical and rational than those that apply in Argentina, and they show the very praiseworthy aspiration of giving an honest industry total protection without affecting its industrial and commercial freedom.'

Official statistics showed there to be 3,600 hectares of vineyards, with 445 producing cellars. By 1910, the figures had increased to 6,100 and 559, respectively. In 1909, oenology courses were introduced for the first time at the Faculty of Agronomy at Montevideo University.

The early winemakers were, for the most part, producing wine for family needs and those of immediate neighbours. Most of the vineyards were planted close to the capital Montevideo, where almost half the population lives. There was little feeling, or demand, for the concept of quality wine. The rebirth of the industry has been dated by one author to the arrival from Catalonia in 1930 of winemaker Juan Carrau Sust. With two partners, he established the Santa Rosa company, also in Colón, which was to revolutionise winemaking in the country and to increase basic quality.

Notwithstanding this, American grape varieties and hybrids dominated production with their high yields and 'different' taste. The buoyant nature of the domestic market, with per capita consumption doubling and tight controls on the importation of competing products, meant that there was little pressure on producers to improve quality. Such was the situation, when the Uruguayan government decided that the country should join Mercosur. This would make necessary a dramatic reorganisation of the wine industry, so that it could survive in the face of new competition, particularly from Argentina and Chile. The decision to reorganise was the more noteworthy in view of the fact that the domestic market for wine was very healthy, with per capita wine consumption at over 30 litres per head – and rising. In addition, internal consumption matched internal production. The situation might appear very sound.

The three directions this reorganisation would take have already been mentioned: raising awareness of, and pride in, Uruguayan wines on the domestic market; improving the overall quality of the wines; and seeking a range of export markets.

With regard to raising the image of wine within Uruguay, there were two forms of competition, first from other drinks, such as beer and Coca-Cola, and secondly, with the arrival of Mercosur, from wines from other countries. Whilst the slogans used have varied, their tenor can be judged from a small car sticker I was given, which was produced by INAVI. Despite the fact that this is no larger than a visiting card, it bears three distinct messages, 'El vino es mejor', 'Uruguayo y natural' and 'Bueno para el corazón'. 'Wine is better', 'Uruguayan and natural' and 'Good for the heart'. Each of these has its particular appeal! From the beginning, stress has been laid on the natural product that is the local wine; the original slogan, used on radio, TV and in a poster campaign, was, 'Take time; ours and natural'.

A further sign of increased confidence in the domestic wines is the number of roadside hoardings that can be seen on the main road to the north, exhorting the motorist to visit one of the neighbouring wineries. With so many of the vineyards, and wineries, being so close to the capital, this could prove to be a powerful tourist attraction. However, any promotional moves seem to have been on an individual basis; surely there must be a potential for a jointly promoted *route du vin*, with accompanying explanatory map and booklet?

With regard to improving the quality of the wine, a number of steps were taken. The first of these was to forbid the use of foreign wine names for Uruguayan wines as early as 1993 – and Uruguay claims to be the first country in South America to have taken this step.

Secondly, and most importantly, there has been a long-term plan to change the composition of the local vineyards from being dominated by American varietals and hybrids, to being mainly composed of *vinifera* vines. In many ways the climate is similar to that of Brazil, with excessive humidity being the major problem. It is for this reason that American and hybrid vines were so widely planted in the two countries: they are more resistant to rot and mildew. Recent treatment techniques introduced in the vineyards have, however, increased the resistance of European vines to these two scourges.

As a result of government subsidies, a programme of replanting is under way, which is set to change the balance of the vineyards. Between the years 1984 and 2002, total production of grapes for winemaking is set to increase by a third. In the same period, production of *vinifera* grapes will also have doubled, whilst that of the Isabella, or Frutilla, will have fallen by a third and that of hybrid grapes will have remained largely constant. At the same time, there will be a change in the quality of the composition of the *vinifera* vineyards. Varieties of lesser quality, such as the Folle Noir, the Ugni Blanc and Hamburg Muscat will be grubbed up and replaced by the Tannat, Merlot, Cabernet Sauvignon and Cabernet Franc. It is interesting that three-quarters of new plantings will be in just these three varietals – all of them red. Indeed more Cabernet Franc is scheduled to be planted than Chardonnay.

However, it is recognised that wine-drinking habits cannot be totally changed, they can only be developed. It is for this reason that there will still be substantial plantings of hybrid grapes and the Hamburg Muscat. They give the wines that have been widely drunk for generations, and will continue to be so.

A further move to upgrade the status of quality wines has been the creation of the term VCP, which stands for *Vinos de Calidad Preferente*, or Preferred Quality Wines. Basically, these must be made from quality *vinifera* grapes and be sold in 75 cl bottles, or smaller. In addition they must have a minimum strength of 10.5° and match up to a number of other standards. The production of these wines is also tightly controlled and the label is only granted after analysis of the wine by INAVI. The twin stated aims of the category are to stimulate the category of fine wines and to defend the status of domestic wines against imported ones.

The corollary of the VCP status is that those wines that do not fill its requirements may be sold only as VC, or Vino Común. Whilst much of this quality of wine has historically been sold in demi-johns, and more recently, litre tetrapacks, it means that any wine sold in a litre bottle, no matter what grape it is made from, *vinifera* or hybrid, is automatically VC. Whereas in Brazil, for example, you know that a wine at this level is made from hybrid grapes, in Uruguay there is a very good chance that it will not.

Uruguay claims to have the strictest wine laws of all the Mercosur countries. As a small country, it seeks to protect itself. If a grape variety is mentioned on the label, it must account for a minimum of 85% of the wine. (This is in line with EU regulations.) In addition, if a geographical source is mentioned, the wine must all come from that source. In effect, this can pose some problems, for a number of wineries source their grapes from different parts of the country and this means that they should all have separate identities if they are shipped into the EU.

Chaptalisation is only permitted for certain *vinifera* grapes and the limits vary from vintage to vintage. The one serious problem that has not been addressed by the legislation is that of yields. Most Uruguayan vineyards are on very fertile soils and unless preventative measures, such as severe pruning or green harvesting are carried out, yields will be very high. One grower, admittedly with some shame, told me that he had achieved 40 tons of Merlot per hectare. Such figures can only lead to reduced quality, and a lack of varietal character is apparent amongst many cheaper quality wines.

An important influence within the industry itself has been the establishment of a number of small groups of growers who work together to improve viticultural techniques. These groups, which are called CREAs, will typically include small independent growers, merchants with vineyards and an agronomist. They visit each other's vineyards and wineries on a regular basis, discussing mutual problems and how to solve them.

With regard to the promotion of the wines overseas, the first faltering steps of a presence at Anuga in 1989, have been followed by a more regular presence at wine fairs around the world. The year 2000 saw the launch of a drive on the British market, with a small budget having been granted for, initially a three-year public relations campaign. In this Uruguay's speciality grape variety, the Tannat, will largely feature.

All these efforts are overseen by INAVI, which perceives itself to have a threefold role: to control the production of grapes (not just those for winemaking, but also those for table consumption); to control the quality of wines; and to promote their sale not only in Uruguay, but also in foreign markets. It is funded by a precept on the sale of all wines. Whilst it is answerable to the Minister of Agriculture, it operates as a private company. In effect its powers are wide-ranging, for it is also responsible for the supervision of all imported wines as well as domestic ones, it has the power to fix the base prices for grapes at vintage time and it can support the market, if growers cannot sell their grapes. It controls a team of 40 inspectors. This, in a small country like Uruguay, represents a great deal of power!

How successful are their efforts? As has been said already, the domestic market is active with current annual consumption standing at 32 litres per person per year. This is the second highest figure, after Argentina, outside Europe. In Argentina wine consumption has been declining rapidly, whilst in Uruguay it is increasing.

As far as export markets are concerned, the increase in sales could be said to be startling. In 1994, approximately 170,000 litres of wine were exported, much of it in bulk. Now sales are 90% in bottle and, in 1999, more than three million litres were sold. However, these figures can be misleading, because more than half of this last figure was accounted for by shipments to Brazil, to satisfy a demand for red wine, which local producers were unable to meet in one particular short vintage. It is not at all clear that this will be ongoing business. What is clear, however, is that in 1994 Uruguay exported to just five countries; in 1999, it exported to more than 25, of which seven shipped more than 10,000 cases.

One problem that has occurred on certain export markets is that of image. A small number of companies have tried to answer a need by competing at the bottom end of the market. Uruguay is a country with comparatively high production costs and its cheap wines do not represent good value for money, the quality is not there. As a result the image of all Uruguay's wines has suffered. A good example of this is the British market, where sales in 1998 were less than half those the previous year, because many consumers had been disappointed in their initial taste of Uruguayan wine. Now there is a more concerted approach to the market. For Uruguay to succeed internationally, it has to present a quality image. The quantities of wine that it has to offer are comparatively small; markets can absorb them at reasonable prices, if the quality is there.

In today's competitive wine race, Uruguay is a late entrant. For it to feature as more than a short-lived novelty item, it must have something to offer consumers. Its marketing is featured around the Tannat grape. Admittedly, in Uruguay, this appears to be supremely versatile, being capable of offering a broad range of styles from fresh and fruity wines, made by carbonic maceration, to full bodied heavyweights, achieved with long maceration and new oak. It is also a great variety that goes well in blends with the Bordeaux trio of Cabernet Sauvignon, Merlot and Cabernet Franc. For the wines of Uruguay to succeed, they must represent quality and value for money at the level at which they offer themselves.

Perhaps two other signs that Uruguay has arrived on the international wine scene are the arrival of flying winemakers and joint ventures. The former have been involved in companies, such as Castillo Viejo, Juanico and Juan Carrau, making wines mainly for European markets. Joint ventures range from an agreement for co-operation with the Chamber of Agriculture of the Gironde and the Pyrenées-Atlantiques (presumably on the question of their mutual interest in the Tannat grape), between vine nurseries in France and in Uruguay and in the field of winemaking between Castillo Viejo and a French group with interests in Bordeaux and Madiran, Juanico and Château Pape-Clément and Juan Carrau and major Spanish group Freixenet. These relationships have all come about very recently and these, and others in the pipeline, suggest a nascent global interest in Uruguay and its wines.

Uruguay, as a country, is approximately a quarter larger than England, though with a population of just over three million. Of these three million, almost a half live in the capital Montevideo. From this it can be gathered that the interior of the country is lightly inhabited. Livestock ranching accounts for 90% of agricultural land.

The expansion in the country's population, came as it did in much of South America, towards the end of the nineteenth century. Immigrants to Uruguay came predominantly from Italy and Spain. They brought with them a love for wine and the knowledge of how to make it. However, for the most part, they were not very sophisticated people. As a result, most of the early vineyards were established close to the centres of population, particularly Montevideo.

At the end of the nineteenth century, 58% of the vineyards planted were in the two departments of Montevideo and adjoining Canelones; today the figure is 77%, though there has naturally been a move out from the immediate city suburbs. In all, 92% of the vineyards are in the four departments bordering the River Plate. These areas have not been selected for qualitative reasons, but rather because they gave ease of access to the market. There are over 3,000 different vineyards on the register, averaging in size, rather less than five hectares. Most of these are run by the members of the families that own them as part of a smallholding, which might include fruit trees and livestock. The largest wine estate is that of Dante Irurtia, with 340 hectares at Carmelo, near Colonia.

Despite the small size of vineyard holdings, as has already been said, co-operative cellars are of little importance; the trade is dominated by the merchants. There are more than 300 of these, though only 37 are of a size to consider exporting. For most of them this means the dramatic change from producing ordinary wine in demi-johns for the domestic market, to concentrating on quality varietal wines for export. In terms of size a third of the bodegas produce 70% of the wine.

The Uruguayan climate is predominantly maritime, with four distinct seasons, an average temperature of 18°C and 1000 mm of rain per year. This comparatively high rainfall, often at vintage time, is the biggest climatic problem faced by growers in Uruguay. Mildew, black spot, oidium and dead arm are all common. Viral diseases, such as leaf-roll, are present particularly in older plantings of Tannat.

Vines are trained on trellises and the lyre system has become widespread in a bid to minimise the effect of the damp. Whilst there has been much recent planting, the majority of vineyards are more than 20 years old. Of the current area under vines, hybrids account for 25%, the Isabella and the Tannat for 20% each and an assortment of Muscats for 11%. What might be termed as classic European varietals make up 10%. The balance is made up of less-than-classic varieties from Europe. The total production of wine in Uruguay is approximately 90 million litres – of which, in 1999, three million were exported.

The importance of the domestic market is reflected in the proportion of styles of light wines that are made: 33% is red, 30% is *clarete* (deep rosé), 25% is rosé and just 12% is white. The *clarete* style is only produced at the level of *vino común and* generally has some residual sweetness achieved by the incorporation of Hamburg Muscat into the blend.

What are the important names to look for in Uruguayan wines?

Bodegas Castillo Viejo. Owned by the Etcheverry family, this company is based in San José, to the north-west of Montevideo, and is one of the most outward looking in Uruguay, with export sales in 14 markets in Europe and the Americas. This is mainly under the brand name Catamayor. The Australian winemaker, John

Worontschak, has also made wine for them for a British super-market chain. They have an important presence on the domestic market, where they recently launched an upmarket presentation of table wine in a litre bottle at a premium price.

They have 130 hectares of vineyards which are the sole source for grapes for their wines. Their future plans include a joint venture with a French group to create a new 75-hectare vineyard and winery, nearby at Mal Abrigo. This will produce only red wines and will represent an investment of US$3 million. The winery has two pneumatic presses and wide use is made of both American and French oak.

Wines I have particularly enjoyed: Sauvignon Blanc 1999, Tannat/Cabernet Franc 1998.

Ariano Hermanos S.A. This company was established in 1927 by two Italian immigrant brothers. They planted eight hectares of vines outside Montevideo. Now the company has 110 hectares of vineyards in production, 40 outside Montevideo and a further 70 in Paysandú department in the north-west of the country. About 10% of their grape needs are bought in.

Wines I have particularly enjoyed: Selección 1998 (a 50% Cabernet Franc, 30% Tannat, 20% Syrah blend).

Bruzzone y Sciutto. This company was established in 1888 by Cayetano Bruzzone and José Sciutto, immigrants from Piedmont. The bodega was built originally in what must have been the countryside some 13 km outside Montevideo. Now it has been absorbed in the urban sprawl and one of its two vineyards lies on the approaches to Carrasco airport.

In all the company owns 120 hectares of vines: 90, producing mainly table grapes and table wines in Montevideo and a further 30 in the centre of Uruguay in the department of Durazno. This second vineyard, El Carmen, was purchased in 1997 specifically for the production of quality wines, as it has stony soils and there is an important difference between daytime and night-time temperatures. The intention is to construct a separate winery there as a joint venture with a French partner. The company was one of the first to recognise the need for the production of better wines and they joined a group importing virus-free noble varieties from France.

They have also just begun selling barrel-aged wines. Their quality wines sell under the label Padre Barreto, a priest, oenologist and tireless promoter of the merits of Uruguayan wine. In the interests of ecumenism, Bruzzone y Sciutto is the only winery in the country permitted to make kosher wine!

Montes Toscanini. This company has a 12-hectare vineyard at Juanico, in Canelones, producing Cabernet Sauvignon, Merlot, Tannat and Sauvignon Blanc, and about 12,000 cases a year of fine wine aimed at export markets. For their top-quality Selección Personal wines, they use new American oak barrels.

Cesar Pisano e Hijos S.A. This company describes its products as *artesanía en vinos finos*, which they themselves translate, I think rather weakly as 'fine handcrafted wines from Uruguay'. In some ways this is the most individual wine producer in Uruguay and bears witness to what can be achieved in a comparatively short time. As recently as 1991, 95% of their production was sold locally in demijohns; now this accounts for less than 5% of their business.

Señor Pisano and his three sons, who all work in the business, have 15 hectares of their own vineyards in production and a further 15 coming into production. In addition they buy grapes from a further seven or eight local growers. These last grapes account for about 30% of their production.

The family's aim is to produce a broad range of high-quality wines in small quantities, generally in lots as small as 5,000 bottles. Thus, at present they have 15 different wines on the domestic market and a further 15 on export markets. Another example of their individuality is that in the 1999 vintage they made eight different styles of Tannat.

They believe firmly that quality starts at the vineyards, which are the responsibility of the son Eduardo (his brother Gustavo sees to the winemaking and the flamboyantly moustached Daniel is in charge of export sales). Yields should be of no more than 12 tonnes per hectare and bunch thinning is carried out at *véraison* in order to achieve this. Premium prices are paid for the grapes that are bought in order to achieve optimum quality and they all pass through a sorting table on their arrival. In their own vineyards they concentrate on Tannat, Cabernet Sauvignon and Merlot for reds and

Chardonnay, Sauvignon Blanc and Gewürztraminer for whites. Coming into production are Pinot Noir, Syrah and Viognier.

The cellar is an interesting mix of the old and the new, a Bucher pneumatic press lies beside traditional *pupitres* for the production of sparkling wines, Slovenian oak vats, locally assembled in 1924, overlook new oak casks from François Frères in Burgundy. To achieve the sought-for individuality, there are as many as 72 epoxy-lined concrete fermentation vats, some as small as 250 litres. The cellar is the kingdom of father Cesar Pisano, who also produces the preserved mushrooms served at lunch. This is a family business in its most traditional Italian expression.

The quality of the wines reflects the care that has gone into their production and Pisano wines are well-worth seeking out.

Wines I have particularly enjoyed: Brut Nature *Méthode Traditionelle* (made from Pinot Gris and Chardonnay), Cabernet Franc Rosado 2000, Merlot/Tannat 1999.

Corporación Vitivinícola Plaza Vidiella. In 1874 Francisco Vidiella established the first wine bodega in Uruguay and this company still bears his name. At present it is passing through the difficult process of trying to transform itself from being mainly a supplier of table wines into one of fine wines. Its vineyard estate is of 115 hectares, of which two-thirds are planted in noble varietals and it is replanting about seven hectares each year. In the cellar, the first French oak casks have been bought and experiments are being carried out with barrel-fermented Chardonnays and oak-aged red wines. Coupled with this change in the nature of the wines that they produce is a realisation that they need to export.

This is a very ambitious company and the young winemaker is making good wines. This may well be a name for the future.

Dante Irurtia. This company has the largest vineyard estate in Uruguay, with 340 hectares at Carmelo, some 235 km west of Montevideo, close to where the River Uruguay flows into the River Plate. Here there are good draining sandy soils on mineral-rich sub-soils. Its first vintage was as long ago as 1913 and for the past 55 years it has concentrated on improving the quality of its plantings. In all it has plantings of 15 different *vinifera varietals* including such comparative rarities for Uruguay as Viognier and

Malbec. The company, established almost a 100 years ago, has at least eight different ranges of wine aimed at different sectors of the market. Some of their wines tend to be very traditional in style. At the top, is the Reserva del Virrey, which offers a Tannat and a Chardonnay aged in French oak. At the entry level is Dante's Red, a Tannat/Nebbiolo blend.

Vinos De Lucca. The De Lucca family arrived in Uruguay from Piedmont at the beginning of the twentieth century and planted vines at Colorado to the north-west of Montevideo. The family is now represented by the third generation Dr Reinaldo De Lucca, who studied oenology in France at Montpellier University. He is another producer who believes in restricted yields and his red wines are very concentrated. Not afraid to experiment, Dr De Lucca's 40-hectare estate includes such novelties as Marsanne and he has used his French training to make some excellent Syrah-based wines.

Establacimiento Juanico S.A. This company has an interesting history. It used to belong to ANCAP, the Uruguayan monopoly for fuel and alcohol, but was sold to a company outside the wine trade. It is perhaps the most aggressive company in Uruguay's wine world and its Santa Teresa wines in tetrabrik and range of Don Pascual varietals are widely seen on the domestic market. In export markets their sales have ranged from basic-priced own-label wines for supermarket chains up to their prestigious barrel-aged Preludio, a blend of up to five varieties sold in a series of individual lot numbers.

Based in the town of the same name, 35 km out of Montevideo, Juanico has an extensive estate with buildings dating back to the 1840s.

Bodegas Leonardo Falcone. This company was established in 1886 at Paysandú, the second largest city of Uruguay some 370 km north-west of Montevideo on the banks of the River Uruguay. The company owns two vineyards to the east of the city totalling 40 hectares. These supply all its grape needs. Perhaps its best wine is Abuelo Domingo, an unoaked Tannat made from 100-year-old vines.

José Luis Filgueira. This winery and 43 hectares of vineyards have belonged to the Filgueira family since 1927 and the original bodega is 80 years old. However, the family made its money from medicine and treated it as no more than a hobby until the current Sra. Filgueira said she would take it in hand – and spend some of her husband's money. So far, she admits to having invested two million dollars and she has a state-of-the-art winery to show for it, with state-of-the-art machinery. She claims that it is technologically the most modern winery in Uruguay with a Bucher press, rotary fermenters and self-emptying tanks. Whilst this description might be challenged by the new Juan Carrau winery at Cerro Chapeu, there is no doubt that it is very impressive, with the old concrete vats having been converted into wine bins and a barrel-cellar. In addition, Caterina Viña Migliardo has been poached from Santa Rosa as winemaker.

The aim is to become totally organic, with the first such wines on stream for the 2001 vintage. Sra. Filgueira has also stated that she will never let her wines be chaptalized.

So far, so good. Currently the problem seems to lie in the vineyards, where the yields are admitted to be excessive. As a result the wines that I tasted all lacked depth and complexity. This is a problem that can be solved with better vineyard management and an aimed-for yield of no more than 14 tonnes per hectare. As the plan is to sell these wines solely on export markets, it is probable that we shall see much of them in the future.

Los Cerros de San Juan S.A. This is one of the historic wineries of Uruguay with a history going back to the early eighteenth century when the Jesuits first planted vineyards on the current site, near the attractive historical town of Colónia. It is a very large estate where cattle raising is probably more important than wine production. In 1872 a massive stone wine cellar was constructed, harbouring large oak vats of Nancy oak, which are still in use. The company, at that time called the Compañía Rural Bremen, shipped its produce by sailing boat from its own quay to Montevideo. The property was taken over in 1988, by the brothers Alvaro and Alfredo Terra Oyenard, from a family of Basque origin and they have raised the quality and the image of the wines. Of particular interest are the top of the range Cuna de Piedra wines, which have been aged in French oak.

Bodega Carlos Pizzorno. This can be truly described as a boutique winery, but it is one that has decided that its future lies in fine wines. Originally from the Canary Islands, the family is now in its fourth generation in Uruguay and they sell their wines under the brand name Don Próspero. Their vineyards produce both table grapes and wine grapes, the latter all European varietals. This is a winery setting out on the quality path, with stainless-steel and new American oak casks beginning to make an appearance. For red wines, the winemaker, Marcelo Laitano, relies on wild yeasts, for whites he uses cultured ones.

Its best wines are an 80% Tannat/20% Cabernet Sauvignon blend and a Merlot rosé. This is a small winery where effort and enthusiasm deserve to be rewarded.

S.A. Vitícola Uruguaya. This is the oldest wine company in continual operation and it is very proud of its history and its traditions. Indeed it is probably the most traditional winery in the country. It was founded, as an agricultural conglomerate, in 1887 in order to give work to those unemployed as a result of the enclosure of the grazing lands and has belonged to the Arocena family since 1910.

The winery is situated at La Cruz, in the department of Florida, almost 120 km north of Montevideo. It sells its wines under the brand name Vinos de la Cruz. In all the estate consists of more than 430 hectares, the majority of which are given over to raising dairy calves for export to Brazil. Polo ponies are also reared, as well as chickens, whose natural output is used as fertiliser in vineyards intended for organic wines. There are 65 hectares of vineyards including some Tannat vines just a year short of the hundredth anniversary of their planting.

The massive cellar, built from granite quarried on the estate, has a storage capacity of more than 1.3 million litres, well beyond current needs. The red wines are fermented in open-top fermenters and much of the ageing is carried out in oak vats.

At present it makes an organic Malbec and full certification as an organic producer is expected for the 2001 vintage. Ninety-five per cent of production is of quality wine, with a quarter of sales going abroad, particularly to Brazil, where it has its own distribution company.

The style of the wines is rather old-fashioned and, to me, the most interesting is probably their Limited Edition Cot Rouge Lacrado.

Viñedos y Bodegas Santa Rosa. This company was founded in 1898 by Juan Bautista Passadore, but was probably at its most influential in the 1940s, when one of its directors was Juan Carrau Sust, who had recently arrived from Spain. The company, then known as the Bodega Hispano-Uruguaya Santa Rosa, became the leading quality wine producer in the country and almost single-handedly created a rapid increase of the consumption of fine wine. In the following decade, it also introduced bottled-fermented sparkling wines to the country and began to look for export markets.

Currently, as well as the brand name Santa Rosa, it uses Château Fond de Cave for blended wines and Anticuario for its top-of-the-range barrel-aged wines. It produces 25,000 cases of bottle-fermented sparkling wine a year, with Jean-Pierre Lédé as a consultant.

The company has 100 hectares of vines planted at Las Violetas in Canelones.

Bodegas H. Stagnari. Pablo Stagnari arrived in Uruguay from Genoa in 1880 and planted a vineyard just outside Montevideo at La Puebla. Now the company has rather a split existence: its newly constructed cellars are in Canelones department, on the main road to the north, while its vineyards are 500 km away at Salto, where Pascual Harriague first planted the Tannat in Uruguay.

The company claims that Salto is ideal for vines with a broad difference between daytime and night-time temperatures and with easy-draining sandy soils. Because of the distance between the vineyards and the winery, the grapes are picked during the late afternoon and trucked down overnight.

Stagnari is one of the most reliable producers in the country and amongst its best wines are its Tannat Viejo, which is aged in cask for two years, and its Gewürztraminer.

Juan Toscanini e Hijos S.A. This company is truly a family affair, being run by three jovial, full-bodied brothers. This family, too, originally arrived from Genoa establishing a winery and the brand La Fuente in 1908. In the early 1980s, they started converting their 75-hectare estate in Canelones department from 'common' grape-varieties to noble European ones, with the emphasis on red varietals such as Tannat, Merlot, Cabernet Sauvignon and Cabernet Franc, though they also have some Sauvignon Blanc, Chardonnay and

Sémillon. They buy in grapes for their domestic sales of *vino común*. In 1999, they produced approximately 35,000 cases of fine wine of which 5,000 were exported to a broad range of countries, including Great Britain, Japan, Germany and Poland. When in full production, they hope to achieve 50,000 cases a year. Of the change in emphasis of their sales, they say, 'It is a long road, but one we have to follow'.

They take great care with their wines, with all the grapes passing over a sorting table. They have two new Diemme pneumatic presses and their French oak casks come from François Frères. In their own words, their wines have 'South American character as a result of Italian philosophy'. To me this means deep fruit flavours and, with the oaked wines, firm tannins. They are certainly one of the more conscientious winemaking families of Uruguay.

Viña Varela Zarranz. This company was originally established in 1933 as Viticultores Unidos del Uruguay and it still sells some of their table wine under the forbidding acronym of VUDU. It has an estate of 110 hectares, 75 hectares of which have been converted over the past 15 years to plantings of noble varietals. The cellars at Joaquín Suarez have a long history in the Uruguayan wine industry as they were originally built in 1888, by Diego Pons, one the great early names. The cellars still use Nancy oak vats dating back to 1903 for ageing their table wines. Like so many of the larger Uruguayan wine companies, this one is in the middle of a difficult, and perhaps painful, transformation. The first trials are being carried out of barrel-fermented Chardonnay, with 20 French *barriques*. White wines only account for 30% of production and I feel this is where they are at their best.

Wines I have particularly enjoyed: Sauvignon Blanc 1999, Unoaked Chardonnay 1999.

Vinos Finos Juan Carrau. The Carrau family trace their origins in the wine trade back to 1752 in their native Catalonia. Whilst he was not the first member of the family to settle in Uruguay, Juan Carrau Sust, a Spanish oenology graduate, arrived in Montevideo in 1930. There, with two partners, he founded the Santa Rosa company in Colón. This expanded rapidly, revolutionising the local wine industry. In 1977, his son, Juan Carrau Pujol, left the company and set up in competition across the road in what had once been the cellars of Pablo Varzi. He was determined just to make fine wines. His early offerings included such exotic names as Chianti Luigi Bonomi and Chablis and Rioja Cava de Varzi.

As the family also had wine interests in Brazil, a cross-border venture was set up with the American group National Distillers and Professor Olmo, of University of California, was briefed to search out a site with the best potential soils and climatic conditions. Finally, after some false starts, the border region of Rivera–Livramento was chosen, as having deep, sandy, easy-draining soils, moderate rainfall and major temperature differences between daytime and night-time.

The family obtained the support of the Uruguayan government for the project, which they declared to be a 'Plan of National Interest'. The company now has 40 hectares of vines planted in the region, which is known as Cerro Chapeu, 'hat mountain', after the peculiarly-shaped local hills, which look like bowler hats. They also have an ultra-modern, hexagonal winery built into the hillside, which is totally gravity-fed, with grapes arriving at the top and the barrel-ageing cellar at the bottom. Such modern techniques as an automatic plunging machine for the fermentation vats are also incorporated. This winery is the first in South America to meet ISO standards.

They have a further 22-hectare vineyard in full production in Las Violetas, in Canelones department, with a further 12 hectares being planted at present and which should be in full production by the year 2004. In both vineyard areas, the vines are planted on American rootstock, in the north because of potential problems with nematodes and in the south because of *Phylloxera*.

The intention is that the two wineries should create separate images for their wines; those from the north being sold as estate-bottled Cerro Chapeu, and those from the south, which might well include some bought-in fruit, as Castel Pujol or Juan Carrau.

The company has always been considered as being in the vanguard of the local industry, being the first to introduce stainless-steel and small oak barrels. It too was the first to realise the importance of export sales with a quality image and in order to help to achieve this it has entered into joint ventures with the major Spanish group Freixenet and with the Bordeaux Lurton brothers. The first fruits of the second liaison were revealed in early 2000, with the launch of Casa Luntro, a 1997 vintage Tannat aged for 18 months in French oak barrels, of which half were new. The aim of the collaboration with Freixenet is less clear, though there is talk of establishing a new vineyard with a production of 100,000 cases per year.

As far as current production is concerned, Cerro Chapeu seems to concentrate on Cabernet Sauvignon, Pinot Noir and Sauvignon Blanc, whilst the 'home' winery at Colón has Tannat, Chardonnay and Merlot.

Viñedos y Bodegas Bella Unión. The vineyards of this company are situated as far away from Montevideo as you can get, whilst still staying in Uruguay. They are in the extreme north of the country 690 km from the capital, where the River Cuaraim, which provides the frontier with Brazil and the River Uruguay, that with Argentina, meet. Basically, the region has a history of growing sugar cane, but with a collapse in the sugar industry, the government financed the planting of vineyards to provide alternative employment.

The vineyards were originally planted in 1975 without grafting, but suffered from *Phylloxera* and were replanted in 1981/2. The company was originally a co-operative body, but is now a quasi-governmental organisation. It has 100 hectares of vines for wine production and a further 30 for table grapes. Annual wine production, solely from its own vineyards, apart from small purchases of Tannat, is approximately 1.5 million litres. It claims that it controls approximately a quarter of the domestic wine market. Its wines, which sell under the brand name Calvinor, get no cask ageing and as a result tend to be soft and commercial. First trials with barrels are being made with some wines of the 2000 vintage.

In order to approach export markets, two marketing groups have been created. The first of these is **Bodegas del Plata**, where a number of larger companies, who already sell under their own label, have come together in order to offer a small range of wines under a joint brand name, Costas del Plata, in quantities large enough to interest major foreign buyers. Initially, they have available a Tannat, a Merlot, a Cabernet Sauvignon, a Sauvignon Blanc and a Chardonnay/Sémillon blend, under the regional appellation of Rio de la Plata.

At the moment, on a more humble scale, is a group called **Vinicultores Exportadores del Uruguay**. This has as members 13 growers from Canelones county, who own between them 250 hectares of vines, 75 of them planted in noble varieties, Tannat, Merlot and Cabernet Sauvignon, suitable for top-quality wines. They claim to produce 6% of Uruguay's total crop. On export markets they sell through **Sunybell S.A.**, under the brand name Del Mar Dulce. Their first wine is a Tannat 2000, but they also will have a Cabernet Sauvignon and a Merlot available.

Do the wines of Uruguay have enough potential to make this the next 'in' wine-producing country? This is the question that Clive Coates poses in the question at the beginning of this chapter. The next sentence rather suggests that he thinks that they have not, or at least compared to the wines of Argentina and Chile. What does Uruguay have in its favour? The first advantage must be a sound, and increasing, domestic market. Moreover, it is a market that is showing an increasing appreciation for quality wines. Whilst there is no doubt that there has been some penetration of the market from both Argentina and Chile, this has not been at the expense of domestic wines.

The second advantage is that quality production is dominated by red wines, where, at present there is a global shortage. The Tannat is a versatile grape, and this is backed up by new plantings of Cabernet Sauvignon, Merlot and Cabernet Franc. Increasing use of oak barrels also points to a widely understood need for quality. In the Tannat grape, Uruguay has something that is distinctive. Neighbouring Argentina has seen the merits of promoting the Malbeck and the Torrontés as being wines distinctive to that country; the Uruguayans are hoping that they can do the same for the Tannat.

Thirdly, this is a country where the government, from the president downwards appears to be interested in giving not just moral support, but also financial aid. This is a recent decision, but one that must be welcomed. However, Uruguay is a small country and its resources are limited. It will find it very hard to compete against the budgets of the other New World wine-producing countries.

What are the potential problems? One of them must be the climate. Whilst most New World wine-producers can rely on long, sunny, ripening seasons, with needed water being available through irrigation, in Uruguay, there can be rain throughout the year and it is common at harvest. This means that much more care has to taken to create the healthy grapes that are needed for the making of fine wine.

In addition, most of the existing vineyards in the country were planted where it was most convenient for the growers. There was no concept of seeking out the ideal soils and locations. Most were planted on heavy clay soils close to the capital, Montevideo, to cut down on distribution costs. It is only in the comparatively recent past that thought has been given to researching such questions and it is probable that, in the future, vineyards may be planted in totally new regions. The impetus for this may come as a result of joint ventures with international companies. They are unlikely to want to invest in planting vineyards on unsuitable soils. Moreover, wider exposure to modern winemaking techniques introduced by visiting winemakers can only lead to improved quality in the wines.

The most important problem in the mind of the buyer of South American wines for Britain's largest supermarket chain is that few people know where Uruguay is. Indeed an early Uruguayan own-label wine sold by a British supermarket chain was called Pacific Heights. As Uruguay is on the Atlantic coast and the country is the flattest in South America, with the highest vineyards being at no more than 300 m above sea-level, this showed either supreme ignorance on the part of the company's marketing department, or, and I hope not, it was an attempt to pass off Uruguay as a Chile look-alike!

If you couple this with the fact that few people will recognise the Tannat as a grape variety, then you have difficulty in persuading the consumer to pick the bottle off the supermarket shelf. Personally, I am not convinced that these are major problems. However much the vineyard area in Uruguay expands, the country is never going to be a major producer of wine and there is, in Britain at least, a large enough body of consumers with an inquisitive instinct to always want to seek out anything new. It is then that the problem arises. If the first purchase of Uruguayan Tannat represents bad value for money, it is probable that the customer will not buy a bottle of Uruguayan wine again. Indeed, this is a problem that has already come up. In the initial surge of interest in the wines of Uruguay, considerable quantities were shipped into Britain by supermarkets at low prices in order to achieve a specific retail price. Frankly, the wine was bad and it put many people off Uruguayan wine for good.

There is a keenness on the part of a number of Uruguayan merchants to export, but most of them have little appreciation of how competitive such markets as the USA and Britain are. They see the success of New Zealand, a country with a similar production figure, selling wines at high prices. They would like to achieve something similar. To do this, the Uruguayans must discipline themselves. They must only export top-quality wines; they must weed out rubbish. There is some recognition of this on the part of the producers and an Exporters' Group has been set up in a bid to set, and consummate, quality targets. Sadly, within a matter of weeks of its establishment, one of the most important members had to be suspended, because he went off at a tangent. Here lies a potential major problem. It needs just one major producer to break ranks for a market to be destroyed. The image of Uruguay on international markets is, at present, fragile; it would not take much to destroy it. Its successful future will depend on a great deal of self-discipline.

Whilst no one would be happier than I would if my discovery were to become the next 'in' wine-producing country, I am not sure that a firm enough base has yet been established for this to be likely. What Uruguay does have in its favour is a will to succeed, a supportive government and a wine industry that is in the process of transforming itself. Once it has established a solid place for itself in the world's wine hierarchy, success seems certain. However, this might take a long time and eagerness to succeed must be balanced with patience.

Venezuela

Venezuelan rum is very good; recommended
brands are Cacique, Pampero and Santa Teresa.
There are four good local beers: Polar (the most
popular), Regional (with a strong flavour of
hops), Cardenal and Nacional (a *lisa* is a glass of
keg beer; for a bottle of beer, ask for a *tercio*),
Brahma beer, lighter than Polar, is imported from
Brazil. There are also mineral waters and gin.
Now there is a good, local wine in Venezuela.
The Polar brewery has joined with Martell
(France) and built a winery in Carora.
Footprint South American Handbook, 2000

In the world of wine, there is much that is *terra incognita* and, since first deciding to write this book, there have been many moments when I have felt that that the task is too much for me. As an initial move I wrote to the commercial attachés of all those countries where I thought that wine might be made. Many did not reply, some denied that there was any wine made in their country, though subsequently they have proved to be wrong. Some of the most unlikely ones proved to be the most helpful and amongst these I would like to single out those of Peru and Venezuela as being the best. The latter even sent me a photocopy of an article of the launch of a new range of wines from Venezuelan vineyards.

Of all the countries in this book, Venezuela shares with Cuba the title of being the least likely wine-producing country, yet it is one. Here I must state that I do not consider as a wine-producing country one that imports concentrated musts, from say, Chile or Italy, and then makes wines. I consider wine as only being made from the fermentation from the juice of fresh grapes. In Venezuela, it is certain that there has been much domestic wine available on the market, but this has not been made from fresh grapes. Indeed, the almost tropical climate is in no way conducive to growing grapes – however, it does happen and wine even by the most rigorous definition is made.

It is the climate that poses the biggest problem for the ambient temperature gives the vine no rest – it has no dormant period during the year. At its least productive, it produces two crops a year and in the state of Zulia, around the city of Maracaibo, where the annual average temperature is 27.5°C, with a day/night difference of only 8°C, and a humidity of 72%, there are as many as three vintages a year. Interestingly, there are distinct differences between the qualities and yields of each season's vintage.

Notwithstanding all this, Venezuela has a long, but scarcely successful, history of wine production. As in all Latin-American countries, it is the church that encouraged the earliest plantings and here there are records of the Jesuits making wine early in the sixteenth century. Early writings speak of vines being planted as shade plants in Caracas. In the twentieth century commercial vineyards existed between 1920 and 1938 in the state of Carabobo, just to the west of the capital and between 1938 and 1974 in the state of Lara.

It is in this last state in the foothills in the Cordillera de Mérida to the east of the oilfields of the Lago de Maracaibo that Venezuela's one genuine winery can be found.

Bodegas Pomar were created partly as the result of the introduction of prohibitive duties on imported wines and spirits in the early 1980s. In order partly to protect its interests in the market, the French brandy company Martell, together with a French vine nursery and the Grape Institute at Barquisimeto University, decided to carry out trial plantings of wine-grapes. This was done at El Tocuyo, some 50 km to the south of Barquisimeto, the Lara state capital. This was a region that had produced table-grapes, for 50 years or more, but the project came to nothing because of difficulties in purchasing land, so they began to look elsewhere. In the meantime, a further partner had been brought in, Cervecería Polar, which has approximately 80% of the domestic beer market in Venezuela and is the fifth largest brewery group in the world. (Their nearest rival uses the rather defeatist advertising slogan 'Try the other one'!) The name 'Pomar' is a contraction of Polar and Martell.

In due course, the tax regime changed, Martell was bought by Seagram, who had little interest in the project, and the French vine nursery withdrew; the brewers were left as sole owners.

The winery is in the charming colonial town of Carora, which has a beautiful main square overlooked by the oldest social club in Venezuela, a pretty little cathedral and a house where the liberator Bolívar spent not just one night but three! The vineyards are at Altagracia, in the lee of the Sierra de Barragua, some 25 km away. This is arid, cactus, country, where goat farming appears to be the only alternative living. The vines are planted on sandy, easy draining soils and are drip-irrigated with water coming from artesian wells. Annual rainfall is about 650 mm per year, split between October/December and April/May. *Phylloxera* is not a problem, but powdery mildew is. After intensive testing it is apparent here that a number of classic grape varieties cannot produce wines with any colour. These include Cabernet Sauvignon, Merlot and Grenache. The reason for this has not been fully discovered, but it is thought that some viral infection is to blame. However, on a 'waste not, want not' basis, these have been blended off and sold as rosé wines. Those that are particularly successful are the Tempranillo, the Petit Verdot and the Syrah. Historically, any other problem wines have been distilled into brandy. For white, and sparkling, wines the Chenin Blanc, Maccabeo, Sauvignon Blanc and Malvoisie are grown.

Interestingly, the company has gone back to El Tocuyo, which is higher and where there are bigger differences between day and night temperatures, to plant an experimental vineyard in conjunction with a local landowner. So far, six hectares have been planted here, with 22 varieties, including such novelties as Primitivo and Sangiovese, and eight different rootstocks.

The company claims that it controls directly 85% of the total production of *vinifera* grapes in the country. In addition, 5% of its needs are met by buying in grapes from the few independent growers, mainly in the Maracaibo region.

No money has been spared on the construction of the winery; the initial cost was US$22 million and investment is continuing, even though it is running at approximately half of its capacity. There is a broad range of stainless-steel tanks of varying size and 400 new barrels, of both French and American oak, have been bought. Current production, split almost equally between still and bottle-fermented sparkling wine is running at about 55,000 cases a year.

The winemaker is Bill Swain, who, for eight years, had his own winery in Oregon and has also held major winemaking posts in Napa, Mendocino and Washington State.

Its leading commercial brand of still wine is Viña Altagracia, which appears as red and white wines. Interestingly, its labels give not just a vintage year, but also a month, to distinguish between the spring and autumn harvests. The bulk of its sparkling wine is bottle fermented, spending a minimum of 14 months on the lees. The intention is to produce a Reserva, which will spend a further year in bottle. It is advised on this side of production by the Champagne company, Louis Roederer.

In addition, it produces a downmarket *frizzante* from Maccabeo and Moscatel grapes, by injecting carbon dioxide into the wine.

Since the winery was first built, the tax situation has changed and the importation of wines and spirits is now much freer. This means that Bodegas Pomar finds it hard to compete with wines from Chile and Argentina, at the bottom end of the market and, indeed, the Venezuelan government has objected officially to 'dumping' on their market. This has led to a shift in emphasis in its product range. Over a number of years, it is likely that the Viña Altagracia wines will be phased out and be replaced by a range of single varietal wines and upmarket blends. The first of these, a straight Tempranillo, was released in August 2000, and was followed by a Syrah. In cask awaiting bottling there is a range of blends of varying permutations of these two varieties and Petit Verdot.

To back up its sales, the company has a very active PR machine and an opulent office building in Caracas. There are also facilities for receiving tourists at the winery and these number about 4,000 a year. The company does also have the agency for a number of prestigious imported wines and spirits and it is difficult to see how the company could continue to exist without these. Even with them, I have the impression wines are the expensive, and prestigious, plaything of a phenomenally wealthy brewery.

What this does show is that even in the most difficult climatic conditions, good wines can be made. However, this does not come cheaply and I believe that the wines of Venezuela are better than those of Cuba, because the resources behind them are bigger. In both cases, however, it seems that their sales will largely be restricted to their domestic markets. Indeed, in Venezuela, the wine industry is so specialised that there is no special legislation to control it; the only thing that applies is general commercial law.

The wines made by Bodegas Pomar are not novelty items, aimed at the curious tourist. They are good wines in their own right and will stand comparison with those of better-known wine-producing countries. However, because of the climatic problems, it seems unlikely that their production will ever rise much above 100,000 cases a year, enough to satisfy the domestic market, but not enough to excite international supermarket buyers!

Conclusion

━━━━━━━

Now this is not the end. It is not even the
beginning of the end. But it is, perhaps, the end of
the beginning.
Winston Churchill, 10 November 1942

Writing about any aspect of wine is not easy, for it is in a constant state of flux and development. Anything that is written today may be out of date tomorrow. The situation is exacerbated in a region so politically and economically sensitive as Latin America. We have seen how in both Chile and Argentina development has been hampered for almost a decade by political reasons. Totalitarian governments in both countries have led to calls for their products, including wine, to be boycotted. Interestingly enough, however, many Chileans credit General Pinochet with creating the conditions that have led to the recent renaissance of the Chilean wine industry.

One way of seeing how countries have progressed, or not, with regard to wine production, is to look at figures. Here are the comparative production figures in hectolitres, for the harvest of seven countries of 1997 and for that of 80 years earlier, 1917:

	1917	1997
Argentina	5,100,000	13,500,000
Chile	3,250,000	4,549,000
Brazil	420,000	2,743,000
Uruguay	200,000	1,028,000
Peru	190,000	111,000
Bolivia	60,000	20,000
Mexico	6,000	1,524,000

These figures illustrate graphically the fluctuations that have taken place. Two countries are now producing less than they did 80 years ago and there are startling increases in Mexico, Brazil and Uruguay. What is particularly interesting is the comparatively low figure for the increase in Chile and the fact that whilst we might consider all these countries as recent arrivals on the scene, they are, in fact, more venerable than we might have imagined.

Whilst there may be certain resemblances between the wine industries of some of the 10 countries dealt with in this book – one example is the influence of the cold currents of the Pacific on the vineyard regions of Mexico, Peru and Chile – there is much more that separates them. If there is to be any form of classification, then Paraguay must be at the bottom of the league. What wines that are made there are produced under very difficult conditions and consumption appears to be mainly in those communities where they are produced. I have the impression that they are made, in large part, to remind the immigrants from Europe of their traditions. I find it significant that a major supermarket in the centre of the capital, Asunción, cannot find room for any Paraguayan wine on its shelves.

Whilst the producers of wine in Cuba have export pretensions, there is little doubt that the majority of their production is firmly aimed at the burgeoning tourist trade. There, too, the climate presents major problems and growing grapes is carried out under very difficult circumstances. However, their Italian backers seem prepared to sink important sums of money into the project and, in Cuba itself, they have a captive market in a monopoly situation.

In some ways, Venezuela is a different problem. It has a sub-tropical climate, like Cuba, with up to three grape harvests a year. However, despite the important market for both rum and beer, there is a tradition of wine drinking, not just with the affluent classes. There is, too, a local 'wine' industry that creates its products from imported musts. Bodegas Pomar appears to be the only company dedicated to producing wine from fresh grapes. The investment that its parent company, the Polar Group, has made, and is continuing to make, has resulted in wines of some quality. However, production costs are comparatively high and, at the lower end of the market, it has been very difficult to compete with wines imported from Chile and Argentina. Indeed, there have been allegations by the Venezuelans of dumping on their market. The result of this is that Bodegas Pomar has taken the decision to concentrate its efforts on up-market wines, both still and sparkling.

It is certain that there is plenty of spare capacity in the winery. Do the wines have any export potential? My answer must be a guarded, 'No'. There always seems to be an importer prepared to try introducing wine from anywhere that it is produced, but, to me, the image of Venezuela is far away from wines. One hears of vineyard developments in such diverse countries as Thailand and Korea. Their wines have yet, as far as I know, to arrive on the British and American markets. At least, in the case of Thailand, there are enough Thai restaurants to support some imports. There is Thai beer on the market, though I note that it is brewed under licence in Germany. Somehow, I feel that we are not yet ready for Venezuelan wine.

Peruvian and Bolivian wines certainly have been, and probably still are, available in Britain, but the wine industry in both countries is struggling, as the figures above show. However, there are distinct differences between the two countries. I feel that Bolivia has the potential to produce top-quality wines. The vineyards in Tarija have an ideal climate, there is plenty of water for irrigation, and agrarian reform has produced a new class of *campesinos*, with pride in what they produce. The remoteness of the vineyards does pose some problems with regard to shipping to the wider world, but there is an outlet to foreign markets through the port of Arica in Chile. The main problem would seem to be a lack of interest by the government in supporting the industry and of capital to enable it to develop. The country has signed an agreement, which means that ultimately it will join the Mercosur, South American Common Market. On the face of it, this would present the domestic wine industry with further competition from the wines of Chile and Argentina. However, it is already estimated that half the wine drunk in the country has been imported illegally, mainly from Chile, so things would not change too much! Bolivia does produce quality wines and there must be a market for the highest wines in the world!

Whilst I have guarded confidence in the future for the wines of Bolivia, I am less happy about the future for those of Peru. As I write this, Mr Fujimori has just discovered that his air ticket to Tokyo is a single and not a return. There are some who say that, whatever his limitations, he was the one person who could hold the economy together. The country and its economy are in a mess. The agricultural reforms have not had the success that they did in Bolivia. First cotton and then asparagus were going to be the crops to bring work and money to the countryside. As you drive south on the Pan-American Highway from Lima, the abandoned fields of asparagus bear witness to the failure of that vision. Having run the land they were given into the ground, the peasants now rely on charitable hand-outs for their existence.

The production of both wine and pisco is largely fraudulent; cane spirit, flavourings and colouring are useful ingredients. The government is well aware of this, but chooses to do nothing about it. There are honest companies; the wines of Tacama have sold at Fauchon in Paris and Harrods in London, but they find it hard to earn enough money to buy the modern equipment that they know they need to compete on the markets of the world. They cite the government of Uruguay as an enlightened example of what can be done. In a country with the problems of Peru, those of the wine trade have a low priority. It will be a struggle for the hardy few to survive.

I wish I could be optimistic about the international future for the wines of Brazil, but having been quite successful in both the American and British markets, a decision appears to have been taken to abandon exporting and concentrate on the domestic market. It is true that the biggest company, the co-operative Aurora, saw its export sales fall by 90% in just one year, due to losing just two customers. The government's unwillingness to sign up to the World Trade Organisation's agreements, has all but closed the doors to the markets of the European Union. It does have on its doorstep an enormous population at present unused to wine, but I am uncertain whether the producers have drawn the right conclusions from all this. The decision has been taken to concentrate on home; Brazil is best for Brazilian wine. Whilst it is true that wine consumption is rising (from a very low base) and that with a population of more than 150 million people, even a small rise in consumption can put a strain on a limited production base, it seems foolhardy to close the door on exporting. The competition on the domestic drinks market is cut-throat with powerful breweries and a strong spirits lobby. Are the wineries strong enough to compete? I find it interesting that some of the multinational groups have taken a step backwards from producing wine in Brazil. It is interesting also that the Brazilian Embassy in London suggested that, for information on the wines of that country, I should contact an

organisation called ABRABE. The e-mail address of this organisation interestingly enough is cachacadobrasil! Do they really have
interest in promoting the wines?

Of course, the main problem that Brazil has is that, within its vast
land-mass, there is no place that is ideal for the production of wine.
Research has shown that the Frontera region, up against the
Uruguayan border, is as close to the ideal as there is, but this is still
at a distance – as it happens both literally, as well as metaphorically.
The largest winery sends its wines more than 1,500 km to be
bottled – and then brings them back for the local tourist industry!
On the other hand, the Serra Gaucha, the centre of the current
industry is a landscape of hills and small properties, scarcely an area
to encourage large-scale production. American hybrids dominate
and the co-operative cellars take what they are offered. Sadly, as
things stand at the moment, I cannot envisage Brazil taking on a
major role in the world's repertory company of wine, though there
are certainly some wines that deserve a wider audience than just in
Brazil itself.

Uruguay has similar climatic problems to those of Brazil and, in
comparison, it has a minute domestic market. Yet, in Uruguay, the
wine industry is thriving whilst in Brazil patently it is not. How
has Uruguay managed to achieve its success, however limited that
currently might be? First of all, Uruguay has the advantage of being
small and compact. This creates much easier circuits of distribution,
particularly when half the population lives in the capital,
Montevideo. Secondly, the country has the smallest proportion of
indigenous population existing in South America. There are less
than 2% of the population left who can claim native American
roots or descent from African slaves, though their tradition lives on
in the local *candombe* music. The corollary is that the country has
the highest proportion of European immigrants in the continent.
These have mainly come from Spain, Italy and Germany and they
have kept up their tradition of wine consumption, which, per
capita, is among the top 10 in the world. Whilst a large part of
Brazil is in the tropics, where a cool beer or an iced rum might prove
attractive, Uruguay has a climate much more conducive to wine
drinking.

What has made it stand out, though, in all the wine countries of
Latin-America, has been the enlightened policies of its government.
This has provided planned support for the wine industry, its

campaign being channelled in three directions. First of all, there has been funding for the replanting of vineyards with the finest European varietals, at the expense of American vines and hybrids. The country has also been fortunate, that its history has granted it the Tannat and given it a quasi-exclusivity. That this should be a red grape is an added bonus at a time when we are told that drinking red wines is so good for us!

The second part of the campaign has been to extend the existing love of the Uruguayan for wine and convert this into a pride in Uruguayan wine. With the country's entry into Mercosur, there was a real danger that the industry might be annihilated by the giants from Argentina, with much lower production costs and economies of scale. In the event this has not happened. Slogans, such as 'Uruguayan wine, ours and natural', conjured up enough images in the mind of the consumer, to enable him to resist being seduced by wines from the other side of the River Plate. At the same time, a shortfall in red wine production in Brazil has opened up a substantial, though perhaps short-lived, export market.

The third aspect of the campaign has seen the release of money to enable campaigns to be started in certain potential markets, such as Britain. The problem is that Uruguay is, and never will be anything but, a small player in the field of wine. The budgets that the government has been able to allocate are minute compared to those of countries like Chile. However, they were met by some producing companies with a kind of euphoria. They were going to meet with instant success overseas. This will not happen unless the country can produce good, distinctive, wines at the right price. The Tannat grape should help them to do this, but it is not the only answer. The country is on the right road, but it will not be a straight road and it will be a rocky road. Not all the companies that have set their hearts on a future in exporting are going to succeed, but good luck to those who do.

Mexico is another producing country that inspires me with confidence. As in Brazil, there is an enormous domestic market; as in Brazil, the actual per capita wine consumption is very low, but different solutions are being sought. In Mexico wine is only drunk by the wealthier middle classes and they, largely for reasons of perceived prestige, are happier being seen to drink French wine rather than Mexican. However, the wineries of Baja California have other markets much closer to them than Mexico City. Los Angeles is less than three hours drive away. Ensenada and Tijuana, the two most important centres of the wine industry, are major tourist centres for Californians wanting to go abroad, with the minimum amount of difficulty. It is true that tequila and beer might prove to be greater attractions than wine – but the Cetto plant in Tijuana attracts more than 100,000 tourists a year and the wineries of the 'three valleys' are wakening up to the tourist potential. All things Mexican seem to be fashionable.

Of the two largest wineries, Domecq seems to be under-utilising the undoubted marketing strengths that it has around the world. Somehow, I feel that it has underestimated the potential of its Mexican wines. Whilst one can understand that their importance is minute when compared to the Domecq brandies, one has to consider that sales for brown spirits are falling, whilst those for wines are increasing. On the other hand L.A. Cetto is beginning to create a global image for itself. Whilst the initial sales of Cetto wines, may have been seen to be novelty items, the wines are now standing on their own merits on the shelves of European super-markets and in restaurants. One of the potential problems for Mexican wines is that there is not much depth in term of potential suppliers. After Domecq and Cetto, there are Santo Tomás and, possibly, Casa Madero, and a handful of boutique wineries. That is not much on which to build a worldwide reputation. Perhaps Cetto will come to be known just as Cetto, rather than as a Mexican wine!

There is one other problem that is already facing the producers of Baja California; that is the question of resources. The success of the state government in using tax incentives to attract assembly industries to the region means that there are now excessive calls being made upon not just manpower, but also on such resources as water. Whilst low-cost labour in the vineyards of the Guadalupe Valley can be replaced by machinery, the water that is a necessity for irrigation cannot. The calls that industry is making on the water of the aquifer that flows under the valley means that some artesian wells are running dry and that there are salinity problems with those which are flowing. So far, this is a problem that no one is willing to face up to. The riches that the *maquilladores* are bringing to the valley blind the authorities to other potential difficulties. Notwithstanding this, the Mexican quality wine industry appears to be vibrant and has grounds to look forward to a prosperous future.

This leaves me with the two greats of the Latin American wine industry, Chile and Argentina. As they say in the exam papers, 'Compare and contrast'! Whilst, in Britain, we might think that the wine industries of the two countries are very similar, in fact it is surprising to see just how different they are. The first thing to say is that the Chilean wine industry would not exist without exporting; the domestic market is not a sound one. Per capita consumption in 1991 was 29.5 litres, now it is just 13.1 litres. In Argentina, too, there has been a serious fall from 55.01 litres in 1991 to 40.99 litres in 1997. However, this fall is solely in the consumption of ordinary table wine; during the same period the consumption of fine wine has increased from 7 litres per person to just over 9 litres. This is a healthy sign and mirrors what is happening in other long-established wine markets, such as France. If we go back to the figures quoted earlier in this chapter, during the past 80 years, wine production in Chile has only increased by a third, whilst in Argentina, despite the fact that it is now much lower than it has been, it has more than doubled.

A parallel fact that has to be taken into consideration is that of populations; that of Argentina is 34 million people, that of Chile is approximately 14 million. So, in Argentina 2.5 times as many people each drink three times as much wine as in Chile! For Chile, as far as wine is concerned, it is export or die; for Argentina, it is export and we live better. It is generally considered in the world of exporting that you need a healthy domestic market to support healthy export markets.

As Hubrecht Duijker has said in his book, *The Wines of Chile*, 'Economic recovery began in the second half of the 1980s, and continued after a national referendum in 1988 heralded the return of democracy. The return of civilian government meant that Chilean wines were once more welcome the world over. In 1989 exports rose by around 66%, with a further 50% in each of the next two years – and that growth has continued. Two figures show how spectacular that increase has been. In 1988 the country exported 17.3 million litres of wine; ten years later it had risen to 230 million. This explosion was at least as impressive in money terms; from $35 million to $503 million.'

These figures are truly impressive and what makes them even more impressive is the fact that this vertiginous increase has not been achieved at the expense of quality. If anything, Chilean wines are now more reliable than they were 10 years ago. It is on the two basic aspects of quality and price, which together represent good value for money, that Chile has managed to extend its markets so rapidly.

In their detailed study entitled *The World Wine Business,* the Dutch Rabobank divides wine into five classes: from the bottom up, Basic, Premium, Super-premium, Ultra-premium and Icon. For 'new wine countries' it allocates the top end of the Basic segment and Premium and Super-premium. Interestingly enough, the top two segments are restricted solely to 'old wine countries'. A number of wineries in Chile are not satisfied with this exclusion, and largely led by foreign investors, have determined to produce 'icon' wines in Chile. Is this just pretension on their part, or are there ambitions justified? It is perhaps too early to say.

This rapid expansion in sales has meant a rapid increase in the planting of vineyards. Where has the land come from? First, it has come at the expense of other products; grapes are now perhaps the most valuable agricultural cash crop. It is worth a grower's while to grub up apple trees and plant vines. Secondly, and more importantly, it has been by extending the area producing fine wine. In the north, the Limarí Valley, which had only been considered good enough for the production of Moscatels for distillation into pisco is now a premium area, where a major wine brand, Francisco de Aguirre has established itself. In the south, too, Cauquenes and the Bío-Bío Valley, which were though to be good for nothing but basic wine from the País grape, now have been selected for planting by such as Kendall-Jackson and Viña Gracia. Thirdly, there has been a broadening of the traditional vineyard areas, often out into subsidiary valleys and up the hillsides. Projects such as Caliterra are in existing vineyard areas, but in areas where it was considered uneconomical to grow vines. Errázuriz has expanded down the Aconcagua Valley in its search for new sites. Whilst the rich floor of the Central Valley is still at the heart of Chilean viticulture, more challenging zones are being developed. This should help quality. It is sometimes difficult to realise that the first vine in the Casablanca was not planted until 1982 – and the person who did this was thought to be a fool and a madman. For too long, making wine in Chile was not enough of a challenge.

How far can Chile go? If I had all the answers to this question, this book would be worth many times the cover price. There is no doubt that there are limitations on land, but if current prices can be maintained, there is plenty of scope for change of crop use. What is potentially a bigger problem is the availability of water for irrigation. In some areas, such as Casablanca, this is already a problem. In other areas, such as Cauquenes, dry-farming is possible, but this is at the expense of yields and the ultimate cost of the wine.

Is Chile flexible enough? So far it has concentrated its export sales on just four varietals, Cabernet Sauvignon and Merlot for red wines and Chardonnay and Sauvignon Blanc for white wines. Whilst I do not have any statistics, I would be surprised if these account for less than 85% of the country's wine exports. This poses two problems. Until now the novice wine consumer has largely been content with these names on the label. As he becomes more sophisticated he will be able to look elsewhere, and will Chile be able to satisfy that demand? Secondly, we have seen that there has been a glut of Chardonnay on world markets, with a consequent collapse in prices. This seems to have occurred because of over-optimistic planting programmes around the world; because of a rapid increase in demand for red wine for health reasons and partly because of a growing boredom on the part of wine-writers with this variety. There is supposed to be a group of wine-writers in London, who call themselves the ABC Club, the Anything But Chardonnay Club. All this poses the question as to whether, in a time of glut, the Chileans can compete with, for example, the production costs of the Australians?

With the dominance of these varietals, which on world markets have now become little more than commodity wines, Chile has been in a strong position, but is it going to have ready its reserve line of attack, when the time becomes necessary? What is going to be distinctive about the wines of Chile? Uruguay has its Tannat, Argentina its Malbec and Torrontés. Chile talks vaguely of its Carmenère, but 330 hectares is not a very solid base on which to build a defence. As the Rabobank report says, 'Increasing demand, however, will not make the wine industry less competitive; the market has become demand driven and will continue to be so.' Will Chile have the answers to that demand?

Chile is fortunate in having a broad range of export markets. Whilst I was there last, disquiet was being expressed as a result of a fall in sales to the British market during the previous six months. Was this a sign of greater malaise? I think not, and the fall was small enough to be the result of just one promotion by a major super-market chain being moved by a week. However, there is some disquiet amongst some of the largest companies in Chile as to what the future might hold for them. Is this why some of them have invested in wineries in Argentina?

How can Argentina be compared to Chile? First of all it has to be said that whilst Argentina produces approximately three times as much as its neighbour, it only exports approximately half as much. Only half is described as 'fine' wine and a third of the 'fine' wine is exported in bulk as opposed to bottle. Argentina, then, is a long way behind Chile in the world of exports. However, the size of the Argentine domestic market has led to greater investment by the major multinational companies in Argentina than in Chile. This can ultimately only have beneficial results for export markets.

It also has one other major potential disadvantage. The rigour of the Pinochet regime in Chile created the soundest economy in South America, though this has largely been at the expense of the income of the workers. This is something that Argentina cannot match. Whilst the government of President Menem introduced an economic reform programme in 1991, which tied the Argentine peso to the American dollar, this has not proved adequate for what has the reputation of being one of the most volatile economies in a continent of volatile economies. An explosion appears to be imminent and may well have happened by the time this book appears. Whilst a devaluation of the peso, for example, might help exports, a period of financial instability, at a time when so much investment is being made, could be disastrous.

What are the potential strengths of the wine trade in Argentina? The first one is the almost limitless amount of land available for planting. In turn this means a lower initial investment is needed. The land available consists of two kinds. First of all, in such cooler climate areas as Río Negro and Tupungato, the current lack of viability of fruit such as apples and pears, means that orchards are available at low cost. However, on a broader scale, land is there for the taking. It appears that less than 5% of the land of Mendoza Province is used and that for most of it there is no shortage of water for irrigation. There is also plenty of land available in the Calchaquíes Valley in Salta Province and there have been tax incentives in the less economically developed Catamarca Province. Climatically, whilst Argentina may be hotter than Chile, there are few potential problems, with the exception of hail. These factors make the country attractive for foreign investors. Of the Californians, Kendall-Jackson is present in both countries and Cuvaison has just bought a property south of the city of Mendoza. Guest consultants, such a Michel Rolland, seem happy to earn money on both sides of the Andes!

One big advantage that Argentina has is the range of grapes that have historically been used for its wines. The grapes that have been popular for so long in Chile are of comparatively little importance in Argentina. All together they account for less than 12% of the area under vines, whilst in Chile, they account for well over half. In addition, Argentina has its two *speciality* grapes, the Malbec(k) and the Torrontés. Whilst I have reservations about the ability of the latter to be a world-beater, I have none about the former. The fact that it is now being planted widely in other South American countries shows that its potential is being recognised. Argentina, then, has less to lose in the event of varietal fatigue.

As the Rabobank report says, 'The new opportunities seem to have surprised many Argentine wine makers, prompting wineries to invest more than $US400 million over the last four years to introduce new processing technologies and replace low quality vines with both classical and high quality local varieties, such as Malbec. These new initiatives are fully geared towards the export markets, and are largely initiated by foreign companies; as a result the ownership structure is changing. Exports of premium wines are expected to increase fast, for the time being mainly to the UK, USA and Japan. Further cooperation, however, is required to enhance access to global markets.'

It is interesting that, internationally, Argentine exporters seem able to obtain slightly higher prices than their colleagues in Chile, and it is not easy to see why. In some ways they have been fortunate to arrive late on the fine wine scene. They have been able to move directly to the right techniques in the vineyards and in the wineries, without having expensive periods of experimentation. As one example of this, I would suggest that the oaking of wines, through the 'inner-stave' treatment, appears to be a more highly developed art in Argentina than it is in Chile.

As the Rabobank report has pointed out, Argentine fine wine exports are highly dependent on just three markets, the United States, the UK and Japan and the last of these is mainly bulk wine.

Between them the United States and the UK accounted for 47.9% of the sales in value. Further markets need to be identified and attacked to diminish any potential harm that might come through falling sales.

In the ever-expanding world of wine, Latin America must play an important part. At the moment, apart from Chile and, to a lesser extent, Argentina, it is largely unexplored. There is enormous room for expansion in sales; possibly in Chile, certainly in Argentina, Mexico and Uruguay. I have faith in the future for the wines of Bolivia and would like to have it in those of Peru. I am sure that the companies operating in Brazil, Venezuela and Cuba will find what they seek in their domestic markets. As for Paraguay, it has long been an isolationist country; for the wine consumer, this is happy news!

Glossary

———

alcool Blanc (Fr.) – Colourless spirit, generally distilled from fruit.

arroba (Sp.) – Weight of approximately 10 kg.

Asti method – See Sparkling wine.

Botrytis (Lat.) – Bunch rot. *Botrytis cinerea* is the rot needed for the production of many of the world's greatest sweet wines.

bocksbeutel (Ger.) – A dumpy bottle with a flat front and back, traditionally used for the wines of Franconia.

cachaça (Port.) – A colourless spirit distilled in Brazil from sugar cane.

campesino (Sp.) – Peasant, countryman.

Charmat – See Sparkling wines.

chips – A method of giving an oaky taste to wine by putting oak chips in with the grapes.

Haut-Pays (Fr.) – Literally 'High Country', in wine history the region of the Upper Dordogne Valley, whose wines were exported through, and often blended with, the wines of Bordeaux.

inner-stave – A method of giving an oak taste to wine by assembling inside a stainless-steel tank a 'tree' of oak barrel staves.

leafroll virus – A viral infection of vines that delays the ripening of grapes and also cuts down yields.

maquillador (Sp.) – Lit. 'One who applies make-up'. In Mexico it is a term applied to assembly plants established in Baja California, under favourable tax schemes.

méthode champenoise (Fr.) – See Sparkling wine.

méthode traditionelle (Fr.) – See Sparkling wine.

négociant (Fr.) – Merchant, one who buys wines from growers to sell, generally under his own label.

oidium (Lat.) – Powdery mildew.

parral (Sp.) – A method of training vines on pergolas traditional in South America. It helps protect the grapes from being burnt by the sun, as it gives extensive leaf cover.

Phylloxera (Lat.) – A louse that attacks the roots of vines and is capable of devastating a vineyard. Native American vines are resistant to it, so, generally, European vines are grafted on to American rootstock.

pileta (Sp.) – Vat.

rauli – A native Chilean tree, whose wood has historically been used for the making of wine-vats there. This tended to give a foreign taste to the wine. It has now largely been replaced by stainless steel.

sparkling wine – In South America, there are four main methods of producing sparkling wine. The finest wines are generally made by the *méthode champenoise* or *méthode traditionelle*. This is the method used in Champagne in France whereby the secondary fermentation takes place within the bottle. An alternative, and more widely used, way of making wine is the *Charmat* or 'tank' method. In this, the secondary fermentation takes place in bulk, in a tank, and the wine is bottled under pressure. The third way, used in Brazil, is the 'Asti' method, taking its name from the sparkling wines produced in Italy. In this the wine must is chilled and stored until needed. There is often only one fermentation up to about 7% and then the wine is bottled under pressure at low temperature. The fourth and cheapest way of making sparkling wine is by carbonation of a still one.

tinaja (Sp.) – A large earthenware jar, or vat, of Moorish origin, used for storing wine. It has rounded shoulders and a narrow bottom.

vin bourru (Fr.) – Lit. a 'gruff' wine. New wine, often turbid looking.

vinifera (Lat.) – From the *vitis vinifera* family of vines, as opposed to such American families as *rupestris*. All noble European varieties are *vinifera*.

Bibliography

The general section includes those works that have been used throughout this book. There are also lists for each of the separate countries.

GENERAL

De Blij, Harm Jan, *Wine Regions of the Southern Hemisphere*, Rowman & Allanheld, Totowa, New Jersey 1985.

Galet, P., *Précis d'Ampelographie Pratique*, 4th edition, Paul Déhan, Montpellier 1976.

Hidalgo, Luis (ed.), *La Viticultura Americana y sus Raíces*, Ministerio de Agricultura, Pesca y Alimentación, Madrid 1992.

Johnson, Hugh, *World Atlas of Wine*, 4th edition, Mitchell Beazley, London 1994.

Johnson, Hugh, *The Story of Wine*, Mitchell Beazley, London 1989.

Jullien, A., *Topographie de Tous les Vignobles Connus*, Mme. Huzard, Paris 1816.

Montorgueil, Georges, *Le Vin à Travers l'Histoire*, Établissements Nicolas, Paris 1924.

Montorgueil, Georges, *Monseigneur le Vin*, Nicolas, Paris, 1924.

Morewood, Samuel, *Philosophical and Statistical History of the Inventions and Customs of Ancient and Modern Nations in the Manufacturing and Use of Inebriating Liquors*, William Curry Jnr and Co., and William Carson, Dublin 1838.

Robinson, Jancis, *Vines, Grapes and Wines*, Mitchell Beazley, London 1986.

Robinson, Jancis (ed.), *The Oxford Companion to Wine*, 2nd edition, Oxford University Press, Oxford 1999.

Sempé, Raymond, *Étude sur les Vins Exotiques*, Féret et Fils, Bordeaux 1882.

South America 1989, Tour of the Wine Districts of Chile, Argentina, Brazil, Institute of Masters of Wine, London 1989.

Stevenson, Tom, *The New Sotheby's Wine Encyclopaedia*, Dorling Kindersley, London 1997.

Visit to South America – 12th to 27th September 2000, JMH & RCB, Laymont & Shaw, Truro.

Guide books from Footprint and Lonely Planet.

Decanter Magazine.

ARGENTINA

Argentina's Wine Industry, INV, Mendoza 1964.

Brasco, Miguel and Checa, Elisabeth, *Manual del Degustador Inteligente, 1998*, Cuisine et Vins, Buenos Aires 1997.

Buzzi, Fernando Vidal and Foix, Augusto, *Mendoza, las Terruños del Sol*, Editorial Foix Frères S.A., Mendoza 1994.

Buzzi, Fernando Vidal and Foix, Augusto, *Argentina, Vineyards, Wineries and Wines*, Morgan International Ltd, Buenos Aires 2000.

Dengis, Jorge, *Manual del Vino Argentino*, Albatros, Buenos Aires 1994.

Denman, James, *The Vine and its Fruit*, Longmans Green, and Co., London 1875.

Estadistica Vitivinícola 72–74, INV, Mendoza 1975.

Diagnóstico Sobre la Situación Vitivinícola en la Argentina, Primera Reunión Técnica para Productores, Bodegas y Viñedos Valentín Bianchi, San Rafael 1997.

Navarro, Dr Emilio Maurin, *Contribucióal estudio de la historia vitivinícola argentina*, Buenos Aires, n.d.

Queyrat, Enrique, *Los Buenos Vinos Argentinos*, 2nd edition, Hachette, Buenos Aires 1974.

Los Vinos Argentinos en los Mercados Exteriores 1976, INV, Mendoza 1977.

Young, Alan, *Wine Routes of Argentina*, International Wine Academy, San Francisco 1998.

Vinos y Viñas Magazine.

'The Wine-List of 1884 Restaurante' – Francis Mallmann, Mendoza.

BOLIVIA

Bluske Sagarnaga, Ivan, *Origen de la Vitivinicultura Boliviana*, n.d.

Bluske Sagarnaga, Ivan, *El Singani un Producto Ecológico*, n.d.

BRAZIL

Albano do Amarante, José Osvaldo, *Vinhos e Vinícolas do Brasil*, 2nd edition, Summus Editorial, Sao Paolo 1986.
Falcade, Ivanira and Mandelli, Francisco (eds), *Vale dos Vinhedos, Caracterizaçao Geográfica da Regiao*, Universidade de Caxias do Sul/EMBRAPA, Bento Gonçalves 1999.
Lona, Adolfo Alberto, *Vinhos, Degustaçao, Elaboraçao e Serviço*, 3rd edition, Age Editora, Porto Alegre 1998.
Miranda, Fernando W., *Arte de Vinho*, Senac, Rio de Janeiro 1997.
Subcomissao Mista Vitivicultura, *Estado di Río Grande do Sul*, Bento Gonçalves 1998.

CHILE

Chile – Report of a Visit to Chile by the Institute of Masters of Wine, Institute of Masters of Wine, London 2000.
Del Pozo, José, *Historia del Vino Chileno*, Editorial Universitaria, Santiago 1998.
Duijker, Hubrecht, *The Wines of Chile*, Spectrum, Utrecht 1999.
Leon Victor, E. (ed.), *Uvas y Vinos de Chile*, Sindicato Nacional Vitivinícola, Santiago, 1947.
Matthass, Jürgen, *Wines from Chile*, Qué Más, Amsterdam 1997.
Read, Jan, *Chilean Wines*, Sotheby's Publications, London 1988.
Sanchez, Francisca M., *Guía de Vinos de Vinos de Chile*, Editora de Publicaciones S.A., Santiago 1994.
Sanchez, Francisca M. *et al.*, *Guía de Vinos de Chile Año 2000*, Paula Comunicaciones S.A., Santiago 1999.
Harpers, The Wine & Spirit Weekly.

MEXICO

History of Casa Madero S.A., Monterrey, n.d.
Thomas, Hugh, *The Conquest of Mexico*, Hutchinson, London 1993.

PARAGUAY

Dyck, Cornelius J., *An Introduction to Mennonite History*, 3rd edition, Herald Press, Waterloo, Ontario 1993.

PERU

Cobo, Bernabé, *Historia del Nuevo Mundo*, Madrid, 1653.
de la Vega, Garcilaso, *El Inca*, Comentarios Reales, Caracas, 1617.
Crónicas y Relaciones que se Refieren al Origen y Virtudes del Pisco, Banco Latino, Lima 1990.
Galver, José, *Ocucaje y El Regente*, 3rd edition, Lima 1970.
Shaw, Thomas George, *Wine, the Vine and the Cellar*, 2nd edition, Longman, Green, Longman, Roberts, & Green, London 1864.
Rotondo Donola, Francisco, *El Conocimiento del Vino*, Bodegas y Viñedos Tabernero S.A.C, Lima 2000.
Tacama, Ica, Peru, Viña Tacama, 1997.

URUGUAY

De Frutos, Estela, *Conocer para Valorar*, Ediciones Trilce, Montevideo 1995.
De Frutos, Estela and Beretta, Alcides, *Un Siglo de Tradición – Primera Historia de Uvas y Vinos del Uruguay*, Ediciones Santillana, Montevideo 1999.
Galanti, A. N., *La Industria Vitivinícola Uruguaya*, Montevideo, 1919.
Instituto Nacional de Vitivinicultura, Uruguay, Création, Objectifs et Fonctionnement, INAVI, Las Piedras 1996
Réglement Vitivinicole du Mercosur, INAVI, Las Piedras 1997.
Vino & Crianza Magazine.

CONCLUSION

The World Wine Business, Rabobank International, Utrecht 1999.

Index of Wineries and Brands

═══════

General Index